D0487493

Birds in Surrey 1900-1970

1 (overleaf) *Dartford Warbler* at the nest, taken in the early 1900s. This is reproduced from a plate in Kirton's *Nature Pictures* published in 1910. It is almost certainly the first photograph ever taken of this species (*Richard and Cherry Kearton*)

Birds in Surrey
1900-1970

edited by Donald Parr
assisted by a Committee of the Surrey Bird Club

Photographic editor : D. M. T. Ettlinger F. R. P. S.

B. T. Batsford Ltd. London

First published 1972
© Surrey Bird Club 1972

Text printed in Great Britain by
Northumberland Press Ltd, Gateshead, Co. Durham.
Plates printed by Richard Clay (The Chaucer Press) Ltd, Bungay, Suffolk
Bound by Hunter & Foulis Ltd, Edinburgh
for the publishers B. T. Batsford Ltd.
4 Fitzhardinge Street, London W1H OAH

ISBN 0 7134 0329 2

Contents

THE VICE COUNTY OF SURREY

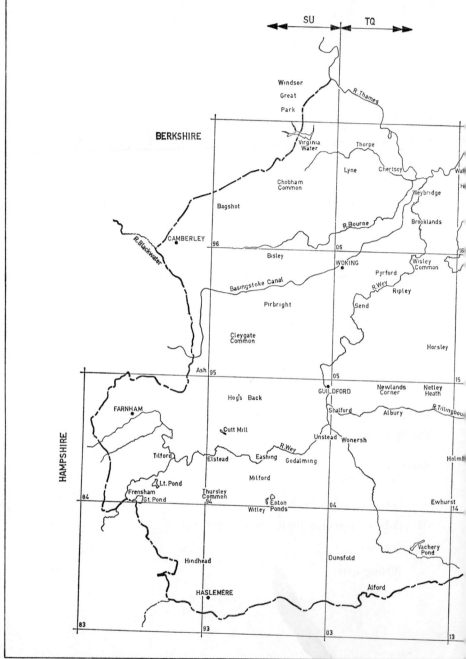

Reproduced by kind permission of John Bartholomew & Son Ltd., Edinburgh

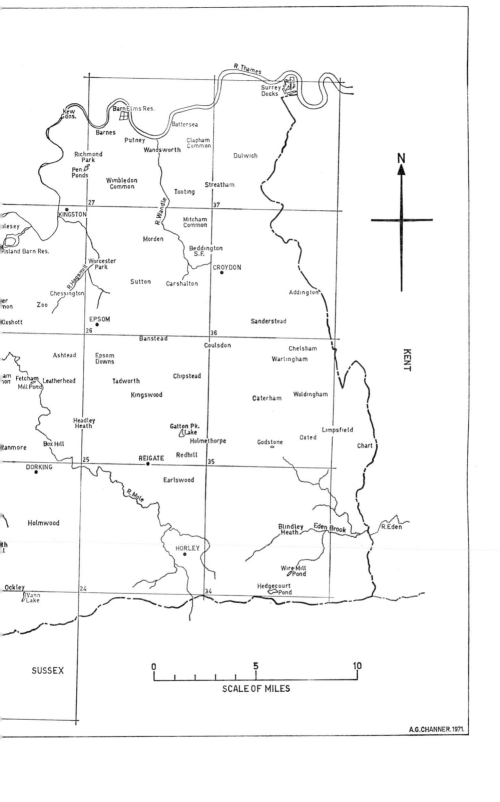

R. Thames

Surrey Docks

Kew Gdns.

Barn Elms Res.

Barnes

Battersea

Putney

Wandsworth

Clapham Common

Richmond Park

Pen Ponds

Wimbledon Common

Dulwich

Tooting

Streatham

27

37

KINGSTON

Mitcham Common

R. Wandle

Morden

Beddington S.F.

CROYDON

olesey

Island Barn Res.

R. Hogsmill

Worcester Park

Sutton

Carshalton

Addington

Chessington

Zoo

EPSOM

26

Banstead

36

Coulsdon

Sanderstead

er non

Oxshott

Ashtead

Epsom Downs

Chelsham

Warlingham

am hon

Fetcham Mill Pond

Leatherhead

Tadworth

Chipstead

Kingswood

Caterham

Woldingham

Headley Heath

Gatton Pk. Lake

Holmethorpe

Godstone

Oxted

Limpsfield

Chart

anmore

Box Hill

25

REIGATE

Redhill

35

DORKING

Earlswood

R. Mole

Holmwood

Blindley Heath

Eden Brook

R. Eden

th l

HORLEY

Wire Mill Pond

Ockley

24

Vann Lake

34

Hedgecourt Pond

KENT

N

SUSSEX

0   5   10

SCALE OF MILES

A.G. CHANNER. 1971.

The Illustrations

The Plates

Maps

Preface

In 1900 John A. Bucknill published *The Birds of Surrey* and to the present time that work has worthily served as the only fully systematized account of the birds which have been recorded in the county. It is known that Charles Howard Bentham began to write an ornithology of Surrey in mid-century and it is regrettable that when the work was completed he was unable to find a publisher and that the manuscript was never traced after his death in 1968. In 1957 *The Birds of the London Area since 1900* was published by the London Natural History Society and included coverage of that part of Surrey within a radius of 20 miles of St Paul's Cathedral.

It was not, however, till the 1960s were well advanced that the idea that something should be be done about a new county ornithology, began to germinate in the minds of several members of the Surrey Bird Club. Eventually it was decided that an effort should be made to produce a new ornithology of Surrey. Approaches were made to leading ornithologists in the county, promises of support and help were forthcoming and a Book Committee under the chairmanship of D. Parr was formed in 1968. The members of this committee were D. Griffin, P. B. Lowe, D. Parr, Mrs J. D. Parr and J. A. Sage, to be joined later by R. Allison, A. G. Channer, R. H. B. Forster, A. J. Holcombe, R. G. Lees, and J. J. Wheatley. Most of the tedious and laborious work of abstracting records and searching the literature fell to this committee and it is a measure of the members' enthusiasm and determination that within four years of the inception of the work the new *Birds in Surrey 1900—1970* had come into being.

The area with which we are concerned in this publication is the vice-county of Surrey. The vice-county system dates from 1852 when H. C. Watson listed 18 provinces, 38 sub-provinces and 112 vice-counties in *Cybele Britannica* (3:524-8), the object being to fix areas of roughly equal size by dividing the larger counties into two or more vice-counties and so fix for all time, recording areas for natural history purposes. The vice-county boundaries of Surrey (No. 17) were those of the administrative county taken from an atlas published in 1844. In 1938 a joint committee of the Botanical Society and the Systematics Association decided to recommend the continued use for recording purposes of the original Watsonian vice-county boundaries and they became thus, firmly established (Dandy, 1969). At present the National Grid generally takes precedence only where biological recording on a national scale is concerned. It is also fortunate that the vice-county of Surrey as established, was the recording area used by Bucknill in 1900, although the Local Government Act (1888) had created the County of London and administrative Surrey had by 1900 lost some 25,000 acres to it. The present work therefore deals with the same recording area that Bucknill considered. The extent of the vice-county is clearly delineated on the map on pp. 6-7. The three separate sub-recording areas mentioned in the text (West, South and LNHS) are shown on the map incorporated in Appendix III.

Bucknill's work dealt with a total of 268 species. The species given by him which do not have a place in this work are for the sake of completeness listed in Appendix I (p. 272). This book includes 27 species that did not figure in Bucknill's and it is heartening that it is in the number of regular breeding species that the greatest gains have been made. In 1900 there were 95 species breeding regularly in the county; since then two have become extinct (Corncrake and Stone Curlew), three are now of doubtful status (Quail, Long-eared Owl and Wryneck), whilst one, the Wheatear, now breeds only irregularly. On the credit side, however, the county has gained no less than 14 regular breeding birds (a few of which bred irregularly or doubtfully before 1900). These are the Great-crested Grebe; three duck—Mandarin, Gadwall and Tufted; the Canada Goose; three birds of prey—Buzzard, Hobby and Little Owl; three waders— Little Ringed Plover, Curlew and Redshank; the Collared Dove, Black Redstart and Grey Wagtail. Many species have declined appreciably in numbers and in some cases to the brink of extinction, as for instance the Red-Backed Shrike and Wryneck. The chats have all declined, as has the Nightingale, while some like the Woodlark have been subject to considerable fluctuations in numbers and the Dartford Warbler has provided a striking example of violent status changes mainly due to climatic factors. Certain breeding species have prospered—the Kestrel, Great Spotted Woodpecker, Magpie, Grasshopper Warbler and Goldfinch to mention but some species whose status in 1970 was much higher than in 1900. Appendix II (p. 274) presents in summary form an assessment of the past and present breeding strength of the birds in the county. It remains impossible, however, to pronounce on the question of the general impoverishment of birdlife in Surrey (i.e. an overall reduction in breeding numbers where habitats have not changed) because of lack of sufficient information and the problem of assessing status at 'abundant' level. However, some ornithologists who have lived in Surrey for a considerable time are convinced that there has been such a general impoverishment.

In considering the changes that have occurred in the present century, a number of factors call for particular mention and the foremost of these is urban growth. The population of Surrey in 1901 was 2,012,744 of which 1,359,195 lived in the county of London. The population of the administrative county together with the London boroughs falling within the vice-county in 1970 was all but three million. London has spread enormously and many species that bred freely on the inner commons and at such places as Dulwich, Kew and Richmond have been pushed relentlessly further out. Fortunately the Green Belt Policy initiated in the 1930s was in time to prevent complete swamping of many open areas by urban development. The larger towns such as Dorking, Guildford and Reigate also expanded and residential properties proliferated in the remoter country areas. However, with development came the building of reservoirs in the Thames Valley, the digging of gravel pits and creation of sewage farms, all of which formed new habitats which birds, particularly duck, gulls and waders, were quick to exploit. The further expansion of railways and the rapid rise of the motorbus and car revolutionized public transport and many formerly quiet and undisturbed areas became subject to public pressures and some species of birds suffered as a consequence. The relaxation of commoners' rights and the decline of sheep grazing on the downs began to result in vegetational changes in many areas and again species dependent on open habitat encountered a new threat. The increasing use of pesticides after the Second World War added to the hazards and by the end of the 1950s some species, for instance the Sparrow Hawk and Barn Owl, had become almost extinct as breeding birds in the county. Happily with the voluntary ban on the use of dieldrin on spring-sown wheat this last threat appeared to be abating at the time of writing.

The climate too has had effects on bird populations in the county. In the review period there have been four winters with a prolonged cold spell (defined for this purpose as 30 or more consecutive days with daily maximum temperatures 37°F or below at Kew)—1916/17 (32 days), 1939/40 (39 days), 1946/47 (38 days) and 1962/63 (56 days). In this last winter the cold spell was probably the longest and most severe since 1813/14 and there was a period of nine days of continuous frost from 17 to 25 January. The 1962/63 winter severely reduced the population levels of many resident species but most of the commoner ones quickly recovered. In the last four decades of the review period there has been a tendency for summers to be wetter and cooler, this to the possible detriment of species such as the Red-backed Shrike. Finally the growing popularity of birdwatching as a hobby and the increasing expertise of birdwatchers in searching out and identifying difficult species has also been a factor in the number of records published, particularly since the Second World War.

Two national research projects sponsored by the British Trust for Ornithology and begun in the 1960s call for comment at this point. The first was the Common Birds Census which was started at the request of the Nature Conservancy in 1961. Its purpose was to investigate the status and numbers of birds, particularly the commoner ones, by means of breeding season censuses on a nationwide scatter of sample plots. The data from census plots in Surrey proved an invaluable source of reference where an evaluation of population levels and recent changes were concerned. It should, however, be borne in mind that the 19 Surrey plots were censused for different periods of time (only one was covered for a ten-year period

(1960/69), that Woodpigeon and House Sparrow were excluded and that results were expressed in terms of occupied territories and not breeding pairs (Griffin, 1970).

The second project was the preparation of an Ornithological Atlas of Britain and Ireland. A survey was planned to cover the five years 1968-72 on the basis of species breeding, probably breeding and possibly breeding within each ten kilometre square of the National Grid. The Atlas, it should be understood, makes no attempt at quantifying breeding populations. Thus a species with one record of confirmed breeding in any of the years 1968-72 merits the maximum registration as does a species that breeds abundantly every year. The results for Surrey for the period 1968-71 are presented in Appendix III (p. 276). The Atlas survey is something of a blunt tool so far as Surrey is concerned but nevertheless a useful reference base.

The chapters in this book are the work of some of the members of the Book Committee and the authorship of each is shown. Mrs J. D. Parr gives some modern historical illuminations, traces changing attitudes to birds in Surrey, introduces prominent personalities from the past and present and sets the scene. R. H. B. Forster gives a comprehensive account of the geology of Surrey. P. B. Lowe describes the reservoirs which have had such a dramatic effect on gull and duck numbers visiting the county, pays particular attention to the Queen Elizabeth II Reservoir and also describes the larger lakes, ponds and gravel pits. J. J. Wheatley shows the extent and importance of rivers and wetland habitats in the county. D. Parr describes the varied nature of commonlands in the county, shows their importance for many of the more interesting and attractive species for which Surrey has long been renowned and expounds on the pressures that are changing the face of many of the open spaces in the county. J. A. Sage explains the factors that have influenced the woodland cover of the county and the significance of woodland for the county's avifauna. Finally A. J. Holcombe gives a fascinating insight into the complexities of bird movements through the county and their pattern throughout the seasons.

Pressure of space prevented the inclusion of chapters on two major habitats extensive in the county, viz. the built-up urban/suburban areas and agricultural Surrey. The former subject was very adequately dealt with in *The Birds of the London Area since 1900* as far as the metropolitan area is concerned and readers seeking more background on the subject are referred to that work. Any chapter on agricultural Surrey, however, would have been severely circumscribed as very little systematic work has been done on bird distribution in agricultural areas. A few of the Common Birds Census plots were situated on agricultural land and give some indications of bird populations in that habitat (Griffin, 1970), but none of these was on the extensive weald-lands in south east and central Surrey. Some of the agricultural lands in the south west of the county, particularly around Alfold and Dunsfold, in an area of high unkempt hedgerows, coppices and small fields, have very large bird populations including many species of warbler and Nightingales but large areas of the Weald do not apparently have high bird densities and in many areas only the commoner hedgerow species are found. Further research into the birdlife of agricultural Surrey is called for and reference to certain species in the systematic list, as for instance the Redshank, Lapwing and Corn Bunting might suggest that the results could be surprising. Fortunately Surrey has been spared the worst effects of 'prairie' farming as practised in many eastern counties.

The systematic list was largely written by D. Parr who accepts responsibility for any errors or omissions and the evaluations of the records in respect of the list as a whole. Substantial contributions to the list were made by D. Griffin, Mrs J. D. Parr, J. A. Sage and J. J. Wheatley all of whom also made detailed criticism of a draft of the list. Other contributions, no less valued, were made by R. Allison, Miss P. M. Bond, R. H. B. Forster, P. B. Lowe and I. S. Robertson.

The list includes reports on 271 separate species of which 121 have been proved to breed since 1900 (Appendix II). The status given for breeding species has been determined very broadly as follows:

Irregular/extremely scarce	:	intermittent (not recorded breeding every year)
Very scarce	:	one—five breeding pairs recorded or estimated annually
Scarce	:	six—15 ... ...
Moderately common	:	16-200 plus ...
Common	:	over 200 breeding pairs estimated
Very common	:	annually—undefined but relative categories
Abundant	:	tive categories

Generally speaking the sources of the more important records are given but to prevent tiresome repetition many references to *The London Bird Report*, the *Surrey Bird Report* and *The Birds of the London Area since 1900* are omitted. The Committee has lent heavily on this last work where records in that part of Surrey falling in the LNHS recording area are concerned and is glad to acknowledge here its indebtedness to that work.

The order and nomenclature used in the list is that of the *Check-List of the Birds of Great Britain and Ireland* published by the British Ornithologists' Union in 1952 and the list incorporates amendments and additions notified in *Ibis* 98:158-69 and 113:420-3. It is unfortunate that the new British Ornithologists' Union check-list had not been published at the time of the preparation of this work. The vernacular names used in the list are those adopted by the editors of *British Birds* (B.B. 46:1-3). Vernacular and scientific names of trees and plants follow Clapham, Tutin and Warburg: *Flora of the British Isles, 1952*.

It is difficult in a work of this nature to mention by name all the many persons who have given help and assistance during the course of research and preparation. The Book Committee's thanks are particularly due however, to the following: Miss C. M. Acland for personal records, abstracts of *The Field* and the loan of many volumes of *British Birds*, Miss P. M. Bond for detailed abstracting of the Haslemere records and help with the systematic list, A. G. Channer for the maps and the BTO Atlas summary, R. H. B. Forster for providing the basic information on which the Atlas map is based, P. A. D. Hollom for personal records and helpful criticism of an early draft of the systematic list, Cherry Kearton senior for permission to reproduce the photograph of the Dartford Warbler (frontispiece), Cherry Kearton junior for the loan of the nineteen volumes of the diaries of his uncle, Howard Bentham. These diaries have proved an invaluable source of information particularly for the early years of the century when very little systematic recording was done. His observations covered particularly the eastern North Downs, the south east corner of the county (including Hedgecourt and Wire Mill Ponds) and the commons around Thursley and the Frensham Ponds. The Committee is extremely grateful to Mr Kearton and to Mrs Bentham for making the material so readily available. Further, thanks are due to R. G. Lees for preparing the gazetteer, D. Melville for material on the Charterhouse Collections and records, O. Polunin for providing other Charterhouse material and information on the Stafford Collection, Miss M. Parker for the loan of the books of her father—Eric Parker, R. Price for legal advice and D. M. T. Ettlinger, FRPS for acting as photographic editor with the onerous task of collecting and sorting the splendid photographs that illustrate this work. About half the photographs in the book are of types of habitat mentioned in the text and were taken in Surrey, the other half is of some representative birds. The majority of these were also taken in the county and all the photographers have a strong Surrey connection—people who live or have lived in the county or have done much photographic work there. We are very grateful to them all for contributing to this work.

The Forestry Commission and the Metropolitan Water Board kindly supplied information and the following also contributed personal records: F. V. Blackburn, G. Douglas, R. M. Fry, G. H. Gush, A. J. Holcombe, C. Ogston, D. Parr, H. E. Pounds, Miss D. Powell, M. J. Rayner, L. J. Raynsford, D. K. J. Withrington and J. J. Wheatley. Finally the Editor wishes to record his thanks to his wife Joyce without whose constant help, advice and support this work would not have been completed.

Donald Parr   December 1971

2 (top) *Leith Hill*, the highest point in Surrey (*D. M. T. Ettlinger*)
3 (bottom) *The front slope of Ranmore Common*. Formerly a breeding site of the Red-backed Shrike (*D. M. T. Ettlinger*)

Abbreviations used in the text

BB	*British Birds*
BTO	British Trust for Ornithology
BOC Bull.	*Bulletin of the British Ornithologists' Club*
c.	circa (about)
CNHS	Charterhouse Natural History Society
GP(s)	Gravel pit(s)
LBR	*The London Bird Report*
LNHS	London Natural History Society
PCGS	Purley County Grammar School
R.	River
RSPB	Royal Society for the Protection of Birds
RSPCA	Royal Society for the Protection of Animals
SP(s)	Sand pit(s)
SF(s)	Sewage farm(s)
SEBR	*South Eastern Bird Report*
SBC	Surrey Bird Club
SBCQB	*Surrey Bird Club Quarterly Bulletin*
SBR	*Surrey Bird Report*
The Handbook	*The Handbook of British Birds*, 1938, revised 1943
Zool.	*The Zoologist*
Walton Reservoirs	include Chelsea and Lambeth and Knight and Bessborough sections
Walton Group of Reservoirs	includes the Walton Reservoirs, Island Barn Reservoir and Queen Elizabeth II Reservoir

4 (top) *The Devil's Punchbowl*, Hindhead. (*F. V. Blackburn*)

5 (bottom) *Ash Ranges*, near Pirbright. Frequent fires have a devastating effect on heathland vegetation as this photograph shows. (*D. M. T. Ettlinger*)

A Modern History of Birds and Man in Surrey

Joyce D. Parr

The London working man in Victorian times who belonged to what Mayhew described as the respectable bird-keeping classes, with a couple of cages of Surrey-trapped Nightingales in his room and the Surrey Bird Club members seeking recreation at Newlands Corner, Surrey's best known Nightingale haunt, on a summer evening in 1970 have this much in common—an interest (albeit in the first case an unrecognized one) in the birds in Surrey. It is with this direct interest, rather than the relationship between birds and man and the changing environment, that this chapter generally deals, for the latter is treated elsewhere in this book. The two concepts only converge in the 1940s when an interest in birds became associated with measures for conservation (although nearly a hundred years earlier Alfred Smee of Beddington had an experimental garden and his son, who was especially interested in birds, observed the importance of habitat and encouraged Nightingales to breed in the garden by the provision of trees and shrubs).

However, Alfred Smee and his son were somewhat out of their time. For most people in Surrey, in most of the last century, birds were there to be eaten or put in cages or used for other purposes; they were there to be kept as pets or used for falconry; they were there to be trapped or shot, for pleasure or profit. It was only towards the end of the nineteenth century that new attitudes towards birds became apparent, although a curious ambivalence had been evident for some time.

Apart from the usual game birds, species taken in Surrey and eaten included the Skylark and the Wheatear (both considered great delicacies), the Coot which was a delicacy to some palates and the Green Woodpecker which could be palmed off as a 'delicious wader'.

Among the song birds caged the Nightingale was the most highly prized. In the London street markets mid-century the best birds sold at a pound. The London bird-catchers thought that Surrey Nightingales were the best. Other birds caught in Surrey for song included the Skylark, Woodlark, Goldfinch and Linnet. Large numbers fed the London market each year but the mortality rate was high (e.g. for Nightingales, on the street markets, over 50 per cent). The Hawfinch was frequently kept as a cage bird although its song in a cage was poor.

Birds were also trapped to make artificial sport and large numbers of Surrey Starlings were sold for shooting at four pence each; Surrey House Sparrows were captured in their thousands for the same purpose or as playthings for children—price a penny each.

The ornamental uses of birds in Victorian England are better known and Surrey birds were in great demand for millinery, etc. At one time there was a fashion for firescreens made of owls and a Surrey dealer was happy to supply the market. And for your drawing-room show-case or collection a well-known taxidermist of Churt, one Smithers, about the middle of the century could supply anyone at any time with a Dartford Warbler. There was also some demand for birds' nests, complete with eggs, as from Shirley Woods. Egg-collecting became fashionable about this time.

In addition to caged birds there were other birds kept as pets and if Surrey sportsmen/naturalists had tame Snipe, sandpipers and Woodcock, this is no more strange than the twentieth-century New Wildfowler's keeping back-garden Grey-lags. Species popular as pets and given freedom include the Bullfinch, Barn Owl, Tawny Owl and Kestrel. The Kestrel was a favourite and was often used for non-professional falconry.

Not a great deal of information is available on professional falconry but Epsom Downs appears to have been the main area used for the sport. About 1873 the great professional falconer John Barr was hawking there and the English Falconry Club (1878) made use of the downs, particularly for Rook-hawking with a Gyr Falcon. Hawking after Herons was practised in Surrey until quite late in the nineteenth century.

Bird-trapping was carried out in various ways, the most usual being with a clap-net and call-bird mainly to take live small species. Pole-trap and other gin-traps were also commonly used for the larger species, destroying them cruelly. Son of the Marshes (of him anon) tells of seeing Tawny, Barn, Long-eared and Short-eared Owls all swinging together on a Surrey gamekeeper's dog-kennel. Bird-liming, another very cruel practice, was also employed, not by local people according to the Son of the Marshes, but only by professional bird-catchers. In fact most bird-trapping was done for commercial purposes and the bird-catchers from London were mainly responsible.

There were not the same profits to be had from shooting as from trapping; however, in a poor county by-passed by the Industrial Revolution 'the sale of Woodcock would buy the children's shoes'.

Shooting for sport was a popular enough pastime but up to about 1870 it was done the hard way. However then, when the battue became fashionable, bags were not really large and Surrey's reputation as a shooting county was not great.

But there was yet another 'pleasurable' purpose in shooting birds in Surrey—that was in the cause of ornithology. The sportsman/naturalist tradition was not new and it is not surprising, in view of general attitudes prevailing, that the new observational nature studies should to a large extent become allied with this tradition (although Gilbert White himself, who had given the impetus to these studies, was as far removed from being a sporting man as it is possible to be). The early ornithologists of Surrey were generally not specialists but all-round naturalists. Those who were taxidermists were probably the most interested in birds. Most notable among these naturalists were those in the 'Godalming group' headed by Edward Newman (Rusticus) who was editor of the *Zoologist* from 1843-63, the *Zoologist* being probably the most important journal to emerge with the spate of new natural history publications. The group included the well-known taxidermists, William Stafford and his mentor Waring Kidd. Members of the group contributed nature notes to a variety of publications and some of these notes were published in book form under the title—*Letters of Rusticus on the Natural History of Godalming* (1849). That the Nightjar was common enough in the area in those days we can have no doubt for in the book we read 'on Highdown Heath Mr Stafford shot 47 in a very short space of time'. From a different part of the county Edward Blyth (Zoophilus) contributed many notes to various periodicals on the birds of Tooting.

An interest in natural history was spreading fast and various societies were formed in the county. The oldest of these still in existence is the Holmesdale Natural History Club (1857). (However the present Guildford Natural History and Literary Society can trace its origins to the educational provisions in the Guildford Mechanics' Institute (1834) and Literary and Scientific Institute (1835)). In these societies microscopy seemed to play a large part; however, some did begin to record birds as well as acquire a collection. Apart from the Surrey Natural History Society these societies were local and most commonly accepted Gilbert White's idea of maintaining a general parochial history of nature and antiquities.

Outside the mainstream of the emergent Surrey ornithology were the 'woodland people', the charcoal burners and plyers of woodcraft, who lived close to birds and had a considerable knowledge of them (for example they knew the Ring Ouzel to be a regular and common migrant in outer Surrey early in the nineteenth century) but whose observations went mostly unrecorded.

The 'woodland people' were discovered by Son of the Marshes (Denham Jordan, 1834 (?)—1920), the first writer of popular natural history in Surrey and a leading one of his day. He wrote his books in his head and dictated them to his editor Mrs Owen Visger, for he was a humble painter and decorator destined to die in the Union Infirmary at Dorking (after his death they likened him to Thoreau). Consideration of the Son of the Marshes leads us from the first three quarters of the nineteenth century into the last, when Surrey assumed many of the 'modern' characteristics which concern us—Bird Protection Acts came into force in 1880 and 1894, there was rapid urban expansion and overspill from London, suburban railway lines proliferated making it possible for Surrey to become the 'playground' of Londoners and the military authorities began to use the Surrey heaths for training. Son of the Marshes belonged to both old and new worlds. He moved into Surrey from the north Kent marshes (hence his pseudonym) at the middle of the century and began to observe the wildlife of the county by day and by night at all seasons. He spoke scathingly of many of the naturalists of the day. 'A two-foot rule and a measuring tape backed by the best library in the world will not make a naturalist'. Although he wrote about the north Kent marshes and other forms of life besides birds, his books contain many acute observations on birds in Surrey. In Son of the Marshes is reflected changes in people's attitudes towards birds. Some time or other he released the birds he kept as pets except for one Tawny Owl. It is not clear when he laid down his gun but towards the end of the century he observed, 'I can honestly say that any real insight I may have into Nature and her ways began when I made that exchange [field glasses for gun] myself'. In some ways his thinking was along lines general in the late 1960s. For instance he saw that habitat rather than protection was most often the key to bird populations where *small* birds were concerned and observed that the decline of the Nightingale at the end of the century was due to loss of habitat to building rather than to bird-trapping (the Wild Bird Protection Acts were largely ignored). In fact he considered the Goldfinch to be the only species to suffer in status because of the activities of the bird-catchers. This is not of course to say that he approved of bird-catching, far from it, but that he understood about population dynamics. He deplored the killing of birds of prey but gave up hope of trying to explain to gamekeepers why they were troubled by 'varmint'.

For Son of the Marshes all living things praised the Supreme Creator. But for Alfred Lord Tennyson (1802-92) who walked the Surrey heaths in his later years there was a stumbling block—it was Tennyson himself who wrote of 'nature red in (tooth and) claw'. But Tennyson's nature poems showing his general love of nature had a considerable influence in the country and many people came to see nature in a new light through him. However, despite some felicitous phrases about birds and a poetry tally of about 60 species, it has to be admitted that Tennyson was not great at ornithology.

Of the many poets associated with Surrey who have written about nature, none can be described as truly Nature poets and only George Meredith (1828-1909) who lived at Box Hill for the last 40 years of his life gives us true poetry of real birds (and yet we should record that he had another side which seemed alienated from Nature). In well-known poems Meredith 'captures' the Skylark and the Nightingale but it is Love in a Valley (1878), an exposition of Meredith's philosophy of earth ('For love we earth, then serve we all'), set it would seem in a valley at Box Hill, that a universal significance is assumed by real birds of Surrey.

> Lovely are the curves of the white owl* sweeping
> Wavy in the dusk lit by one large star.
> Lone on the fir-branch, his rattle note unvaried,
> Brooding o'er the gloom, spins the brown eve-jar.†

Before we pass on to the twentieth century there are a few more observations to be made. F. D. Power had begun watching visible migration from his garden in Brixton in 1874 and was eventually (he continued his study to 1909) to give the first well-documented account of the phenomenon (as observed inland) in the country. In c. 1882 a fossil bird was found in a new railway cutting/tunnel at Park Hill, near Croydon—*Gastornis klaasseni*—the first bird of Surrey yet recorded. The beginnings of the Haslemere Educational Museum, which was to become essentially a living nature museum, date from 1888; the museum soon acquired a bird collection.

In 1889 William Stafford died leaving a superb collection of Surrey birds. Charterhouse School bought a cross section in 332 cases for £400 and this was to be the basis of the Charterhouse Museum. One assumes the collection was admired by the young Julian Huxley whose father was a master at the school during the last decade of the century. However, Sir Julian Huxley's (autobiographical) *Memories* of this time were of being in the field, bird-watching in south west Surrey and it was for example at Cutt Mill that he discovered for himself the 'secret' of the Snipe's feeding habits.

In 1894 Clemence Acland aged four began bird-watching in Surrey at Woodmansterne, her father aiding her identifications by reading details of birds to her. About 1898 what may have been the first wild bird sound-recording was made in Surrey. It is not quite clear who made the record but it was of the Nightingale's song in the Limpsfield area and one George Wickham was mainly instrumental to having it broadcast in Canada where people thought it was marvellous.

Meantime Sir John Bucknill (1873-1926), himself an old boy of Charterhouse, was preparing the first book on the birds 'of' Surrey, more it would seem from examination of skins and notes from various correspondents than from personal field observations. *Birds of Surrey* (1900) was published when Bucknill was 27. Two years later he was posted abroad and remained abroad for the rest of his life. In *Birds of Surrey* he left

* Barn Owl
† Nightjar

behind a work which was no mean achievement and which, if rather ambient in style, inspires confidence in his judgements.

On 1 January 1906 Howard Bentham started keeping a diary. In it he was to record in the greatest detail over 60 years of bird observations made for the most part in Surrey. Howard Bentham was born in Croydon in 1883 and began bird-watching during his boyhood. In the early 1900s he met Richard Kearton who, together with his brother Cherry, was one of the early nature photographers. (Much of the Keartons' early photography was done in the Caterham area.) Richard remained in Surrey while Cherry went abroad in 1908 and it was with Richard Kearton that Howard Bentham collaborated. Up to 1916 they spent a great deal of time photographing the Dartford Warbler on the outer Surrey heaths. In those pioneer days Howard Bentham noted that the Dartford Warbler's irides were reddish and came to the conclusion that the descriptions in the bird books of the day giving the colour as yellow (various shades) were made from the examination of dead specimens. When Bentham began active service in 1916 this era came to an end and an injury to his shoulder in the war which prevented him from carrying heavy equipment put an end to his photography. (After the war Bentham married Richard's daughter Grace.)

In the period up to the First World War the grosser offences against the Wild Bird Protection Acts came to an end and field ornithology became established. Bentham became a regular contributor of notes to the new magazine *British Birds* (1907). Witherby's Marking (Bird Ringing) Scheme was launched in 1909 and in 1910 Howard Bentham and Clemence Acland were both ringing birds in Surrey.

In 1910 Eric Parker (1870-1955), the Surrey naturalist writer, moved from Weybridge to Hambledon. The garden of his new home, Feathercombe, he regarded as a bird sanctuary. Very rich in birdlife it was in those days. Forty years later Eric Parker was to write of the birds of the countryside which had gone from his garden. The general impoverishment of the Surrey countryside, particularly the loss of hedges for nesting birds, was something which recurs time and again in his writings.

Before the First World War Julian Huxley studied the courtship of the Great Crested Grebe at Frensham Great Pond. Although his published researches were made elsewhere, it may be that the idea of the interaction between the environment and social behaviour was first conceived at Frensham.

In 1913 the London Natural History Society was formed by the union of two Victorian societies, one, the North London Natural History Society previously operating within a radius 20 miles from St Paul's Cathedral north of the Thames. Immediately the new society took in the area within the same radius south of the Thames and so the London Natural History Society embraced a large part of Surrey. Although there were some ornithologists in the society, ornithology had not yet arrived; however the scene was set for the realization of considerable ornithological studies in Surrey in the 'London area'.

The modern trends which began in Surrey towards the end of the nineteenth century continued between the wars. London expanded another five miles or so into Surrey although a halt was called when the Green Belt became a reality in 1938 and the increase in motor traffic and the development of the stockbroker belt brought continued pressures to bear on the countryside. At the same time there were certain developments that were good from an ornithological standpoint—reservoirs, sewage farms and then gravel pits expanded rapidly to meet the needs of urbanization.

In 1921 the Rev W. W. Shaw produced a paper on the birds of the Haslemere district, one of the few proper accounts of birds in any part of Surrey in that period. In 1923 R. O. Blyth began recording birds in Surrey (he had started bird recording in 1899) and in that year he ringed a Whitethroat at Frensham which was to be the first overseas recovery of a Surrey bird (of any species). In 1970 he was still watching birds in Surrey and pointed out that he was by no means the senior member of the British Ornithologists' Union! In 1927 E. M. Nicholson pioneered common bird census studies with a census of a 40-acre plot near Haslemere.

In the 1920s Phyllis Bond who was voluntary assistant curator at Haslemere Museum for many years and also P. A. D. Hollom began bird watching in Surrey. P. A. D. Hollom focused attention on the ornithological importance of sewage farms early in the 1930s from his own watching at Brooklands SF where he was observing many 'unusual' waders.

In 1929 Clemence Acland returned to Surrey after an absence of nearly sixteen years and began lecturing on birds, mainly to schools. From then on, Surrey was to remain her base and she was still taking an active interest in the birds of the county in 1970.

In the 1930s the Ornithological Section of the London Natural History Society expanded rapidly and in 1936 the first *London Bird Report* (separate from the *London Naturalist*) was published. In the same year the society started an Ecology Section and we note that in the *London Naturalist* for 1936 C. L. Collenette made a plea for the preservation of bracken as bird cover in Richmond Park. Five years later the Ecology Section began a survey of Bookham Common which was still going strong in 1970. As a sustained amateur effort it is unique. Although the survey essentially involves team work, during most of the period a large amount of the ornithological work has been carried out by Dr Geoffrey Beven. This survey has made a considerable contribution to conservation thinking not only in the county but in the country.

H. F. Witherby lived in Surrey for a time during this period and maintained a bird sanctuary at Graciouspond Farm near Chobham. Visitors to the sanctuary were taken on a kind of nature trail and Howard Bentham recalls a visit to the sanctuary on 18 May 1935 when he was shown the nests of Woodlark, Little Owl and Tawny Owl.

Bird census work, sewage farm bird-watching, the bird report and the nature trail may belong to the modern world but in the 1930s the 'old' was not dead. One of the last of the great taxidermists, P. J. Mountjoy, re-organized and mounted the birds in the Charterhouse Museum during the mid-1930s. However most of the Stafford Collection had been destroyed about 1930 and in 1970 it was but a remnant, only the Baillon's Crake being with any degree of certainty one of the birds in the original collection.

Although egg-collecting had decreased somewhat after the First World War, it was still very much alive in the 1930s. While Eric Parker was editor of *The Field* in 1934 there was considerable correspondence in that paper on the subject and a correspondent made the point that the robbing of eggs by collectors was particularly noted in Surrey. Eric Parker himself was full of antipathy towards egg collectors. He was in fact an early conservationist of the 'first orthodoxy'.

Whatever the real effects of the Second World War on the birdlife of Surrey, Eric Parker was in no doubt. The Surrey War Agricultural Executive Committee was anathema to him. 'There are no birds in the fields today', he wrote after the war blaming the policies of this committee but prophesied that 'common sense will return, with (it) the sight and song of birds'.

Certainly bird-watchers proliferated after the Second World War although it was not until 1956 that Harold Dickinson succeeded in getting ornithologists together to form a county ornithological society. In 1957 the Surrey Bird Club was founded. There were several changes in major offices in the early years but the first president was Sir Norman Boyd Kinnear and the first vice-presidents—Phyllis Bond, Howard Bentham, Richard Homes and Guy Mountfort. Later Howard Bentham was to become president and Clemence Acland a vice-president. P. A. D. Hollom served on the Records Committee from the Club's inception and was still in office at the end of 1970. The first *Surrey Bird Report* had been published for the year 1953 on the initiative of Phyllis Bond supported by the Haslemere Natural History Society; it covered the area outside the LNHS range; however the reports for 1954 onwards recorded the whole of the vice-county (except for a tiny fraction of 'inner London'). The Surrey Bird Club took over publication of the number for 1957. The Surrey Bird Club (and the *Surrey Bird Report*) made steady but not spectacular progress over the years for many difficulties were encountered.

On 28 April 1968 Howard Bentham wrote in his diary, 'Cuckoo heard— three Swallows'. There is no entry for 29 April. Howard Bentham died that day. He was at his home in Tadworth only a few miles from his birth place. He left behind a record of birds in Surrey which will never be equalled. Many of his notes have been published and he extended the frontiers of ornithological knowledge both for Surrey and the country as a whole. These notes include observations of birds rare in Surrey, of the Dartford Warbler and Stonechat and of various phenomena including early and late nesting, autumn singing, mimicry and unusually large clutches. It is strange to note though that he often considered birds in territory as 'too numerous to count' and one wonders why he did not take a transect. Species he observed sunbathing include the Grey Wagtail, Turtle Dove and Barn Owl, a testimony to his watchfulness and patience. He entered up his diaries with meticulous attention to detail and he was ever scrupulous, not being afraid to correct an entry (as happened only rarely, mostly in the early days) if the need arose. As an ornithologist of Surrey, Howard Bentham was peerless. It was known that he had written a book on the birds of Surrey but on his death the manuscript could not be traced.

P. Bruce Lowe, an active and founder member of the Surrey Bird Club became its president on Howard Bentham's death and by this time the Club was well fulfilling its functions as a county ornithological organization.

Finally we may ask how much progress there has been in Surrey over the past 150 years in attitudes and actions towards birds? In fact it was just as legal to shoot a wintering Jack Snipe in Surrey in 1970 as it was when Son of the Marshes described the beginner's target of the mid-nineteenth century when the species was much more plentiful. Taking of birds for aviculture (and some Surrey local fanciers' clubs show British birds) was legal if under Home Office licence (but no figures from the Home Office could be supplied). However to a very large extent birds in Surrey are protected by the Wild Bird Protection Acts and as far as abuses of these acts are concerned, Surrey is probably no worse and most likely rather better than the run of counties in Britain. Certainly when pole trap cases were being investigated at the end of the review period, there being some in all the neighbouring counties, as far as could be ascertained, Surrey was without stain. It is thought unlikely that there is much illegal trapping and although egg-collecting does still exist in the county it is not practised to any great extent and the southern counties' zoologists' ring is reported to have broken up. Nevertheless even a little after the end of the review period the Tawny Owls' nest box on the RSPB bird reserve at Barfold Copse was robbed and in European Conservation Year (1970) a Hobby was shot in Surrey.

The Surrey Bird Club is increasingly concerned with conservation and is working in close cooperation with the Surrey Naturalists' Trust. Nonetheless in European Conservation Year there was only one bird reserve as such in the county—15 acres of Barfold Copse—together with a few areas named bird sanctuary such as Selsdon Wood and a few privately owned nature reserves. There were no national or local nature reserves set up under the National Parks and Access to the Countryside Act, 1949.

However the increasing strength of the Surrey Bird Club, the Surrey Naturalists' Trust and the RSPB in Surrey is a sign that we can expect increasing pressure directed towards the preservation of specialized bird habitats and that conservation policies, caring and creative, will increasingly be pursued.

The writer is aware that very many people who have contributed to the ornithology of Surrey have not been mentioned in this chapter. The inclusion or otherwise of names rests arbitrarily on the story as here presented. The writer is grateful to all those, including officials of the RSPCA and RSPB, who have supplied information for this chapter.

The Geology
of Surrey

R. H. B. Forster

Surrey owes much of the variety of its scenery and its natural history to its geology.

Part of the county lies in the Weald which is a classic example of the effects of denudation, but the dominant feature in the architecture arises from the belt of chalk, about 1,000 feet thick, which covers the whole of the northern part of the county, though it is overlaid by other formations in the extreme north. The southern edge of the chalk forms an impressive scarp running from east to west across Surrey.

The south of England has been subject to a series of rises and falls in level so that for long periods it has been below the sea and at other times it has been dry land. In the Cretaceous period Surrey lay at the bottom of a great inland sea stretching from Scotland to Russia and the purity of the chalk that was laid down during the later stages indicates that few rivers flowed into the sea so the surrounding country was probably desert. At the end of this period Europe and Asia were convulsed by great earth movements; the Alps were formed and the chalk, in what is now the Weald, was raised in a great dome which, in the region of Crawley, may have been about 2,500 feet above the present sea level. A rise in water level probably protected the lower parts of the chalk to the north and south of the Weald but the central dome was severely eroded so that the softer formations were exposed. During this period the London Clay and associated formations were laid down.

A drop in the level of the sea was followed by another rise in water level. There was still enough of the dome left to form an island and traces of the sea shore line can be seen in the deposits of sand and gravel on the 600-foot contour at Headley and Netley.

As the sea dropped again, long ages of heavy rainfall caused rapid denudation of the softer parts of the Weald. Enormous masses of rock were carried away by the ancestors of the Rivers Mole, Medway and Wey in the north and by the Arun, Adur and Ouse in the south. The depression that has been left, which lies between the North and South Downs, is designated the Weald. The word 'Weald' is derived from Anglo-Saxon and means forest but it is also applied to other forms of wild, uncultivated country. In the particular case of the tract of country embracing parts of

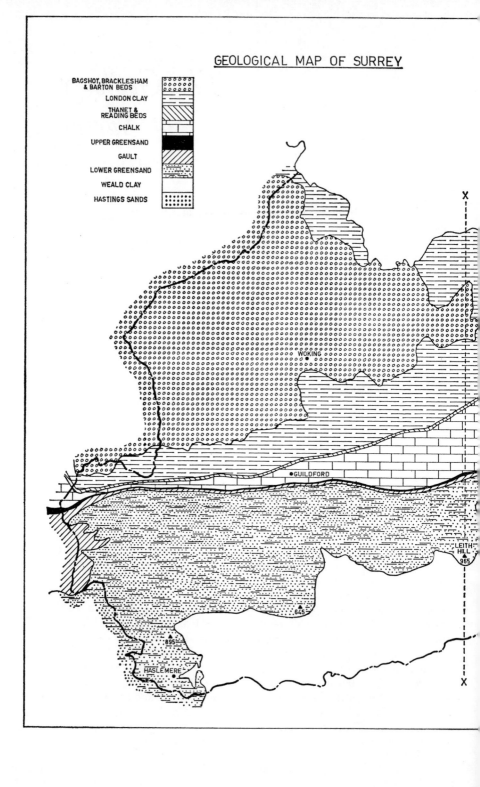

GEOLOGICAL MAP OF SURREY

BAGSHOT, BRACKLESHAM & BARTON BEDS

LONDON CLAY

THANET & READING BEDS

CHALK

UPPER GREENSAND

GAULT

LOWER GREENSAND

WEALD CLAY

HASTINGS SANDS

WOKING

GUILDFORD

LEITH HILL ▲965

▲645

▲895

HASLEMERE

X

X

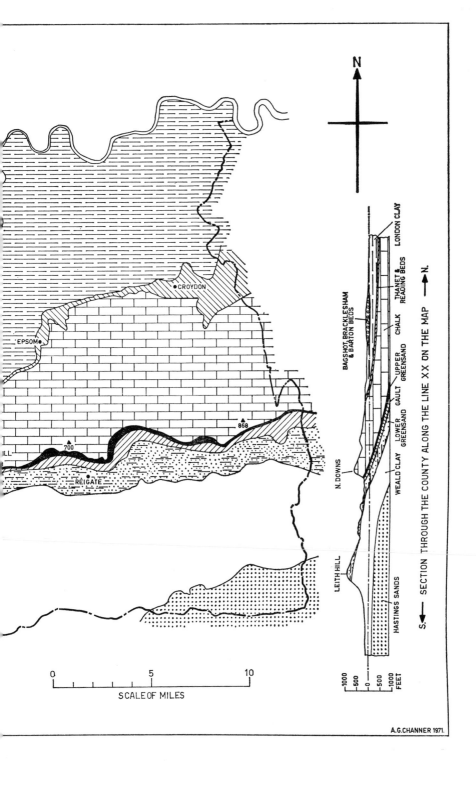

N

CROYDON

EPSOM

700

868

REIGATE

N. DOWNS

LEITH HILL

SCALE OF MILES

0   5   10

BAGSHOT BRACKLESHAM
& BARTON BEDS

LONDON CLAY

THANET &
READING BEDS

CHALK

UPPER
GREENSAND

GAULT

LOWER
GREENSAND

WEALD CLAY

HASTINGS SANDS

1000
500
0
500
1000
FEET

S. — SECTION THROUGH THE COUNTY ALONG THE LINE XX ON THE MAP — N.

A.G. CHANNER 1971.

Surrey, Sussex and Kent, the region was known as Andredsweald or the Forest of Anderida. This was a wild, terrifying area with dense, impenetrable forest which made it one of the last regions of the south of England to be subdued by man.

In the remainder of this chapter the various rocks exposed in the county are discussed and they are dealt with in the order in which they were formed, starting at the oldest which were laid down some hundred and fifty million years ago. Readers are also referred to the map on pages 28-9 showing diagrammatically the distribution of strata over the county.

Hastings Sands

This is represented by the Tunbridge Wells Sands in Surrey and covers only a small corner of the county in the south-east around Felbridge.

Where this formation is high and well drained, as at St Leonard's Forest in Sussex, it forms heathland but where it occurs in Surrey it is generally low lying. It is sufficiently retentive of moisture to hold ponds as at Wire Mill and Hedgecourt which are surrounded by typical damp oakwoods and the very fertile agricultural land around Lingfield.

Weald Clay

This formation in the south of the county outcrops about a quarter of the county's surface. It extends from the eastern boundary of the county in the Crowhurst area to Haslemere in the west. The texture of the soil is nearer to sand than clay but it is almost completely impermeable to water.

The natural climax vegetation on this base is damp oakwood, dominated by the Pedunculate Oak (*Quercus robur*) often in association with Silver birch (*Betula pendula*), Alder (*Alnus glutinosa*) and other species. There is frequently a shrub layer of Hazel (*Corylus avellana*) which was until recently coppiced regularly.

The Lower Greensand

There are four divisions in this series. These are, in order of age, the Atherfield Clay being the oldest, as follows:
  1. Folkestone Sands
  2. Sandgate Beds
  3. Hythe Beds
  4. Atherfield Clay

Folkestone Sands

These consist of about two-thirds fairly coarse sands and the formation stretches across the whole length of the county. A large part of the outcrop is covered by heathland as at Limpsfield, Reigate Heath, St Martha's Hill, the Thursley group of commons, Crooksbury, Farnham and Frensham.

Sand extraction is a valuable industry and some of the deposits in the east are of national importance as they consist of very pure silver sand which is used in the manufacture of refractories and glass. Elsewhere the quality deteriorates to that of a poor building sand. The chain of sandpits associated with this outcrop accommodates large colonies of Sand Martins. These are dependent on the existence of an almost vertical cliff face in to which they can tunnel. Collapse of a cliff face is liable to occur with weathering so the colonies are usually confined to pits actually in production where new vertical faces are constantly being created. There is some evidence to suggest that the higher grade silica sand faces are most resistant to collapse.

From the natural history point of view it is fortunate that the Folkestone Beds do not lend themselves readily to farming and that vast areas have been permitted to remain as heath. On this very porous formation there is a tendency for the soil to become what is known as a podsol. Downward washing removes the humus and clay from the upper layers and carries them below, where they may be reformed into a hard impermeable layer. We can thus have the apparent anomaly of a permeable surface layer becoming water-logged or marshy.

Sandgate Beds

These vary greatly in character throughout Surrey. East of Redhill they contain important deposits of Fuller's earth. Further west they change, first to loamy sands with little stone and later to coarse calcareous sandstone known as Bargate Stone. The soil associated with the latter is highly fertile and yields a rich flora and fauna. This section lies west of Dorking. It is good arable land and much of it has survived against economic pressures leading to a swing to pasture which has been the fate of much of the poorer soils. Further west the character of the land changes again and the deposits are known as Puttenham Beds. Part of Thursley Common and adjoining woodland lies on the Puttenham Beds.

Hythe Beds

These attain great importance in the west of Surrey since they form the dominant heights of Leith Hill, Holmbury, Coneyhurst and Hindhead. In parts of Kent the rock contains lime and when it breaks down it forms a deep loamy soil which is of great value for the production of fruit and hops. However, the remainder of the beds in Kent and those in Surrey are non-calcareous and give rise to woodland and heath. In travelling westwards across the county this formation first becomes prominent south west of Dorking and rises to the summit of Leith Hill. The area has now largely become woodland but vestiges of the original heathland still remain.

Atherfield Clay

This is a fairly insignificant narrow outcrop which differs little from the Weald Clay which it surmounts. It runs from east to west across the county, skirting the south of Redhill, Reigate, Dorking and Leith Hill.

Gault

Gault is an impervious belt of stiff blue-grey clay which was formerly largely rough pasture but since the Second World War much of it has been cultivated. The lake at Gatton Park was formed by damming a stream as it traversed the Gault outcrop. The lake is fed by a clear chalk stream so that very little silting takes place. The Gault outcrop is characterized by the complete absence of beech which cannot exist on the heavy, badly drained soil. Since the Gault is in close proximity to the Chalk scarp face, which supports many magnificent beeches, the contrast is very marked.

Upper Greensand

In many places this forms a horizontal shelf at the foot of the Chalk scarp. The composition of this sandy limestone or malmstone varies and in some districts the presence of glauconite is indicated by a greenish colouring. The soil is characterized by having relatively few trees and by being light and readily ploughed. The average thickness of the Upper Greensand is about 50 feet but in many places downwash from the Chalk scarp lies thickly on the top of the Upper Greensand and its true character is hidden.

Chalk/Clay-with-Flints

From the eastern boundary of the county to Reigate the chalk band varies from five to eight miles in width. Thereafter, running westwards, it tapers away and, between Guildford and Farnham, the Hog's Back outcrop is less than a mile wide.

Until about 2000 B.C. all the chalk was probably covered by forest but this was gradually destroyed, culminating in the Middle Ages, in almost complete clearance which persisted throughout the great period of sheep farming. With the disappearance of sheep and the reduction in numbers of rabbits, grazing control has almost ceased and a rapid growth of scrub is taking place.

On the steep southern facing scarp of the North Downs, cover is thin and a true chalkland succession prevails with hawthorn (*Crataegus spp.*), Buckthorn (*Rhamnus catharticus*), and Blackthorn (*Prunus spinosa*) widespread and local occurrences of Yew (*Taxus baccata*), Box (*Buxus sempervirems*) and Juniper (*Juniperus communis*). In places oak may occur but it cannot develop fully in shallow soil so that it is likely to be superseded by a climax of closed canopy beechwood. In these circumstances most of the undergrowth will be shaded out or starved because the roots of the beech run horizontally close to the surface.

On the northern dip-slope where the surface is fairly level, a considerable part of the chalk is covered with Clay-with-Flints reaching 30 feet or more in thickness and enabling oak to flourish. The farms in this area are largely arable in spite of the heavy soil and the presence of many stones.

The term Clay-with-Flints embraces products of degradation of a wide range of formations. The earliest appears to be composed of the insoluble

6 (top) *Beechwood*, on chalk, Box Hill (*D. M. T. Ettlinger*)
7 (bottom) *Oakwood*, on clay, Bookham Common (*D. M. T. Ettlinger*)

residue from the break-down of chalk and this may have started some seventy million years ago. The flint nodules in this case are broken but unworn. The process was suspended while later deposits such as the London Clay were being laid down but it was resumed with the destruction and redistribution of series later than the Chalk. In these cases the flints have been worn down into small, rounded pebbles. Where the slope is appreciable, erosion has resulted in removal of the clay and the chalk lies just below the topsoil. Here the vegetation is similar to that on the southern facing scarp. At the northern extremity of this chalk strip, the chalk dips below the Thanet and the Reading Beds which form a narrow outcrop. These beds in turn pass under the impervious London Clay.

The permeable Chalk forms a vast sponge and holds enormous quantities of water which at one time overflowed in considerable volume from springs. It was this ready water supply that resulted in the chain of villages following the junction line and stretching from Croydon to Guildford. The reduction of water-level on both north and south faces in ancient times, is very apparent from the numerous dried river beds which form re-entrants. This trend was primarily due to the erosion of the impervious Gault on the south face of the Downs but in recent times the creation of artesian wells has resulted in a large proportion of the water being diverted and has further accentuated the lowering of the water table. In consequence many springs have ceased to exist but at Carshalton the River Wandle takes its source from such a spring and the River Hogsmill is supplied in part from a spring at Ewell. The spring at Fetcham Mill pond was capped and sealed from the ponds within the last decade and now supplies water direct to the waterworks at Leatherhead. On the southern scarp, springs feed the Medway via the River Eden and the water issuing at the Silent Pool near Shere passes to the Tillingbourne Stream.

Thanet and Reading Beds

These formations mark the start of the Tertiary period. The Thanet Beds are composed of fine-grained sands and the Reading Beds consist of sand, clay and occasional pebble beds. In the area under discussion they generally outcrop in a very narrow belt marking the eruption of the springs which were mentioned above. There are a few outliers, notably at the Nower and Cherkley woods near Headley, which are of interest both geologically and botanically.

London Clay

This extensive formation has a full thickness of 300-400 feet. However the erosion which completely removed this clay from the upper part of the Chalk dip-slope has also thinned the clay further down the slope.

In the north-east of Surrey the London Clay has been almost completely covered by the suburbs of London but outside this area it supports pasture, commonland and woodland. The hedges are characterized by a predomin-

8 (top) *Guildford Sewage Farm.* Open settling beds, particularly attractive to waders on passage are becoming fewer as farms are modernised. (*D. M. T. Ettlinger*)

9 (bottom) *Abinger Watercress Beds.* A less common type of acquatic habitat, which attracts a variety of species. (*D. M. T. Ettlinger*)

ance of English Elm (*Ulmus procera*). The clay itself when exposed to air becomes brownish red due to the formation of iron oxides but when it is covered a reducing action sets in and the clay reverts to a blue-grey colour.

From the natural history point of view a number of important areas such as Ashstead, Bookham, Epsom and Effingham Commons and the Prince's Coverts, Oxshott, lie on this formation.

Bagshot, Bracklesham and Barton Beds

This series forms a huge block covering most of the north-west of the county. The Bagshot Beds are about 80 feet in thickness and are composed of fine quartzose sand with local pebble beds, giving rise to light dry soils which are rendered fertile only with great difficulty. The commons at Esher, Oxshott, Ockham and Wisley lie on this deposit and the vegetation is typically heathland with heavy penetration of birch and pine. The Bracklesham Beds are of laminated clay and sand. They give heathland at Pirbright, Stanford Common, Cobbett Hill and Chobham. The Barton Beds consist mainly of sand. They lie between Aldershot and Chobham. Parts of Chobham Common and Bagshot Heath lie on this formation.

Netley Heath Deposits

These are of mixed gravel and sand. They occur at about the 600-foot contour of the North Downs and have been much disturbed by weathering. Their origin has given rise to several theories but it is now generally agreed that they mark the shore line of a sea which surrounded an island rising some thousands of feet above the area now occupied by the Weald. The soil associated with most sandy deposits is acid and this is also true of the Netley Heath Deposits. The basic constituents have been washed out of the soil by the rain water which is itself slightly acidic. In consequence heathland vegetation is usually dominant. This is particularly apparent at Headley and Walton Heaths. Much of the area on these deposits is now wooded, large tracts being given over to forestry and planted mainly with conifers.

River Gravel

Most of the rivers in the county are associated with a flood plain and particularly so are the Rivers Blackwater, Thames and Wey. These deposits are extensively exploited by commercial firms and huge quantities of sand and gravel are extracted annually. As old pits are exhausted many are filled in or used for recreational purposes but new ones continually take their place and form an important natural history habitat for plants and animals. The most important groups of pits occur near Ash Vale on the Blackwater, at Thorpe on the Thames and at Send (Papercourt) on the Wey.

The Reservoirs
and other Waters

P. Bruce Lowe

The vice-county of Surrey covers some 485,000 acres of which about 1,000 are under water. Almost all of the waters were created artificially. The most important both in size and for the birds they attract are the reservoirs in the Thames Valley. There are also the lakes and pools some of which date from the Mediaeval Wealden Iron Industry and perhaps from Roman times. The Frensham Ponds are former monastic stews owned by the Bishops of Winchester and the Pudmore Ponds on Thursley Common are now considered to have originated as peat diggings. Some of the more recent owe their existence to the imitators of 'Capability' Brown and fly-fishermen. The remaining group consists of the gravel and sand pits which have been opened and closed in some cases, since the building boom of the post war years.

The reservoirs of the county are Barn Elms at Hammersmith and the Walton Group which consists of Chelsea and Lambeth, Knight and Bessborough, Queen Elizabeth II and Island Barn. These reservoirs cannot however be satisfactorily divorced from those nearby in south Middlesex and in Essex. Readers are referred to the chapter 'The Reservoirs and Other Large Waters' by R. C. Homes in *The Birds of the London Area* (1957) for a complete history of the London reservoirs.

Permits are issued by the Metropolitan Water Board to members of recognized ornithological societies to visit all reservoirs which are regularly manned. Since the Second World War bird-watchers, together with anglers, have taken increasing advantage of the opportunities lying on their doorstep. The interests of both wildfowl and humans have proved compatible, as most of the duck quickly become used to watchers and anglers and rarely move far when they appear. Thus permit-holders have unique opportunities to study some of the 'difficult' species at close quarters.

The table below gives the dates when the reservoirs in Surrey were inaugurated along with their acreage and depth. The Walton Group of Reservoirs is also depicted on the map overleaf and in the plate facing p.480

A series of small reservoirs alongside the Thames at Lonsdale Road, Barnes were also in use in 1900. These have been sold by the Metropolitan Water Board within the last few years and ceased to be used as reservoirs. One

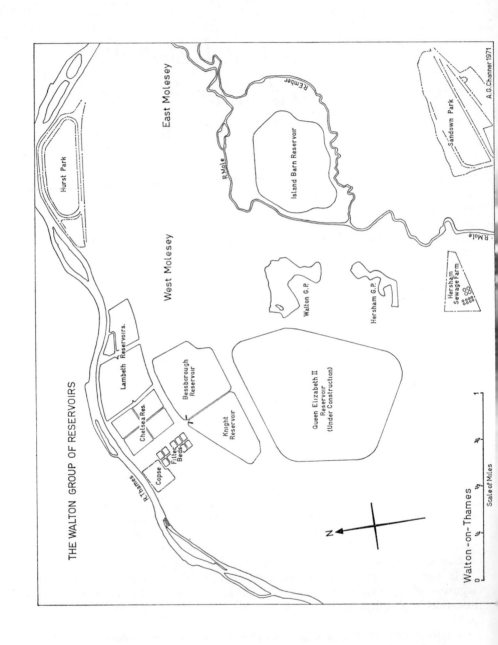

THE WALTON GROUP OF RESERVOIRS

Hurst Park

East Molesey

R.Mole

R.Ember

Island Barn Reservoir

Sandown Park

West Molesey

Lambeth Reservoirs.

Chelsea Res.

Bessborough Reservoir

Walton G.P.

Hersham G.P.

R.Mole

Copse

Filter Beds

Knight Reservoir

Queen Elizabeth II Reservoir (Under Construction)

Hersham Sewage Farm

R.Thames

A.G.Channer 1971

N

Walton-on-Thames

0   ¼   ½   ¾   1

Scale of Miles

Reservoir	Inauguration	Area-acres	depth-feet	
Lambeth (Walton)	1874/1903	72	20/24	(a)
Chelsea (Walton) (four reservoirs)	1877	40	20	(a)
Barn Elms (Barnes)	1896/97	87	14	(a)(c)
Knight and Bessborough (Walton)	1907	52+74	38	(a)(c)
Island Barn (Walton)	1911	121	27	(b)
Queen Elizabeth II (Walton)	1962	317	57·5	(b)

(a) vertical sides   (b) sloping sides
(c) the sides here also incorporate a shelf at water level which is attractive to waders.

Note: Total acreage in 1900—c. 160
         ...   ...   1914— 415
         ...   ...   1970— 763

however still held water in 1970 and supported a wide variety of wildlife including breeding Great Crested Grebes.

Queen Elizabeth II is the largest sheet of water in the county at the time of writing and has been completed for less than a decade. Its construction and establishment demonstrates the importance of a gravel-pit type of habitat and also affords a unique opportunity to trace the development of a biotope. It is therefore described at length and in some detail.

Construction began before the Second World War and had to be suspended in 1939 when the clay 'puddle' had been completed to ground level. At this stage five different diggings had been started and two working gravel pits were in operation on the eastern edge. The two in the centre of the site were deep as the clay used by the contractors came from them but three others were shallow and at times almost dry.

The whole area, then known as the Walton Gravel Pits, provided some 78 acres of varied wetland throughout the 1940s and 1950s. Several pairs of Little Grebe, Lapwing, Snipe, Redshank, Yellow Wagtail and Reed Bunting bred regularly in spite of farming activity and in the autumn the pits were visited by many migrants. Smew regularly visited the pits in winter.

In 1948 the London Natural History Society decided to study the bird populations of four selected groups of gravel workings and the Walton pits were one of the selected sites. K. P. Keywood led a team which carried out the survey the results of which were published in a paper in the *LBR* (Keywood and Melluish, 1953) and the enrichment of birdlife in this type of habitat emerged very clearly.

When construction of the reservoir was resumed in the late 1950s water was pumped out of the pits into brooks running into the Mole and 30 or more acres of shallow pits were exposed. The area was quickly colonized by Little Ringed Plovers and five pairs were present in 1957, although breeding success was low due to disturbance by machinery. From 1958 to 1961 the reservoir site provided a breeding habitat for Lapwing, Redshank and Sand Martins, as well as for Little Ringed Plover and many migrant waders were recorded here.

The winters of 1960/61 and 1961/62 brought interesting changes, as water was allowed to collect in areas on the half completed floor of the reservoir and a gull roost built up under the lee of the west bank, particularly on stormy nights, when tens of thousands of birds, which probably roosted on neighbouring reservoirs in normal weather, took advantage of the new shelter. Dabbling duck were also attracted, particularly Teal and Wigeon, numbers of both species rising to about 200 in February 1962.

When the reservoir was opened in April 1962 the modern high-pressure pumping machinery was not ready and for the purposes of the ceremony, a large volume of water had to be transferred from Knight and Bessborough, rather than direct from the river. This meant that some of the life from these established biotopes was transferred and in consequence, for example, Great Crested Grebes were observed catching fish up to four inches long the following autumn.

Mallard and Teal were quick to exploit the new water and numbers rose quickly. Shoveler appeared in small but growing numbers. By the mid-1960s Mallard concentrations were at times approaching the 500 mark and the normal wintering flock of 400 or so Teal which had previously been centred on Island Barn appeared to divide its time between that reservoir and the new one. Shoveler numbers rose steadily and by 1964 the maximum had reached 70. By 1965/66 the flock was holding together till well into the New Year and beginning to reappear in July. The first count over 100 was on 10 September 1967 when 175 were present and further increases in the following seasons brought peaks approaching the 300 mark. So in less than a decade the new water had become a major wildfowl refuge.

Numbers of wildfowl wintering on the reservoir fluctuate from one month to the next but at the end of the review period between 200-350 Mallard might have been expected normally in mid-winter, with 80-200 Teal, up to 40 Wigeon and, according to the level of the water, as many as 60 Tufted Duck with a smaller number of Pochard, possibly three or four Goldeneye and 40-50 Cormorants.

Queen Elizabeth II is the Board's deepest reservoir and the last to freeze over in hard weather. During the winter of 1962/63, one of the severest winters on record, Queen Elizabeth II was in full operation and the 'last stand' was made there; an ice-free pool about 500 feet wide was maintained near the outfall valve at the north-east corner. Peak numbers were present on 13 January when the reservoir held an estimated 300-500 Great Crested Grebe, 3,100 Tufted Duck and 2,370 Pochard. A few days later the MWB called in contractors to clear the ice from Knight and Bessborough and some hundreds of tons were removed in blocks a foot thick. This greatly relieved the pressure on the birds on Queen Elizabeth II and much of the refugee flock moved across. Over 850 Goosanders were counted as they flew into roost on Queen Elizabeth II on 27 January and seven Bean Geese were present there from 21 to 26 January.

Another feature of this water is the development of the winter gull roost. Already in 1962/63 enormous numbers of gulls, mainly Black-headed, had begun to use the reservoir for roosting. Counts made in 1963 and in the winter of 1967/68 showed that normal roosting numbers were in the range of 50,000-100,000 birds and there was evidence that in abnormal weather conditions numbers approached a quarter of a million. The reservoirs had become almost overnight one of the largest gull roosts in the London area and anyone who cares to take up a position in the Hersham Road at East Molesey an hour before dusk any evening in January will see several hundred gulls pouring over the top of the bank every minute till well after dark.

During the 1950s there was a growing tendency for Cormorants to flock at the Walton Reservoirs before dispersing in spring and after Queen Elizabeth II came into use they began to rest on its towers, particularly the one near the south-west corner. Throughout the day single birds can be seen arriving from the north and north-east, presumably having fed as very few alight on the water. The record number was c. 130 on 28 January 1968.

The older sections of the Walton Reservoirs have always been attractive to the diving ducks. The middle part of the Chelsea and Lambeth has a submerged causeway seven or eight feet below the surface level which supports large numbers of fresh-water molluscs and attracts the diving species, particularly Goldeneye. Since the early 1960s a flock built up here from under 20 to nearly 50. These sections also carry the majority of the Great Crested Grebe in the area and some of the rarer grebes are not infrequently reported.

In the earlier years of this century a number of Smew, sometimes in excess of 100, were recorded at Chelsea and Lambeth but since the mid-1950s the species has largely deserted the Walton Reservoirs.

Until the milder winters of the 1960s Knight with Bessborough was an important Goosander roost and during the 1950s over 100 of these birds were often present by evening in January and February. There is also a flock of Wigeon from November onwards which spends much of its time grazing on the tops of the banks. Sometimes the overall total is between 40 and 50.

Until Queen Elizabeth II was filled, Bessborough was a much favoured Great Black-backed Gull roost, probably the largest to the west of London and some birds still roost or collect there before moving over to the new site at Queen Elizabeth II. Knight and Bessborough were also the deepest of the older Walton Reservoirs and unusual numbers of waterfowl had collected there in such winters as 1937/38, 1946/47 and 1955/56. During January and February 1956 there were two extremely severe cold spells when a closely packed raft of Tufted Duck, Pochard, Goosander and grebes kept an open patch of a few hundred square yards in the middle of Bessborough. Total numbers were estimated at between 5,000 and 10,000 and rarities included 24 Red-breasted Mergansers, both Common and Velvet Scoter and a Ferruginous Duck.

Island Barn Reservoir with its secluded position and sloping sides has been the main haunt of wintering Teal for many years although as already noted they now spend some of their time on the newer reservoir. Island Barn also supports varying numbers of wintering Tufted Duck, Coot and Great Crested Grebe and after the turn of the year a small number of Goosander and Goldeneye. During the late 1960s Black-necked Grebe have been recorded on passage and in small wintering numbers, as well as occasional Slavonian and Red-necked Grebes. At the end of the review period however, preparations were being made for sailing here and the effect of this on its wintering wildfowl will be anxiously studied.

Barn Elms is the most easterly of the reservoirs and it attracts flocks of duck as they come up the Thames, especially the diving species. The shallow water is very attractive to Pochard. Smew now appear there oftener than anywhere else in Surrey and it is the main Surrey breeding site for Gadwall. A sizeable winter flock of Gadwall often in excess of 50 is usually present at this reservoir.

The increasing pressures should be mentioned, for the use of these waters which up to now have been relatively undisturbed wildfowl refuges, for recreational purposes, particularly sailing. The threat to Island Barn, which has already been mentioned, is a warning. In an attempt to meet these demands with constructive proposals, the Nature Conservancy has classified the 300 reservoirs where Wildfowl Counts have been made in the last 10-15 years.

The reservoirs of Surrey have been assigned to the two following classes:

> *Class* 1 (sites of national importance holding an appreciable proportion of the north European or British population of one or more species)
> Barn Elms
> Walton Reservoirs (Knight & Bessborough, Chelsea & Lambeth)
> *Class* 3 (sites of local importance holding populations of 250-1,000 wildfowl)
> Queen Elizabeth II
> Island Barn

Class 1 sites are considered to deserve special consideration and extensive areas of them ought to be set aside as wildfowl refuges. At least one class 3 site ought to be set aside in any one locality as a refuge. As Island Barn is to be used for sailing, it was recommended that Queen Elizabeth II should be kept as a refuge (Hammond, 1968).

All sections of the Walton Group and Barn Elms are regarded of great importance by the Wildfowl Trust and they call for priority counts from them every four weeks from September to March.

Away from the reservoirs the ornamental pools and small lakes of the south London parks provide alternative water surfaces in and on the suburban edge of London. Common species such as Mallard, Moorhen and occasionally Tufted Duck breed on these and in hard weather and at migration times some unexpected records occur. This is particularly true of Pen Ponds in Richmond Park. At one time Goosander wintered here regularly and after an absence of some 20 years a flock returned for several weeks in the 1970/71 winter.

A group of waters in the centre of the county near Cobham deserve some mention. A shallow but good-sized ornamental lake in private woodland at Painshill Park supports a good breeding population including Mandarin Duck, Canada Geese, occasionally Tufted Duck and grebes and rails. Silvermere, barely a mile to the north west has a good growth of *Phragmites* and a small Reed Warbler colony and Mandarin regularly use this water. Boldermere, alongside the A3 at Wisley, is now too heavily disturbed at weekends but Great Crested Grebes were still breeding in the 1960s and the pool was regularly visited by Canada Geese.

The most important lake in the north-west of the county is Virginia Water, half of which lies in Surrey. A large colony of Mandarin Duck established itself on this water by the 1930s and a heronry has been established at the lakeside for very many years. In 1948 it moved to nearby Fort Belvedere on the Surrey border where it has flourished ever since. The lake also supports several hundred wintering Mallard and smaller numbers of Shoveler, Pochard and Tufted Duck. It also provides occasional records of the rarer species including Goldeneye and Goosander. Smew were regularly recorded in the 1950s but there have been no records of the species since 1963 (South, 1971).

Apart from the gravel pits at Send and at Thorpe, near Chertsey, all the other waters of any size lie south of the North Downs. Early in the period under review observers, in particular Howard Bentham, had many interesting records from the ponds in the eastern corner of the county at Hedgecourt and Wire Mill and Frensham in the far west. The ponds at Frensham have indeed been one of the most important ornithological sites in the county, producing a large proportion of rarities. The birdlife of the ponds has been well chronicled by Bentham, Mr and Mrs L. S. V. Venables and ornithologists associated with the Haslemere Museum. Since the Second World War disturbance and public pressure have increased, at all these places (Hedgecourt and Wire Mill as well as Frensham) and their value has declined, although no doubt the alternative attraction of the 'second generation' London reservoirs, the newly created gravel pits and the reservoir at Weir Wood in Sussex have all had their effect.

Gatton Park Lake has always been attractive to wildfowl and it was one of the first places where Canada Geese bred regularly in Surrey but the colony thrived so well that control measures had to be taken and breeding ceased entirely when the military authorities took over the park in the Second World War. Nesting was not resumed for over 20 years. The duck position has been confused in recent years by the release of hand-reared birds by shooting interests.

Vachery Pond was formerly a very important water but information from this site has been limited in recent times. However during the 1960s it has held a steadily growing winter flock of Canada Geese and as many as 100 have been seen flying round the district during the last year or two.

Vann Lake at Ockley is being carefully built up as a private nature reserve by G. B. Blaker. The ponds at Bury Hill and Westcott near Dorking and Fetcham hold small wintering populations of wildfowl, the latter being well known for its grebe and wintering Water Rails, particularly before the adjoining cress beds were filled in.

Broadwater in the Wey Valley south of Guildford supports a winter flock of Mallard and small numbers of Pochard while breeding birds include Great Crested Grebe and Tufted Duck. The ponds at Winkworth have breeding Canada Geese, Mallard, Tufted Duck and Little Grebe and at Enton the ponds carry sizeable winter flocks of surface feeders, large numbers of Canada Geese and occasionally the rarer swans. Waterloo Ponds on the Tillingbourne have an attendant flock of Mallard and a small *Phragmites* marsh adjoining the ponds sometimes holds Reed Warblers.

The small ponds on the Western heaths are on greensand and peat so they are too acid to carry an abundant food supply but they attract small parties of wildfowl, especially Teal, in winter and a few breeding species. Since the Second World War, Teal have nested on the morass at Pudmore and Tufted Duck and Great Crested Grebe have nested on some of the ponds at Thursley and Cutt Mill, this latter site has also held Mandarin and provided a recent breeding record of Wood Duck.

The gravel pits must next be considered. They offer useful but usually temporary habitats for numbers of breeding and migrating birds. Some of the gravel pits in Surrey described in *The Birds of the London Area* have already been filled in. One group which was developed in the late 1950s at Thorpe, will be severely affected by the M3 Motorway and subsequent developments. This will be regrettable in the extreme as in 1969 and 1970 it was the principal breeding station of the Great Crested Grebe in the county and Pochard nested there twice in the mid-1960s.

Worked-out gravel pits at Papercourt (Send) have been landscaped and are used for dinghy-sailing but remain attractive to several species. Wigeon and Pochard have occurred in winter joining the Mallard, Tufted Duck, grebe and Coot which are regularly present. Reed and Sedge Warblers have colonized the lakeside vegetation that has grown up in recent years.

In the Redhill/Oxted district there is an important group of diggings consisting of the sand and gravel pits at Holmethorpe and the Fuller's Earth Union company's pit at Nutfield. Fortunately it seems likely that conservation measures will be taken at some of these pits and at another which is privately owned at Buckland, just outside Reigate. If these waters become refuges in addition to that at the Surrey Naturalists' Trust's small reserve at Godstone, there will be great benefit to many species which will increasingly need cover in which they can breed and from which they can maintain their populations, in this part of the county.

Finally there is an important group of pits in the Blackwater Valley on the extreme western boundary of the county. It includes those at Frimley, Mytchett, North Camp, Aldershot and Ash Vale. Many migrant species have been recorded there in the last years of the review period and breeding species include both Sedge and Reed Warbler, Great Crested and Little Grebe, Canada Goose, Tufted Duck and Little Ringed Plover. Attempts by the Surrey Bird Club and the Surrey Naturalists' Trust to establish an aquatic reserve in this area, however, have so far met with no success.

The Surrey Commercial Docks at Bermondsey in the extreme north-east corner of the vice-county provided some interesting records in the early years of the century. In 1970 they were closed to shipping and at the time of writing were attracting large numbers of duck, particularly Tufted and Pochard and in the autumn and early winter of 1970/71 Shelduck and Scaup had also been recorded there (Grant, 1971).

There remain a number of smaller waters scattered throughout the county which might well, with further investigation, provide interesting records. The Mandarin Duck will, for instance, tolerate very small ponds and watchers should also be on the look-out for its near 'cousin', the Wood (Carolina) Duck, which seems at the time of writing, poised for further expansion in Surrey.

Marshes, Rivers and Sewage Farms

J. J. Wheatley

The river systems make an important contribution to the bird life of the county. Their valleys contain a good deal of damp woodland, rough pasture and marsh and these features often combine to produce a rich mixture of habitat with a correspondingly wide variety of breeding birds within a small area. The bird community of the better parts of these valleys is distinct in balance and composition from that of other watery places, such as the wet acid heaths of the western districts, the sewage farms and the lakes though of course all have, as the commoner birds go, much in common with each other and the county as a whole.

The two largest rivers are the Mole and the Wey. Both are virtually wholly within the county, meandering across from opposite ends of its southern border through, in places, broad flood-plains. Each cuts a deep gap in the North Downs—the Mole at Dorking and the Wey at Guildford —and they reach the Thames within a few miles of one another at Molesey and Weybridge. They are attractive rivers, free of any serious pollution, and the main marshes lie in their valleys.

The catchment area of the Wey includes virtually all the heaths, commons and ponds in the western half of the county. It is a sluggish, rather muddy river under normal conditions, the passage of the water being slowed by many locks and weirs and it is extensively paralleled by canals. In earlier days it was a waterway of some commercial importance, navigable as far as Godalming and with canal connections to Basingstoke and the Arun. Today it is used by a considerable number of pleasure craft, mostly between Guildford and the Thames. The Wey has several tributaries. One rises in north Hampshire and enters the county at Farnham. Another rises in the Sussex hills south of Haslemere, with a branch from Waggoners Wells, and enters at Frensham to join the first at Tilford. Below Tilford the Wey passes through marshes and water meadows which are particularly well developed at Elstead, Eashing, Godalming, Unstead and Broadford. At Shalford it is joined by another tributary which rises south of Ewhurst and then by the Tillingbourne. There is a fine section with much marsh and water meadow from Shalford through Guildford to Pyrford and a little further on, in a sand cliff by the Royal Horticultural Society's garden at Wisley, one of the few riverbank Sand Martin colonies can be found. It connects with the Basingstoke Canal at Byfleet and is joined by the Bourne (which originates in the Virginia Water area) at Weybridge, a short distance from where it joins the Thames.

The catchment area of the Mole is not so large as that of the Wey and its marshes and water meadows are less extensive. The river is too shallow to be navigable for much of its length, giving it a greater measure of seclusion. Its valley is in places well wooded and it has so far proved more attractive than that of the Wey to the Mandarin Duck which is, in the valley, now a common breeding species, locally outnumbering the Mallard. The Mole rises just south of the county border and enters at Horley. From there it follows a wandering course through farmland on the Wealden plain and then, through mature parkland at Betchworth, on to Dorking. There are some gravelly stretches between Dorking and Leatherhead and at rare and irregular intervals the bed has become dry, the river following an underground course. Shingle banks attract the occasional migrating Common Sandpiper and it could well have been on one of these that Son of the Marshes found a nest and four young a century ago. (*Wildfowl and Sea Fowl of Great Britain*). Below Leatherhead the river deepens and there are valuable marshes and damp pastures at Woodlands Park, Slyfields and Cobham. Shortly before reaching the Thames it forms, with the River Ember, the island on which Island Barn Reservoir is built.

The Tillingbourne is a shallow stream of predominantly clear water, different in character from other Surrey watercourses. It rises near Wotton and runs west to the Wey between the greensand hills and the North Downs. The section through Abinger is perhaps the most interesting. There are some small ponds with a little (common) Reed (*Phragmites communis*) and the stream is used to irrigate watercress beds. The area is regularly frequented by Kingfishers and Grey Wagtails and since the cress beds have open water even in hard weather wintering Green Sandpipers have been seen there from time to time. Water Rail and Water Pipits sometimes winter and very hard weather has brought less common species, as in early 1963 when a Bittern spent some weeks there before being found dead at Paddington Pond. There is a little marsh, much overgrown with scrub and attractive mainly to *Sylvia* and *Phylloscopus* warblers.

The Thames forms the whole of the northern border of the vice-county. Being tidal up to Teddington it exposes a large expanse of muddy foreshore and attracts a few migrant waders as well as the resident birds. Oystercatchers, recorded as often as anywhere in a hook of the river at Barn Elms, have several times been seen flying along the river. Gulls are present at all times of the year and some of the less common species have been recorded. The only county records for the Great Skua, Razorbill and Crested Lark come from the Thames and the hardly more common

Arctic Skua has also been seen there. The river supports the largest concentration of Mute Swans in the county. Mallard can regularly be seen on the lower reaches and further up, where there is a certain amount of dispersal from the reservoirs, other water-birds such as the Great Crested Grebe and various duck including sometimes Smew, may be found. There are also many riverside trees, including a good deal of Alder (*Alnus glutinosa*) and these attract tits, Siskins, Goldfinches and a host of other birds in winter, as they do elsewhere, and maintain a good population of the commoner breeding birds.

The remaining watercourses are of no great size. The extreme southeast of the county is drained by the Eden, which runs into Kent. The North River, running into Sussex, drains a small area south of Leith Hill. The Hogsmill rises at Epsom and joins the Thames at Kingston, providing useful relief in a predominantly urban area. The Beverley Brook, rising at Cheam, runs through Richmond Park to the Thames. The River Wandle, polluted and for part of its length piped or enclosed between concrete banks, starts at Croydon and passes by Beddington Sewage Farm and Morden Hall Park to reach the Thames at Wandsworth. There are also a number of stretches of canal apart from those in the Wey Valley. These are in many places derelict and have on the whole more in common with ponds than rivers. The Coot, for example, which is a bird of still and open water, nests on the Basingstoke Canal at Ash. The Surrey Canal, currently threatened with filling, has a certain historical interest since it was from a nearby osier bed that G. Graves (1812) described the nest of a Marsh Harrier found in 1811. His account seems to be the last record of breeding for the county and the only one with a date. The female was shot from the nest.

Some birds are very characteristic of the rivers themselves. The Kingfisher makes its nest-burrow where the banks are high enough and will use quite small streams in woodland if these are suitable. Grey Wagtails are commonly met and have found in the many dams, locks and weirs, a habitat which suits them well. The Little Grebe is more local but nests along the quieter and deeper stretches, notably on the Mole between Leatherhead and Cobham. Others prefer marshes and since none of those in Surrey is really extensive quite small pockets of wet ground can provide a foothold for species which must have such habitat for successful breeding. The Reed Warbler is a case in point. In other counties this species is chiefly associated with the (common) Reed. This is a rather local plant in Surrey and even rather minor stands, as at Abinger and a hook of the Wey by Guildford Sewage Farm, will attract a pair or two. It will, however, nest among other vegetation and the extent of its Surrey distribution is due largely to this. Tall herbage consisting mainly of the Reed Mace (*Typha latifolia*) for example has supported colonies at Guildford and Hersham sfs. Another species, the Redshank, extended its range greatly in the early years of the century but later suffered much loss of habitat and feeding area with the modernization of the sewage farms. For this and other reasons it was much reduced in numbers by the end of the 1960s, breeding very locally on marshes in the Mole and the Wey Valleys. The Yellow Wagtail has for many years been very thinly distributed in the county. It bred regularly on the older style sewage farms and has been lost to most of them following modernization. There were also colonies in the Wey Valley, at Shalford and the water meadows at Stoke, Guildford. Both of these are now extinct for reasons which are not entirely clear—change in the habitat does not seem to have been a factor. There is yet a good sized breeding population at Beddington SF and the species is still found at some of the reservoirs and gravel pits and occasionally elsewhere.

The wetter parts of the riverside marshes are usually dominated by the Reed Sweet Grass (*Glyceria maxima*). This gives way to other coarse grasses such as Reed Grass (*Phalaris arundinacea*), Tufted Hair Grass (*Deschampsia caespitosa*) and to various rushes (*Juncus spp.*) on the drier ground with an often rich mixture of smaller plants. Where drainage ditches run through, there may be scattered bushes—favourite sites for Sedge Warblers. In winter these marshes are sometimes under water and they remain very wet in spring and early summer, drying out considerably and in places completely by the autumn. Beds of Stinging Nettle (*Urtica dioica*), Meadowsweet (*Filipendula ulmaria*) and Alder and willow scrub may form marginal areas, with the whole bounded by a neglected thorn hedge. There is normally little open water—the marsh at Broadford, where Tufted Duck have nested, being an exception. Even over a short stretch the terrain can be extremely varied. The Alders which line so much of the river are often riddled with holes and seem particularly attractive to Lesser Spotted Woodpeckers. Old holes are frequently used by Starlings and Tree Sparrows and the cavities and crevices in larger trees provide sites for Mandarin, Little and Tawny Owls and (particularly in pollarded willows) Tree-creepers. Stock Doves also seem to like these areas and during the summer will fly out from the trees to perform their slow circling display flight over the water meadows. The damp copses harbour Marsh and Willow Tits, Blackcaps and Garden Warblers and other woodland birds.

An example of this sort of ground is at Guildford. On the south side of the town, below St Katherine's, a nettle and scrub marsh supports a considerable population of Sedge Warblers, Whitethroats, Reed Buntings and Tree Sparrows and there is a small Sand Martin colony above the entrance to the railway tunnel. A herd of Mute Swans is present the year round and some nest along the stretch of river which runs through the town. Grey Wagtails frequent the waterfront and Collared Doves mix (in winter) with Siskins in waterside trees by the car park. On the north side of the town, at Stoke, all these species recur together with Lapwing and Snipe which are present throughout the year. A *Glyceria* marsh and rough tussocky grass draws Grasshopper Warblers and occasionally Coot, Red-shank and Teal. Old hedges offer a characteristic habitat to Lesser White-

throats and separate the marsh from rough dry pasture. Pheasant, Partridge, Red-legged Partridge and Meadow Pipits nest and the three species
of woodpecker frequent the adjacent woodland. Swift, Swallows and House
Martins hawk for insects over the marshes and skim the surface of the
river. Altogether around 70 species, almost two-thirds of the birds breeding
in the county have bred or attempted to breed in the Guildford section of
the Wey Valley and Guildford is not alone in having such a varied bird
population within its boundaries. Other valley towns such as Dorking,
Leatherhead and Godalming are similarly placed.

Areas like this attract migrants. Some, like the Whinchat, are conspicuous but others, especially when dispersed over a large area of marsh,
are easily overlooked. Even so species such as the Greenshank, Green Sandpiper, Ruff, Woodcock and Jack Snipe have often been recorded, particularly in the Mole Valley between Leatherhead and Cobham. It is
sewage farms, however, that provide the best migration watchpoints. They
are, for the most part, situated close to rivers to meet drainage requirements
and provide an important water habitat. Although similar to the riverside
marshes in many ways, they have much greater expanses of open water.
In the earlier years of the century they were mostly wet field systems with
substantial areas of marsh vegetation surrounding shallow lagoons. These
were dried out regularly in the course of the operation of the farms and
then provided shallow pools with muddy fringes succeeded by a heavy
growth of weeds, which seeded abundantly in winter. Latterly most of the
farms have been modernized and the wet field systems have been much
reduced. Some have been closed down and partially built over or converted to refuse tips.

Hersham sf, a small farm of 26 acres opened in 1900, was the subject of
an intensive study by D. Parr (1963) and his results, which can only be
described in the briefest detail here, are probably representative of conditions at many others. Little Ringed Plover had nested once, in 1952, and
Lapwing bred irregularly until 1958. About 80 pairs of 21 species bred
annually in 1961 and 1962 and these included a pair of Yellow Wagtails,
ten pairs of Pied Wagtails and a few pairs of Reed and Sedge Warblers,
Reed Buntings and Tree Sparrows. In 1962 the farm had been partially
modernized. The newer part of the farm, with circular clinker beds sur-
mounted by rotating sprinklers, was found to be an important source of
food for birds at all times of the year. Material collected showed that the
clinker contained a complex mass of algae, bacteria, fungi, protozoa and
dipterous larvae. The most abundant animal in samples from the surface
layers was a fly (*Psychoda alternata*) and this formed one of the principal
foods of wintering Starlings—about 4,000 larvae being found in the stomach
of one bird in January. The humus beds, which accept the effluent from the
filters to allow the suspended humus to settle out, were the second most
important food source, developing a rich aquatic flora when wet which
gave way, on clearance, to bare muddy areas abounding in animal life

10 The Walton Group of Reservoirs. An RAF survey photograph. These form the largest
concentration of water in the county (*Crown Copyright Reserved 1961*)

and very favourable to waders. They then dried out to develop a heavy weed cover amongst which goosefoots (*Chenopodium spp.*), bur-marigolds (*Bidens spp.*), Redleg (*Polygonum persicaria*) and the Thistle (*Cirsium arvense*) were important food plants to flocks of seed-eating passerines in winter. The winter population of the farm was on average 1,000-1,500 birds, mainly gulls and Starlings and like other sewage farms Hersham had a good record for migrants.

Interest in the sewage farms was greatly stimulated by P. A. D. Hollom's work at Brooklands SF in the 1930s. He showed that many wader species previously considered rare in Surrey occurred commonly on passage and since the war sewage farms have been intensively watched. Beddington SF is the largest, at about 800 acres. It has been well worked and has added handsomely to the county list. The only Kite, Short-toed Lark, Aquatic Warbler, Richard's Pipit and Little Buntings have been seen there, as have some barely more common species including the Purple Sandpiper, Black-winged Stilt, Alpine Swift, Bluethroat and Lapland Bunting. Gadwall and Water Rail have bred and Spotted Crake have summered. Lapwing and Snipe have bred and very large numbers are sometimes present in winter. In recent years, following modernization, much of it has dried out. An abundance of mice and voles has from time to time drawn many predators. Over 25 Kestrels and ten or more Short-eared Owls have been present in autumn and winter on occasions.

In the early 1950s, when still unmodernized, Guildford SF provided another good example of the potentialities of this sort of farm. A few rarities, such as the Grey Pharalope and Spotted Crake were seen, but the outstanding feature was the wader passage. About 20 species were seen during the decade and the commoner ones came in considerable numbers. Redshank were regularly present from February to August and there were sometimes as many as 60. There were 25 Ringed Plovers one day in May 1959 and 12 Wood Sandpipers in July 1956. Snipe were present throughout the year with up to 600 in autumn. At least four species of tern and many different duck occurred. The farm provided one of the first Surrey breeding sites for the Little Ringed Plover and, as on other farms, Teal, Yellow Wagtails and possibly Redshank, Snipe and Water Rail nested. Up to 1,000 Swifts were present in August. Modernization commenced in 1958 and some of the best Snipe ground reverted to rough grass or was rolled under an expanding refuse tip. As it is now, it still attracts interesting birds, though in reduced numbers. For some years a notice has warned that it is a game preserve, with more justice than might at first appear since Pheasant and Partridge nest among the rank vegetation. Beyond is a car dump and the tip—usually burning—on which grows an assemblage of alien plants which have led it to be rated highly by botanists. Some of the older part of the farm is still in use and Water Pipits winter with fair regularity.

Epsom SF, now closed, produced a series of rarities including the Spotted

11 (top) *Henley Park Lake*. A typical dammed water on acid soil, with resident Canada Geese in the foreground (*D. M. T. Ettlinger*)

12 (bottom) *Hedgecourt Pond, Felbridge*. Recreational use by sailors is an increasing pressure on many waters in the Home Counties, this pressure is now spreading to reservoirs (*D. Washington*)

Crake, Pectoral Sandpiper and Black-winged Stilt in the 1950s. Over 70 Jack Snipe were sometimes present and the breeding list, as with other good farms, included Teal. Unstead SF, notable for the only county record of a yellowlegs and at one time with a large Lapwing colony, is still good. With the declining importance of Beddington and Guildford it now seems to maintain the largest winter Snipe population and is a favourite haunt of Jack Snipe. It also has a good record for other migrants and for breeding birds.

Among the remaining sewage farms the one at Worcester Park is probably representative of those in a more urban area. It is a largely modern works close to a refuse tip, playing fields and allotments. It has proved a useful place to watch the commoner migrants and has about 20 breeding species. As many as 200 Carrion Crows as well as many Black-headed Gulls and Starlings can be found feeding in the modern section and flocks of larks, buntings and finches resort to the older part of the works in hard weather. The once excellent farms at Berrylands, Brooklands, Esher, Leatherhead, Lyne and Molesey have been built over or modernized but there are still farms of the older style at Godstone, Ripley and Woking and those at Camberley, Dorking, Earlswood, Elmers End, Ripley and Wisley have been profitably watched in recent years.

Commons and other Open Spaces

Donald Parr

This chapter embraces land which has been subject to rights of common since 1900 together with 'waste' manorial land not subject to such rights but remaining unfenced and uncultivated within living memory, land once commonland but appropriated for military use during the last hundred years and other 'open spaces' enjoying public access in 1970.

Problems of ownership, access and rights have long beset our commons but with the passing of the Commons Registration Act, 1965, procedures were set in motion to register and safeguard the existing commonland for all time and at the end of the review period the huge task of registration was largely completed although adjudication on rights was still continuing. Many commons are now owned by local authorities or charitable trusts. The National Trust owns 11,000 acres of land in Surrey, much of it commonland.

The nature of Surrey commons is very varied; some, especially those near London are now closely cut grassland; some are in fact woodland but most are open grass or heathland with a varying amount of scrub or tree growth and it is with the last that we will be mainly concerned in this chapter.

Surrey is fortunate in possessing a large number of commons. The total acreage of registered commonland exceeds 28,000 and together with other land open to the public and owned by the County Council and other public bodies the total acreage of such land in the administrative county in 1970 exceeded 33,000 acres. In addition to this over 8,000 acres, formerly commonland and largely in the north-west of the county, are owned by the Ministry of Defence and although used by the military forces are still preserved as undeveloped open spaces.

It is on the outskirts of London that most loss of open land has occurred, in the present century. Homes (*The Birds of the London Area*, 1957) described the transition of many open commons into scrubland or over-managed parkland, the expansion of building development on downland particularly in the 1920s and 1930s and the increasing human pressures on the remaining open spaces leading to deterioration of the habitat. The initiation of the Green Belt policy in the late 1930s and the acquisitions by the National Trust and by the Surrey County Council were however, in time to preserve from development many of the finer stretches of common and woodland in the county including some in a radius of 13-15 miles from the centre of London.

Thus the worst fears of Bucknill who complained in 1900 that Surrey was then fast becoming a vast suburb, were never realized and we may also note in passing that all the commons listed by him and which he no doubt considered of ornithological significance, namely: Wimbledon, Epsom, Ashtead, Bisley, Pirbright, Chobham, Royal, Crooksbury, Puttenham, Thursley, Witley, Dunsfold, Holmwood, Hurtwood and Ranmore are still undeveloped with free public access, if not all as registered commons.

The commons of Surrey have played and continue to play an important part in the provision of refuge habitats for birds and indeed all wildlife and plant life. They fall into three main and distinct groups recognized by the geological formation on which they lie. These are described below.

The first group of commons lie in the old gravel terraces of the River Thames and are typified by those at Barnes, East Sheen, Mitcham and Wimbledon. The proximity of these commons to London has meant that they have suffered most from human pressures. The largest, Wimbledon, still retains open areas of dry heath and grassland with patches of open birch woodland. Of the ground nesting species—Skylarks, Meadow Pipits, occasionally Tree Pipits, Yellowhammers and Reed Buntings still survive in the larger open areas. Woodlarks were reported breeding there in the period of expansion of that species in the 1950s. Redstart, Grasshopper Warbler and Wood Warbler have all nested in the last decade of the review period and Redpolls had newly colonized the birch woods by 1970. The Dartford Warbler last bred there in the 1930s. Barnes Common, which can number Nightingales and the chats amongst its former breeding species, now supports only the commoner 'garden' birds, but Blackcap and Chiffchaff still cling on to its edges where larger private gardens give some measure of quiet. Mitcham Common has now either been degraded by waste dumping or converted into playing fields and is now a shadow of its former self, although it shares with adjourning Beddington sf in occasionally providing a winter territory for visiting Great Grey Shrikes.

The second group of commons is the largest and is associated with the Tertiary beds of the London Basin. These form three sub-groups, the first on the coarser phases of the Bagshot Sands, the second on heavy intractable London Clay and the third on patches of sand and gravel of the Pliocene Age high up on the dip-slope of the Chalk Downs. It is necessary to consider these three sub-groups separately. The first includes the Bagshot Commons which lie on the light sandy soils with some gravel cappings and bands of clay creating damp areas with ponds. There are large stretches of grass heath, heather and Bracken (*Pteridium aquilinum*), stands of Scots

Pine (*Pinus sylvestris*) and open birch woods. Chobham Common is the largest (1,444 acres) and probably the most important bird habitat. The dry areas are dominated by Heather (*Calluna vulgaris*) and Purple Moor-grass (*Molinia caerulea*). The common is now owned by the Surrey County Council and the area is subject to increasing human disturbance by model aircraft and other interests. At the end of the review period the building of a new motorway was ravishing the common and there have been various other soil disturbances by pipe laying. Excessive fires have considerably damaged the habitat and birch is encroaching on the open heath in many places, pine invasion is occurring in the south of the area around Gracious Pond and mixed deciduous scrub is invading other areas. The common has been an area of considerable significance in Surrey ornithology. Curlew formerly bred there (it was last recorded here in the breeding season in 1968). Nightjar and Woodlark are still present in reduced numbers and it was formerly an important breeding site of both the Dartford Warbler and the Red-backed Shrike. Pipits are still common and so are Stonechat. Hobby and Sparrow Hawk might still be seen here and in the winter it frequently supports visiting Great Grey Shrikes and raptors of various species. Its continued importance would seem to depend on some form of management control of the scrub and fire prevention and perhaps restriction of access to certain areas. This group of commons also includes those at Ash, Wyke and Pirbright largely given over to military purposes but possessing some of the finest stretches of mature heather in the county although again fire and scrub invasion, particularly of birch are, as in other areas, growing problems. The avifauna is similar to Chobham's and includes good numbers of Redstarts but because of access restriction, information from the area is limited.

Further to the south, north west of Guildford, are the Whitmoor, Rickford and Stringer's Commons which contain both wet and dry heath communities. Birch, Bracken and pine invasion are causing a rapid diminuation of the open areas here also, with the consequent loss in the variety of breeding birds. Further to the east we might take the Wisley and Ockham Commons as further examples of this sub-group. These are an interesting association of mature pine stands, dry heath areas and patches of bog dominated by rush and sallow. Here the process of pine invasion has been accelerated by a deliberate policy of conifer planting by the present owners, the Surrey County Council, and the whole area is likely before long to become pine forest although at the end of the review period Nightjar, Grasshopper Warbler, buntings and pipits still bred. A similar progression to climax vegetation is taking place on the adjoining areas of Oxshott Heath and Esher Common with the consequent loss of many species of birds.

The second sub-group of commons are those lying on London Clay and include Ashtead, the Bookham Commons, Effingham and Epsom. They are generally wet. Open areas are dominated by Tufted Hair-grass (*Deschampsia caespitosa*) and Bracken with extensive clumps of Gorse (*Ulex europaeus*) particularly on Ashtead and Epsom. Roughly half the area of these commons is covered with climax Pedunculate Oak (*Quercus robur*).

These commons have supported and still support a rich and varied avifauna including (other than essentially woodland birds) Skylark, Nightingale, Grasshopper Warbler, Blackcap, Garden Warbler, Whitethroat and Lesser Whitethroat, Meadow and Tree Pipit, Linnet, Redpoll, Yellowhammer and Reed Bunting. A long-term ecological study was started on Bookham Common in 1941 by members of the LNHS. Thanks to this we know a great deal about the vegetation and fauna composition and changes that have taken place in the last three decades. In 1941 about half the common was open wet grassland with local rush communities and hawthorn and Bracken fringing the woodland. Before 1914 the grassy plains though partly gorse covered, were kept open by grazing by cattle and sheep and the exercise of other commoners' rights. By 1949 all grazing had stopped and since then the grass has become tall and tussocky, there has been a vast increase in shrubs (particularly hawthorn, sloe and rose), Bracken and saplings of oak, Ash and birch; in fact by 1967 oakwood covered 250 out of the 380 acres of the area being studied. The changes in the bird community in the open area of the common have been detailed as follows: Snipe ceased to breed in the 1920s, Stonechats and Whinchats disappeared in the 1930s, Linnets have become scarce, Skylarks ceased to breed in the 1940s and Tree Pipits declined from 12 pairs in 1948 to nil in 1955 (Beven, 1971).

During the Second World War, 111 acres of Epsom Common and 166 of Ashtead Common were ploughed for agricultural purposes. This cultivation had ceased by 1959 and the land was allowed to return to the wild. The ground has quickly reverted to type becoming dominated by Tufted Hair-grass, with extensive clumps of gorse, bramble, willow herb, thistle and rush in the wetter areas. The bird communities on these two commons are probably now as rich as they were in pre-war times although the Nightjar has gone and Stonechat has become irregular but for some species, as for instance Grasshopper Warbler and Reed Bunting, numbers have increased. A serious threat here however is, as at Bookham, the spread of scrub, especially of sallow, thorn and saplings of birch and oak. The danger remains that unless either fire or some form of management policy intervenes much of the remaining open areas of both Ashtead and Epsom Commons will progress to oak woodland and an open commonland bird community will give way to a closed woodland community.

The third and final sub-group of the commons we are now considering are those lying mainly on the gravels on the dip-slope of the Chalk and in some cases extending onto the Chalk itself. These include, from west to east, Merrow Downs, West Clandon and Albury Downs, Netley Heath (largely woodland), Hackhurst Downs and Ranmore Common. East of the Mole Gap are Headley and Walton Heaths, Banstead Downs and Heath, Burgh Heath, Park Downs and the Epsom and Walton Downs. Other significant areas further east are Coulsdon Common, Kenley Common and Riddlesdown. The true downland areas as at Merrow and Albury are subject to heavy scrub growth except where the grass is cut or regularly swiped. The open grassland, where not too heavily disturbed, supports Tree Pipits and Yellowhammers and the transitional scrubland habitat a rich variety of warblers particularly Garden Warbler, Blackcap, Whitethroat, Grasshopper Warbler and Willow Warbler. Newlands Corner, the popular 'open space' overlooking Albury Downs, is still one of the best places to go to hear Nightingales.

Very little true commonland remains on the dip-slope running from Albury to Ranmore, the land being largely woodland but where areas are cleared for replanting, heather along with other ground shrubs re-asserts itself here and there and such species as Nightjar, Tree Pipit, Yellowhammer and even Stonechat regain a temporary footing.

Headley Heath lies on well-drained sandy gravel giving a vegetation of heather, gorse, light scrub and birchwood. This common is now owned by the National Trust and managed by a Management Committee. Its Report for the years 1955-63 described the spread of birch on the sandy soil and of thorn and dogwood on the chalky areas, dating back to the time when commoners' rights fell into disuse, a more recent contributory factor being top soil disturbance caused by military vehicles in the last war. A serious fire in 1956 razed 250 acres of the heath but a good recovery was made. The Management Committee has taken steps to halt the spread of scrub and even to clear certain areas. The Report also described the vast increase in the number of visitors to the area, particularly at weekends in the summer. The heath has an interesting ornithological history which is well chronicled. Dartford Warblers last bred there in 1939 and in 1970 Stonechats did so again after a long absence. Despite the human pressures on the area, it was still supporting an interesting community which in 1970 included Meadow Pipits, Tree Pipits and Yellowhammers. The Cuckoo, Nightjar, Whitethroat and Nightingale decreased in the 1960s but some species including Turtle Dove, Tree Pipit, Garden Warbler, Spotted Flycatcher, Linnet and Redpoll have been reported as increasing and Wood Warblers bred at the end of the review period. It is a hopeful sign that despite the pressures on this popular spot a varied bird community can still maintain itself.

Walton and Banstead Heaths are similar in character to Headley. A large part of Walton Heath was lost to agriculture during the Second World War and another part became a golf course but is still able to support a varied avifauna including the Nightjar. Further to the north lie areas of commonland on the Chalk at Epsom and Walton Downs. This is largely short fescue pasture and is subject to much trampling and disturbance and of little interest ornithologically. An area of similar grassland adjoining Banstead Heath on the south known as Chussex Plain supports a high population of ground nesting species including pipits, Yellowhammers and Skylarks although breeding success is sometimes affected by mowing. Areas of grassland and scrub on chalk as at Banstead Downs and Park Downs support breeding populations of several species of warblers including Blackcap, Garden Warbler, Whitethroat, Lesser Whitethroat and Willow Warbler and resident species such as Skylark, Meadow Pipit, Linnet, Redpoll and Yellowhammer. Also this area was up to the 1960s a stronghold of the Red-backed Shrike.

Finally in the extreme east of this area lies the cluster of commons, again principally consisting of scrub on downland, at Coulsdon Common, Farthing Downs, Kenley Common and Riddlesdown. These commons provide a good warbler and Nightingale habitat and formerly held the Red-backed Shrike.

The final and probably most important group of commons lies to the south of the chalk ridge mainly on the coarser sands of the Lower Greensand. These commons stretch from the extreme east adjoining Kent, westwards to the Hampshire border and are covered by a considerable range of vegetation. Limpsfield Common in the east is locally dominated by heather, Bracken, gorse and Tufted Hair-grass but mixed deciduous scrub and woodland now cover the larger part of it. As in the other areas the open heathland has suffered greatly in recent years. H. Bentham recorded much of interest from this common including Stonechats, Whinchats, pipits, Red-backed Shrikes (up to seven pairs in the 1930s) and Nightjars. The chats and shrikes have now gone but buntings and pipits still occur and so does the Nightjar particularly in the area of the High Chart. A small common to the south of this area, Blindley Heath (72 acres) is exceptional in that it lies on the Weald Clay and represents a relic area of wet grassland dominated by Tufted Hair-grass. This common supports an interesting bird community of Reed Buntings, Yellowhammers Tree Pipits and Grasshopper Warblers. Some grazing still takes place but is insufficient to prevent encroachment from oak and sallow saplings spreading from the edges of the common.

West of this area are the commons at Redhill and Reigate on which the typical vegetation is heather, Purple Moor-grass, birch and pine. These commons are now much reduced in range. Reigate Heath is partly golf course and despite much pressure from visitors, still supports Tree Pipits, Yellowhammers and in the birch copses, Wood Warblers. Earlswood Common is largely given over to public use and provides little or no undisturbed ground cover apart from scattered clumps of trees and shrubs.

Holmwood Common, south of Dorking, now owned by the National Trust, straddles the clay and greensand; the eastern area on the clay is largely oak woodland and there is a sharp dividing line between this and the western half on the greensand which was formerly heath but now largely swamped by Bracken. Tree Pipits, buntings and the leaf warblers are present in good numbers on this common.

West of Dorking, the Lower Greensand formation widens considerably on to the Leith Hill range on which lie Abinger Common, Hurtwood (an area of 1,670 acres of forest manorial waste now largely woodland) Winterfold Heath, Albury Heath and Blackheath. Blackheath which is owned by the National Trust, holds some fine open stretches of heather with a bird community including Tree Pipits, Yellowhammers and Nightjars; warblers frequent the wood edge areas. Stonechats bred there earlier in the century but there have been no recent records. The heather is mixed with extensive pine stands and the pine (and birch in places) is colonizing the open areas at a rapid rate. A large part of Holmbury Hill in the Hurtwood area was devastated by fire in 1956 and only the larger scattered Scots Pines survived but at the end of the review period birch and oak scrub was regenerating rapidly and Bracken had largely swamped the heather. Dominant bird species in the area in the late 1960s were Willow Warbler, Whitethroat, Wren and Robin. Nightjar, Redstart and Tree Pipit were also present and in the fine late spring and hot summer of 1970 Nightjar numbers were exceptionally high.

In the Rural District of Hambledon in extreme south west Surrey lies the biggest concentration of commons in the whole county, between 40 and 50 in number covering 6,000 acres. Amongst them is the important group centred on Thursley Common and including Witley, Ockley, Royal, Hankley, Frensham and Hindhead. The heather commonland of this general area has provided many of the highlights of Surrey's ornithological history and ornithologists with recollections of these localities from earlier in the century have nostalgic memories of Dartford Warblers, chats and Woodlarks singing from the heather, Red-backed Shrikes in the scrub, Hobbies wheeling over the pine clumps and Curlews calling from the bogs. Although at the end of the review period most of these more interesting species were much restricted in range and reduced in numbers, only the Dartford Warbler was missing and the Red-backed Shrike seriously depleted. The report of the Special Committee of Wild Life Conservation, *The Conservation of Nature in England and Wales* (1947) described the 40 square miles of the Thursley District as containing the best remaining area of low lying Surrey heath, holding valuable and characteristic representatives of a fast disappearing flora and fauna. The area has been subject of much excellent amateur ecological work and of particular ornithological significance was a paper by Venables (1937), *The Bird distribution on Surrey Greensand Heaths*. In this work Venables described the bird communities on the heather commons, the effect of fire in keeping the heaths open and the various phases through which ground that had been burnt, progressed to a climax pine forest stage. He demonstrated the importance of the phase of mature heather association (*Calluna-Erica* with largely prostrate gorse) which requires at least eight years growth to achieve a height of 18 inches to two feet and which then becomes extremely susceptible to fire and seldom lasted long. This growth phase supported the highest number of bird species including particularly

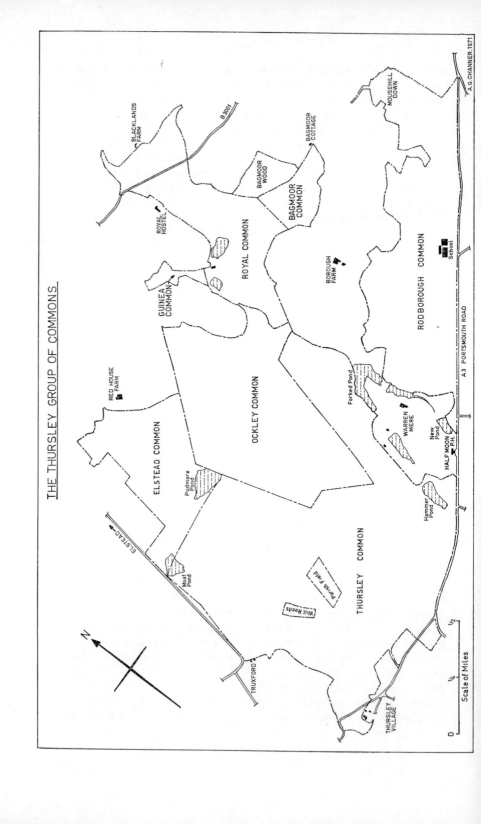

THE THURSLEY GROUP OF COMMONS

A.G. CHANNER. 1971

BLACKLANDS FARM

B 3001

MOUSEHILL DOWN

ROYAL HOSTEL

BAGMOOR WOOD

BAGMOOR COTTAGE

GUINEA COMMON

ROYAL COMMON

BAGMOOR COMMON

BOROUGH FARM

RED HOUSE FARM

ELSTEAD COMMON

OCKLEY COMMON

Forked Pond

RODBOROUGH COMMON

School

A 3 PORTSMOUTH ROAD

WARREN MERE

New Pond

HALF MOON P.H.

Pudmore Pond

Hammer Pond

ELSTEAD

Moat Pond

Will Reeds

Parish Field

THURSLEY COMMON

TRUXFORD

N

THURSLEY VILLAGE

Scale of Miles

0   ¼   ½

Linnet, Tree Pipit, Meadow Pipit, Dartford Warbler and Stonechat. Other species such as Woodlark, Wheatear, Nightjar and Lapwing favoured earlier stages in the recovery phases.

A large area consisting of Thursley, Elstead, Ockley, Royal and Bagmoor Commons has been designated a Site of Special Scientific Interest under section 23 of the National Parks and Access to the Countryside Act, 1949. Bagmoor and Thursley Commons are managed as reserves by the Surrey Naturalists' Trust and Elstead, Ockley and Royal Commons, although owned by the Ministry of Defence, are subject to an agreement between the Nature Conservancy and the Ministry under which the natural history interests are protected. A map of this area is presented opposite.

In considering the commons of this corner, and indeed other parts of Surrey and the changes since 1900, one is struck by the fact that so many have survived. Apart possibly from some extensive enclosures around Hindhead much of the larger tracts of commonland are still virtually intact. What has changed however is their open nature. At the beginning of the twentieth century there were very few trees on the commons—they were kept open by a combination of the exercise of commoners' rights (such as fuel gathering and grazing) and fire. Peat was dug on Thursley Common till the 1920s and many commons were used in both world wars by the military authorities with a devastating effect on the vegetation. With the passing of the exercise of commoners' rights, particularly the cessation of grazing and, in the past 20 years, the decimation of the rabbit population due to myxomatosis, there has been scrub and tree penetration on many commons with a consequent loss of open aspect. Oak and pine in particular, from adjoining woodland, have invaded open areas and much heathland has been completely lost. Excessive fires in some areas appear to have encouraged the growth of Bracken and Rose-bay Willow Herb (*Chamaenerion angustifolium*) at the expense of heather, Purple Moor-grass and gorse. However, extensive areas of open heath still exist and provided action is taken to prevent further spread of scrub and pine infestation, habitats capable of supporting a varied and interesting avifauna will be preserved.

The above paragraphs deal, albeit perfunctorily, with land that, in very general terms, may be classed as commonland in Surrey. One further category deserves mention and that is land acquired and owned by the County Council and managed for the benefit of the public. The Council's first acquisition was Norbury Park Estate (over 1,300 acres) in 1930 and this includes a small section of Fetcham Downs. Many commons have been acquired and other areas have been given to the Council. Other estates so acquired include the Shabden Park Estate and Sheepleas although neither of these areas is particularly noteworthy from the point of view of bird interest.

The County Council has also entered into access agreements with private landowners under the National Parks and Access to the Countryside Act,

1949 and many acres of land particularly on the North Downs at Newlands Corner, at St Martha's and at Puttenham Common are thereby open for public enjoyment. Finally it should be noted that the North Downs, the Leith Hill range of hills and almost the whole of the south west corner of the county fall within the Surrey Hills Area of Outstanding Natural Beauty designated and confirmed under Section 87 of the National Parks and Access to the Countryside Act, 1949. This confers some planning protection and enables the County Council to obtain help from the Government in covering management costs.

A constantly recurring theme in this and other chapters is the alteration in character of certain habitats brought about by vegetational changes, in particular the growth of scrub and the consequent reduction of open heathland. This has been particularly acute in the past 20-30 years. This process, if unchecked, will have a serious effect on the variety of our bird populations. Some attempts at vegetational control have already begun. The Surrey County Council has cleared areas of downland at Newlands Corner, and elsewhere, the Conservation Corps of the Surrey Naturalists' Trust has undertaken much clearance work on the Trust's reserves and on some National Trust land. Some action with the support and advice of members of the Surrey Bird Club was taken in the late 1960s by the Conservators at Park Downs to improve the habitat by clearing leggy scrub and providing an increased wood-edge effect. Beven (1971) has described how a limited programme of scrub control on Bookham Common has over a period of 12 years (1959-70) resulted in certain changes in the bird population of grass scrubland. Increases in numbers of Wrens, Robins, Long-tailed Tits, Nightingale and Grasshopper Warbler occurred. Chaffinch and Yellowhammer numbers remained the same and those of Willow Warbler and Reed Bunting decreased. At least four species—Whitethroat, Yellowhammer, Reed Bunting and Grasshopper Warbler were preserved which would otherwise have virtually disappeared. These instances are only a beginning and the problem of scrub control has barely been touched. There is an urgent need for a dialogue between owners, particularly local authorities, and naturalists and for the former to take active management steps to preserve the open commons.

The commons of Surrey were once the 'waste lands' of the county. We now see them as our rich natural heritage for plants and animals.

The last year of our review period—1971—was European Conservation Year and it would not be inappropriate to draw attention to the need to conserve open heath and common in the county and with these habitats, the birds associated with them.

Woodland, Downland and Parkland

J. A. Sage

Before the influence of human activity, Surrey was extensively wooded and formed part of the primaeval forest which covered the country after the last Ice Age. When man appeared, so woodland was cleared, firstly for growing crops and then with increasing momentum for fuel, building and in fairly recent historic times for supporting the Surrey iron industry. Most woodland in the county has probably at some time been felled and renewed either by natural regeneration or by deliberate planting. In the main where there is natural regeneration the basic nature of the woodland does not change as it is largely determined by the underlying soil type. Planting can cause change however if new species are introduced and in time the flora and fauna can also be affected. The most striking example in Surrey of a species originally planted is the Scots Pine (*Pinus sylvestris*), a native of northern Britain, which was probably introduced into the county at the time of John Evelyn of Wotton in the middle of the seventeenth century. The extent to which this species has naturalized and its influence on the face of Surrey can now be readily seen.

Since the beginning of the present century a number of changes have been observed which have had either direct or indirect effect on the bird life in the woodlands. There has been a steady expansion of suburban London which has overrun some woodlands and approached others so closely that the bird population has been affected. The cessation of commonland grazing and the decimation of the rabbit population by the myxomatosis outbreak of the early 1950s has resulted in an unchecked growth of Silver Birch (*Betula pendula*) and pine saplings on many common margins which consequently have become woodland. This change is creating additional habitat for a few species such as the Willow Warbler at the expense of those restricted to open heathland. In some areas of natural woodland the mature trees have passed their prime and have therefore a declining value as timber. Such woodland is increasingly being felled for replanting to the detriment of hole nesting species. Again species dependent on rather specialized woodland habitat such as the Wood Warbler are affected in some cases.

The most recent figures available from the Forestry Commission show that woodland covers something like 17 per cent of the land area in the administrative county of Surrey. An analysis of the woodland is as follows:

Coniferous forest (including planted trees)	24,000 acres
Broad-leaved forest (including planted trees)	28,000 acres
Scrub	27,000 acres
Coppice	2,000 acres
	81,000 acres

(*Note: figures rounded at source.*)

Private woodland (including that owned by the Surrey County Council) accounts for 73,000 acres and woodland owned by the Forestry Commission 8,000 acres.

For the purpose of this chapter woodland is divided into two broad categories. Firstly high forest where the established growth has existed for many years and the flora and fauna change little unless subjected to outside influence. Secondly coppice and plantation where the equilibrium of the high forest will never be reached.

The paragraphs that follow describe first the woodlands of the high forest (as defined above but excluding those in parkland) and their associated avifauna and then the plantations and coppice in general with their associated avifauna. The woodlands themselves vary a good deal in size, from largely unbroken areas of hundreds of acres down to quite small plots of a few acres. The woodlands are generally dealt with in an order in which west takes precedence over east and north over south.

A number of species—Blue Tit, Great Tit, Blackbird, Woodpigeon, Chaffinch and Jay—are found in all woodland areas. Some widespread species such as the Wren are common where sufficient undergrowth is available to provide food and nesting sites and are not therefore typical of beechwood or conifer plantation in an advanced stage of development. The deciduous woodlands generally support far more birds than mature conifers and the greatest variety of species is often found along the woodland margins when woods merge into other more open habitats. These margins provide nesting and feeding areas both for the woodland birds and for those of scrub and farmland.

The greater part of the woodland in north-west Surrey is on the light dry soil of the Bagshot, Bracklesham and Barton Beds and is dominated by Scots Pine and birch and such woodland can best be seen in the Bisley, Deepcut and Pirbright areas and at Wisley. Where the pinewoods do not form a close canopy birch undergrowth is unchecked. In these woods, predominantly of pine, the Coal Tit and Goldcrest are the most common species throughout the year while in winter, Siskins and in many years Crossbills, feed on the cone crop. Crossbills do occasionally breed. Other breeding species in the woods include the Great Spotted and Green Woodpecker and more unusually the Lesser Spotted Woodpecker. The Sparrow Hawk breeds regularly. The Willow Warbler is common where the birch rather than the Scots Pine is predominant although none of this woodland is favoured by other warblers except possibly the Grass-hopper at its birch scrub edges. In the open parts where the trees are only thinly distributed Tree Pipits and Yellowhammers breed as do the Wood-cock and Nightjar, particularly where there is also heather or Bracken cover. Hobbies breed sporadically in this general type of woodland al-though their preference for nesting is the isolated pine or clump of pines rather than close woodland. On a smaller scale similar woodland is also found in the Esher and Oxshott areas and again on a large scale on the predominantly Lower Greensand areas on the borders of Frensham, Hank-ley, Ockley and Thursley Commons.

The most important woodlands on the London Clay are found at Ashtead and Bookham. On the clay the Pedunculate Oak (*Quercus robur*) is the predominant broad-leaved tree. The numerous insect species attend-ant upon the oak provide sufficient food to support a variety of birds in good numbers. The secondary growth is usually Hazel (*Corylus avellana*), hawthorn (*Crataegus spp.*) and Elder (*Sambucus nigra*) with occasional evergreens such as Holly (*Ilex aquifolium*). Breeding in the oakwoods at Ashtead and Bookham are hole-nesting species such as the Green, Great Spotted and Lesser Spotted Woodpeckers, the Nuthatch, Treecreeper and some species of tit, also warblers including Chiff-chaff, Willow Warbler, Garden Warbler and Blackcap and the Nightin-gale. Woodcock rode over the wood edges and nest regularly, the wet parts of the wood providing suitable feeding grounds.

On the chalk belt, Beech (*Fagus sylvatica*) is the typical tree and beech-woods can best be seen at Sheepleas and on the downs north of Shere at Combe Bottom, White Downs and Ranmore. In this general area Beech is typically associated with Yew (*Taxus baccata*) the berries of which provide winter food for the thrush family. Wood Warblers breed in these woodlands. The beeches provide sites for the hole nesting species and the Spotted Flycatcher is a common summer visitor. In winter the beechmast attracts Chaffinches and Bramblings.

South of the chalk belt the greensand ridges in the centre of the county carry the vast areas of woodland comprised of Winterfold Forest, Hurt-wood, Abinger Forest and Leith Hill. The woodland is varied in character; it is predominantly conifer at Winterfold, there are good areas of beech on the western side of Hurtwood and in the Abinger Forest while the Leith Hill area is typical of the broad-leaved/conifer mixed woodland. These woodlands provide a wealth of habitat including the most important one in the county for the Wood Warbler.

Slightly further south west the principal woodland areas are at Hollo-
ways Heath and Hydon Heath (another stronghold of the Wood Warbler).
The western edge of the county in the Haslemere/Hindhead area (which
includes the Devil's Punch Bowl) is also well-wooded. Among the species
which breed in the area are the Redstart and Crossbill.

A great deal of woodland remains on the Weald Clay but it is inter-
spersed with farm fields as the Weald is the main agricultural area in the
county. However the edges of these woodlands are attractive to many
species as indicated earlier in this chapter. Nightingales are common in
this habitat, particularly in the more westerly Wealden areas of the
county.

The main Forestry Commission plantations are to be found in the areas
of Chiddingfold, Effingham, Hurtwood, Leith Hill, Limpsfield, Ranmore,
Witley and Worplesdon and the Commission further manages certain
privately owned estates. For new plantation the selection of tree species
and the decision whether to include broad-leaved varieties with conifers
will depend largely on the nature of the soil. Conifers provide a short-
term crop as they are fast growing and after thinning any broad-leaved
varieties are left to mature. Mixed plantations in the early years tend to
give the false impression that the varieties planted are completely conifer.
New plantations in Surrey are usually on the site of felled woodland as
there is little opportunity for planting new areas due to competing interests.
Species which may find suitable habitat in the early stages of growth are
the Nightjar and Woodcock. As the amount of cover increases the Yellowhammer, Whitethroat and then Lesser Whitethroat and Grasshopper
Warbler are attracted. D. Parr found at Prince's Coverts, Oxshott, that these
species persisted until the highest growth was about ten feet (in 1964). At
this stage the Nightjar and Woodcock could presumably no longer find suitable nesting sites and were not recorded in 1965. The Grasshopper Warbler
and the Lesser Whitethroat were last recorded in territory in 1966 and
1967 respectively. Whitethroat, Redpoll and Yellowhammer were significantly reduced in numbers in the period 1966-70. In this particular plantation of Norway Spruce (*Picea abies*) the growth of thorn, rose, oak, willow
and bramble was left unchecked and the spruce was completely smothered.
In this condition the plantation was still attractive to some species notably
the Nightingale, numbers of which had doubled between 1964 and 1970.
The dense tangle met the needs of the Garden Warbler but not the
Blackcap. While Prince's Coverts cannot be considered typical of plantation
management it amply demonstrates the value of such a habitat and the
varied avifauna it can support.

Under controlled conditions where the undergrowth is not allowed to
swamp the conifers the trees become dominant and form a canopy which
together with the deep litter of dead Bracken and the lower branches of
the pine saplings which are generally left on the ground, completely
smother the undergrowth. In this condition the bird species remaining are

13 (top) *Holmethorpe Sand Pit*, near Redhill. Working sand and gravel pits provide
    valuable transitional habitats fully expoited by many species of birds. (*D. Washington*)
    14 (bottom) *Papercourt Gravel Pit*, near Send. (*D. M. T. Ettlinger*)

usually the Coal Tit, Goldcrest, Woodpigeon and Turtle Dove.

The coppicing of woodland is now practised much less than formerly and its importance as a habitat is therefore declining. The usual subject for coppicing was hazel growing under oak. A number of oak standards were allowed to remain and the hazel was normally cut on a 10-15 year cycle. The dense new hazel growth with the ready availability of oak leaves made a habitat ideally suited to the Nightingale which was probably the most important associated species. In more recent years there has been a tendency for hazel coppicing to be replaced by chestnut coppicing although only on a small scale. An example of this habitat can be seen at Pebble Coombe to the east of Box Hill.

The downland in Surrey largely follows the chalk formation which extends from the Hog's Back in the west to the borders of Kent in the east. This section gives an overall picture of the downland and its avifauna, dealing also with some of the downland areas which were not covered in the preceding chapter. The entire length of the chalk downs in Surrey is within easy reach of London and provides a recreational area which is justifiably patronized by the public. The penalty of this close proximity to London is that disturbance can reach a level which has a significant effect on the breeding birds. Box Hill is a case in point.

The downs are cut into three sections by the deep river valleys of the Wey at Guildford and the Mole at Dorking. The Hog's Back which is at the extreme western end is a well known Surrey landmark rising to some 500 feet. The chalk ridge here is but a few hundred yards wide and is of particular note because on the arable fields on the slopes it is possible to find Cirl Bunting, Yellowhammer and Corn Bunting in the same area, probably the only place in the county where this is possible.

East of Guildford the North Downs rise steeply from the Wey Gap across Merrow and Albury to Newlands Corner. Merrow Down has long been a favoured haunt of the Grasshopper Warbler even before the population increase of the late 1960s. The ground falls steeply away to the south across Albury Downs to Chilworth. The line of the chalk runs eastwards along the northern side of the Tillingbourne Valley. The northern dip slope of the ridge is overlaid with Clay-with-Flints and at Ranmore, for example the typical acid-loving vegetation—oak and Bracken (*Pteridium aquilinum*) approaches almost to the edge of the scarp. In this central section between the Wey and Mole gaps are Hackhurst and White Downs and at the eastern end, the Denbies hillside. In these areas there is abundant evidence of the encroachment by scrub and the grass, once short, is now generally long and unchecked. The chalkland low flora is in danger of being smothered. The Red-backed Shrike, once a common breeding bird in these areas, is now extremely scarce. The Tree Pipit and Yellowhammer, however, continue to be common breeding species in this habitat.

From the Mole Valley the North Downs rise steeply eastwards to the top of Box Hill. As the name implies there is an important growth of

15 (top) *Ashtead Common.* The middle distance shows a typical Grasshopper Warbler habitat. (*D. M. T. Ettlinger*)

16 (bottom) *Thursley Common.* A Surrey Naturalists' Trust Reserve and a celebrated area for many types of wildlife. The invasion of birch and pine on the heather can be clearly seen. (*D. M. T. Ettlinger*)

Box (*Buxus sempervirens*) with Yew and Beech. The yew berries provide food for the wintering thrushes but in summer the human disturbance of the habitat reduces its attraction for breeding species. Further east from Box Hill the effect of the outwards spread of London becomes more apparent and development has occurred to such an extent that only small areas of downland remain. Colley Hill above Reigate is under the control of the National Trust and the grassland on the upper slopes is kept short by mowing. Tree Pipits and Yellowhammers are well represented here particularly on the steeper slopes where there is less trampling. Areas such as Epsom Downs have been largely cleared of scrub and their value as a breeding habitat has declined.

The growth of scrub on the North Downs is the development of the greatest significance from an ornithological standpoint. The downs had been close-cropped by sheep for centuries and with the decline of the wool trade, once centred in Guildford, grazing was continued by the growing rabbit population until its decimation by myxomatosis in the early 1950s. After so many years of close grazing a complex association of plant and animal had been established which was dependent on short turf. It is probable therefore that there will be a significant change in the face of the downland now there is no natural means of keeping the turf short. Many areas of downland are now subject to scrub infestation and much of the chalk scarp that was previously open grassland is overrun by scrub and is in the very early stages of transition to its climax state of woodland with the attendant change in avifauna. However scrub is a valuable bird habitat and it is desirable to maintain such areas of scrub at an optimum level to meet the nesting and feeding requirements of such species as Grasshopper, Willow and Garden Warblers, Chiffchaff, Blackcap, White-throat and Lesser Whitethroat, Blackbird, Nightingale, Chaffinch, Green-finch, Bullfinch, Yellowhammer and Redpoll.

A pilot scheme of 'scrub maintenance' under the auspices of the Surrey Bird Club and the Surrey Naturalists' Trust is being undertaken at Park Downs, Banstead. Under the scheme, light is admitted to scrub to en-courage ground cover and increase nesting sites particularly of warblers. All the species mentioned above except the Grasshopper Warbler are present on Park Downs where the scrub is in 'good condition'. If the treatment is carried out on a rotational basis the area in 'good condition' can be increased and further it allows for untreated sections which provide controls in the experiment. Scrub control with amenity and nature interests in mind is also being carried out on Farthing Down and Riddlesdown.

In the present century there have been several changes in the downland bird populations, not all of them however explicable by the developments described above. The Wheatear has disappeared as a breeding species and the Red-backed Shrike once well distributed is now a rarity. The Stone Curlew was becoming rare in Bucknill's day but has now gone completely. The Whinchat has long since ceased to breed on the downs. Hooded

Crows which were at one time regular winter visitors can no longer be considered other than vagrant. On the credit side the low scrub and long grass have encouraged a number of warblers, thrushes and finches to breed which would not have favoured the downland habitat when the turf was close-cropped and cover very limited.

Parkland is a more significant habitat in the metropolitan area of the county than in outer Surrey. Again the importance of the park depends on whether it is a 'natural' park with rough grass and woodland or of the 'municipal' type with short mown grass. Some parks are open to, and used extensively by, the public while others have restricted access and are normally associated with large country estates. The essential feature common to all parks is the large (or comparatively large) area of land uncluttered by hedges but having a number of trees which may be more or less isolated.

In private parkland the land is now often intensively farmed but while the trees are allowed to remain many breeding populations are supported. Parkland does not usually hold any unusual species but the abundance of nesting holes in trees attracts Tawny and Little Owls, Stock Dove, Kestrel, Tree Sparrow, Green Woodpecker, Blue and Great Tits. Ground nesting species are found in parks providing suitable cover and only limited disturbance. Municipal-type parks frequently attract ground feeding species such as gulls and thrushes.

Richmond Park is perhaps the best known and watched in the county. Collenette summarized observations up to 1937 and since then records have been published in the annual reports of the LNHS and later also the SBC. The birdlife of the park is of considerable interest, although some of the former breeding species such as Wheatear, Whinchat and Stonechat have long ceased to breed. In 1935 there were 20-25 pairs of Redstart but in 1970 just one pair bred. Meadow Pipits, Skylarks, and Yellowhammers however breed commonly. Tawny Owls and Stock Doves breed in the ancient oaks and in 1967 no fewer than 20 pairs of Kestrels were known to breed in the park.

Equally renowned is Windsor Great Park, the southern tip of which is in Surrey. Within the park are ancient forest, open water and grassland and a good cross section of the breeding birds of the county is present. The Mandarin Duck breeds freely here.

Ashtead Park supports some ground nesting species including Willow Warbler and Whitethroat and the private section has thriving populations of Jackdaws, Stock Doves and woodpeckers which breed in the well-spaced oaks.

The corvids are well represented in Farnham Park, Jackdaws nesting round the castle keep. The Willow Warbler, Chiffchaff and Whitethroat are the common summer visitors and the Nuthatch is frequently recorded. Grey Wagtails can be seen on the stream and Turtle Doves and Collared Doves are increasing. Great Grey Shrike was recorded in 1964 and 1965.

Stoke Park, Guildford provides varied habitats including damp riverside, rough grassland and allotments. Breeding species include Pheasant, Tawny Owl, Stock Dove, Skylark, Chiffchaff, Willow Warbler, Blackcap, Whitethroat, Meadow Pipit, Linnet and Tree Sparrow.

The woodland, downland and parkland of Surrey support in no small measure most of the species which breed or winter in the county. Surrey is better endowed than most counties in the extent of these habitats and it is surely important that we should do what we can to maintain them.

Migration, Roost Fly-lines and other Movements

A. J. Holcombe

Although Surrey has no coastline or mountains, it is possible to observe a considerable amount of bird movement in the county throughout the year. In this chapter all movements will be discussed, not only the spring and autumn passage of birds through the area to and from their breeding grounds elsewhere and the arrival and departure of our summer and winter visitors but also hard weather movements, occasional 'invasions' or irruptions and flights to and from roosts and feeding grounds.

Naturalists and others had long been aware of the arrival, departure and passage of different species of birds in Surrey but surprisingly little work had been done on migration until recent years, with the remarkable exception of F. D. Power's study (1910) carried out in the Brixton area from 1874 to 1909. From his suburban garden there, he noted large migrations, particularly in October; the birds, mostly Chaffinches, Skylarks, Starlings, Rooks, Redwings and Fieldfares, were seen in numbers only when the wind blew from a westerly point, preferably wnw; on such days there would be streams of birds passing steadily wnw into the wind. On very windy days, migrants would pass low over his garden. Power also noted that the hirundines followed a more southerly autumn migration direction. Most movements were seen between 0730 and 1030 hours and on the few occasions when migrants had a following wind, the observer concluded that the wind had changed after they had set out. The spring passage was not very conspicuous.

After this, there appeared W. Eagle Clarke's *Studies in Bird Migration* but this work was not much concerned with Surrey and until fairly recently it was only from the notes of such observers as A. Beadell in east Surrey and later H. Bentham, that we had much information on migration in the county. Beadell recorded the arrival and passage in the Chelsham area and Bentham tabulated numbers of newly-arrived nocturnal migrants found on the Downs in autumn.

It is now realized that nearly all of Power's conclusions were correct, although the constituents of the migration are nowadays somewhat different, there being more Woodpigeons and less Corvidae participating. Many more studies of visible migration have been made, confirming that the largest migrations are seen in autumn when the wind is in a westerly quarter, although there may well be a passage at higher altitudes with following winds or (as Power thought) into different headwinds, the birds remaining unobserved from the ground. The London area in particular has been watched intensively and yet a large number of migrating birds must escape notice altogether. Indeed, we are only seeing a fraction of the complex bird movements that are constantly taking place.

Much of the passage takes place at night and here the trained listener can establish the migration of such species as Curlew, Greenshank, Whimbrel and Redwings, the last being very frequently heard in late October and November and on their return to northern Europe in March and early April. Evidence of nocturnal passage is easily obtained also by visiting such areas as the Downs and commons early on a spring or autumn morning; many passerines such as Wheatears, Whinchats, Redstarts, flycatchers, warblers and thrushes are seen where they do not normally breed and soon afterwards they have moved on elsewhere. In some cases, migrants stay for a few days, more especially in autumn. Certain species migrate by day as well as at night but the hirundines, Swifts and other groups such as corvids and pigeons seem only to migrate diurnally.

In 1960 the London Natural History Society initiated an autumn diurnal migration watch, which was repeated in 1962. These counts, made by numerous observers at different points, established that there is on certain days a broad front migration of birds which have presumably set off from continental Europe at dawn and maintain their general westerly direction as they move inland in this country. In the years 1960-2, the spring passage was also studied and found to consist of small movements to the east or north in late March and April. Some idea of the numbers of birds involved in the autumn visible migration may be gained from the estimate of 4,000,000 passing over the LNHS area during less than seven weeks in 1960.

It was in 1963 that the Surrey Bird Club set up nine Inland Observation Points for the study of bird movements and populations, as a part of a national scheme organized by the British Trust for Ornithology. All birds flying within, or seen flying from, a clearly defined area were to be identified and counted, if possible on a daily basis, throughout the year. This work continued in 1964 with a slightly smaller number of Observation Points. Besides affording many unusual records (such as that of 50 Whooper Swans flying ENE at Chessington on 22 March 1963), these studies reaffirmed the general pattern of autumn passage, starting with warblers in late July, then with hirundines in August and September and finally Starlings, Chaffinches and Redwings in October, as main participants, with lesser numbers of Skylarks and other species.

Observations made in Surrey in 1964, in conjunction with migration watches organized by the Sussex Ornithological Society, encouraged further studies on the Downs in east Surrey, in 1965 and 1966. Counts at these inland sites only provided a fraction of the numbers of migrants seen on the Sussex coast but the October passage was fairly heavy. An interesting fact to emerge here (noted also at Chessington) was that the birds were not always flying into the wind; for example, several hundred Starlings and thrushes moved NNW and WNW with easterly winds on 9 and 10 October 1965. This is an instance of the complexity of the problems concerning migration; the direction and force of the wind are clearly not the only factors, although it is true to say that most visible migrating flocks seem to fly more or less into the wind. Birds were seen on the move in most weather conditions, except continuous rain and thick fog. Migration was occasionally noticeable before and after the passage of frontal weather systems.

This watching on the east Surrey Downs was rewarding in the variety of species, as records of Sparrow Hawk, 'ringtail' harrier, Woodcock, Curlew, Black Tern, Short-eared Owl, Woodlark, Hawfinch and Crossbill show.

Work done using films of radar screen displays in the post-war years has been adding to what was known about the migrations in south east England. The movements are shown to be exceedingly complex and variable, but reveal three main directions of flight: east to west, NNW to SSE, NNE to SSW, and conversely. East to west movements occur in every month, southward movements are commonest in autumn but occasional in spring, northward movements are commonest in spring and rare in autumn; all six movements occur in winter, with 'reversed' movements throughout the year, usually with a more or less following wind. Hard weather flights, from areas affected by snow or frost, have been frequently noted, with corresponding return flights when conditions improved. A feature of the hard weather flights is that the wind is frequently behind the birds as they move away from the approaching snow.

The main point of difference between the radar findings and the theories of Power and others is this: Lack and Eastwood (1962) found that many movements take place with a following wind; and that wind direction has little effect on the spring passage. This is partially explained by the fact that low-flying migrants visible to Power and other watchers in autumn are too near the ground to be picked up by radar and the high-flying birds plotted on the screens are too far up to be seen by observers on the ground, even in good weather.

Radar studies also show that birds have an innate tendency to migrate in a set direction, which is then modified during a sea crossing by a secondary tendency to make for the nearest land. Thus, Chaffinches heading wsw in autumn over Holland and along the Belgian and French coasts have been seen to assume a wnw course at Cap Gris Nez over the English Channel and it is this direction that they are still following when they pass over Surrey.

It was necessary to consider south-east England as a whole in the preceding section, because of Surrey's relatively small size and absence of coastline but now we can turn to detailed records of migrants in our county. Marking of birds by rings has been responsible for our knowledge of the movements of individual birds and over the last twenty or thirty years has added enormously to our information on migration and dispersal.

During 1957 the Surrey Bird Club supported and helped to organize ringing at Epsom and Guildford sewage farms, whilst the lnhs continued to operate very successfully at Beddington sf and individuals carried out ringing at Hersham and elsewhere. The Hersham Ringing Group was founded in 1964 and since then, both the numbers of ringers and the sphere of their activities have increased and it is of interest to note that at the end of the review period upwards of 15,000 birds were being ringed annually in the county. Space does not permit the listing of the individual recoveries, the more important of which have been referred to in the systematic list but it is clear that ringing plays a very important part in providing vital information on the origins of our summer and winter visitors, on longevity and on dispersal generally.

Some of the sightings of unusual species in Surrey are presumably due to the 'overshooting' of the birds' destination, owing to abnormal weather conditions and in particular to strong winds. Seabirds of various species have been reported storm-driven inland, such as Manx Shearwater, Leach's and Storm Petrels, Gannet and auks but these appearances are rare and in general there are, as one would expect, far less records of 'drift' and storm-driven rarities than in the coastal counties.

In winter, however, the advent of severe frost and snow causes very large movements of ground-feeding birds, usually south, sw or west to regions where the food supply is more readily available. In such cases, there is a mass exodus of such birds as Lapwing, Woodpigeon, Skylark and thrushes. For example, 810 Lapwings flew sw in 90 minutes at Weybridge on 27 December 1968; the next day, c. 550 flew west at Ewell in a similar period of time and c. 900 went wsw at Worcester Park in 100 minutes. Fieldfares are also seen in numbers in similar movements; 626 flew west at Ewell on 9 January 1968 and more than 780 flew sw at Worcester Park on 28 December of that year. Similarly, 'hundreds' of this species moved south over Clapham Common on 1 January 1962, at which time c. 2,000 Skylarks flew south at Shirley and thousands likewise at West Molesey.

Certain species occur in the county in abnormal numbers from time to time. These invasions or irruptions have been ascribed to a failure of the food crop and/or population pressure resulting from unusual breeding success elsewhere. One such bird is the Crossbill, normally very few being present in Surrey but which appears periodically in unusually high numbers in suitable habitats throughout the county. There have been numerous invasions of this species in the present century full details of which are set out in the systematic list. Waxwings have also graced the county with their presence in several winters, the invasion of 1946-7 being the largest ever recorded. An influx of the rare Nutcracker into this country occurred in 1968 and a few were noted in Surrey in the early autumn.

From time to time there are increases in the numbers of Jays and other Corvidae and also of different species of tits, whose movements are apparent through suburban parks and gardens (as in the autumn of 1957). A record of 50-60 Jays at Wandsworth Common on 5 November 1965 is noteworthy.

The Short-eared Owl appears in fair numbers in certain winters, when voles and other small mammals are abundant; thus at the end of 1970 there were as many as ten of these owls at Beddington SF.

Many of the visible bird movements are connected with communal roosting. Especially in winter, there are very considerable flights of Starlings, gulls, Woodpigeons, Rooks, Jackdaws, thrushes and finches throughout our area. Most of the Starlings from the suburban districts fly into the centre of London to roost, their flights often being thousands strong. There are well-established fly-lines but birds from areas more than about 14 miles out do not appear to use central London, having some roosts in outer Surrey as at Reigate and Ockham where numbers sometimes reach prodigious proportions.

The enormous increase in the number of gulls in the area led the Roskill Committee to ask for documentation on their numbers and habits, in connection with the siting of the third airport for London; in response to this members of the LNHS and the SBC contributed to a study of gull roosting flights in Middlesex and Surrey (Parr, 1970). With the increasing number of reservoirs, suitable habitat for gull roosts is available and counts made in January 1969 showed that, on those reservoirs in the Thames basin which lie in Surrey, a total of 186,440 gulls roosted, of which most were Black-headed but with several thousands of the other wintering gulls, viz. Common, Herring, Great and Lesser Black-backed. More than half of these were counted at Queen Elizabeth II Reservoir but Island Barn and Barn Elms also held very large numbers of roosting gulls. Most of the information collected concerned evening flights, as these are more easily observed; the morning dispersal to feeding-grounds takes place very early and is usually protracted and on a broad front, whereas the evening flights are more concentrated and channelled in well-defined routes. The birds feed in various habitats: water-meadows, sewage farms, rubbish dumps and ploughed land, for example. At dusk, the gulls can be seen making their way, often in formation, back to the reservoirs.

Gulls from west Surrey are seen to use the Queen Mary Reservoir roost, in Middlesex; some follow approximately the course of the River Wey. The Mole Gap is used by some of the gulls from central Surrey heading for the Walton Group of Reservoirs but the main approach to these is initially from the SE and finally from the east. Barn Elms is approached from a SE direction. The Thames is believed to act as a guide-line to all these reservoirs. The evening flights are frequently of spectacular proportions.

Rooks and Jackdaws have well-known roosts, for example at Titsey, Oxted and Smallfield and formerly at Gatton Park, whilst a roost of Carrion Crows has long been established at Woodmansterne, many of the birds spending the day at Beddington SF. Several House Sparrow roosts exist in hawthorn thickets on the Downs and in winter there are large roosts of several Finch species in certain localities. Other species which commonly form winter roosts are Redwing, Fieldfare, Pied Wagtail (sometimes favouring greenhouses as at Milford and Hersham), Meadow Pipit and Corn Bunting.

Movements of birds to and from roosts complicate considerably the task of the ornithologist in compiling an accurate assessment of migration through Surrey but when regular observations are made at a fixed point, the pattern becomes apparent and when a true migration takes place, it can be recognized as such. Thus, during the morning of 18 October 1958, K. D. Edwards observed at Epsom the following birds moving WNW on a broad front at heights of 40-200 feet, into a wind veering from WSW to WNW.

Cormorant	7	Meadow Pipit	5
Lapwing	9	Starling	243
Stock Dove	6	Greenfinch	19
Woodpigeon	11	Linnet	51
Skylark	748	Chaffinch	6
Fieldfare	66	Reed Bunting	2
Redwing	37		

These birds were no doubt flying low on account of the headwind. By the afternoon there was less movement but Skylarks and Lapwings were still migrating and in the next few days there were many such observations, corresponding well in flight direction and composition of flocks with larger-scale movements recorded at Dungeness on the Kent coast. This is an example of a typical 'good' Surrey migration in mid to late October, on a broad front, into a westerly airstream.

But many birds migrate virtually unobserved. It is by making regular counts locally that one establishes an arrival of migrants. For example, H. Bentham in 1960 found a marked influx of Wheatears, Meadow Pipits, Linnets and Goldfinches on Epsom Downs from late August to early October. During the years 1953-60, the waders at Guildford SF were regularly counted by N. J. Westwood and a clear pattern emerged. The spring passage would begin with Redshank, followed by Little Ringed Plover and increased numbers of Green Sandpiper, after which came Common Sandpiper and the less numerous Dunlin, Greenshank, Ringed Plover and other waders. In autumn, the birds stayed longer and Green and Common Sandpipers were present generally at the same peak period, in late July and August. Snipe numbers were at their greatest in late autumn and early winter and again in early spring. In addition to the customary species, such rarities as Knot, Grey Plover, Sanderling, Curlew Sandpiper and Grey Phalarope were recorded.

A brief survey of the year's migratory movements would be as follows: in January and February, birds are in their winter haunts and only in the event of severe weather will there be any pronounced movements, in which case these will probably be in a direction between south and west; with warmer weather, return movements may be seen. From early March, the first arrivals from the south of summer visitors take place and winter visitors begin to depart eastwards. By the end of the month, several species of summer visitors have arrived and during April the majority of the breeding birds are returning to their nesting-sites. Passage, particularly of waders, continues throughout May and the remainder of the later nesters, such as Nightjar, Swift, Hobby and Turtle Dove, complete the total number of Surrey's breeding species.

The first Lapwings are already coming across the Continent in late June and July and by the end of the latter month some of the other wader species are again passing through Surrey. The first Black-headed Gulls appear in July followed by Lesser Black-backed Gulls in August. Warblers begin to leave in July and then in August and September there is a further generally southward departure of these and also of Swifts and hirundines, whose direction of flight is normally between south and sw. The first winter visitors are here before the last Swallows and House Martins have gone and by mid-October the extensive immigrations, which we have described earlier, are under way; these continue, in a general nw, wnw or west direction well into November. Meanwhile, the winter populations of duck are building up on the lakes and reservoirs and the scene is set for the cold season once more, with the roosting-flights and movements connected with the availability of food.

There remains a great amount of work to be done before the complete picture of migration in Surrey is known. Studies of visible migration from certain vantage-points, counts of birds in places where migrants rest and feed, radar scanning and ringing have all contributed a great deal but there must be many migrants passing through unrecorded and many problems, such as the effect of wind direction and force on the height and intensity of bird movements, remain to be solved. It is hoped that many readers will become interested enough to do some migration-watching themselves; for the study of the autumn passage in particular, there should on certain days be sufficient numbers of birds on the move, to make the figures meaningful. Correlation with data obtained from coastal observatories will be useful. Any site with good all-round visibility would be suitable for a migration-watch, preferably at some height and away from disturbance so that call-notes can be heard, to assist correct identification.

In Surrey, birds at times may seem to follow the edge of the escarpment and have been seen to use the Mole Gap as part of their route but passage is generally seen on a broad front, with little channelling or change of direction. The lakes and reservoirs are good places for the observation of resting migrants, as are the sewage farms and, for 'falls' of passerines, commons and bushy areas should be visited. Many interesting birds occur even in gardens and the writer of this chapter has seen, over the years, Hoopoe, Great Grey and Red-backed Shrikes, Black Redstart, Wryneck, Tree Pipit and Brambling in his suburban garden at Sanderstead, thus showing that there must be considerable migration in that area although no set route is apparent.

An attempt has been made in the preceding pages to show that despite the absence of a coastline the phenomenon of migration is no less a fascinating or absorbing subject in Surrey than in counties endowed with more spectacular natural features. It is hoped that these observations will inspire further research and that in the next few years we will have much more information on this intriguing subject.

The Systematic List

Very scarce winter visitor.
This bird has been recorded in the county 15 times in the present century and almost half the records refer to the winters from 1954/55 to 1957/58 when sightings were made at Barn Elms Reservoir, Lonsdale Road Reservoir (Barnes), Frensham, Earlswood Lake and Walton Reservoirs. No records have been accepted for the county since 18 February 1965 when a bird was found dead at Frensham. Most records cover the period November to April but one bird, first seen on 1 February 1937 at the Lonsdale Road Reservoir, stayed till 5 June 1937 by which time it had acquired full breeding plumage.

Black-throated Diver *Gavia arcticus*

Extremely scarce winter visitor.
There have been eight records of this species in the county accepted in the present century and five of these have been from Barn Elms Reservoir. Other localities where it has been recorded are Hedgecourt, Frensham and Pen Ponds (Richmond Park). The records span the months October to February and the last record in the review period is that from Pen Ponds where a bird stayed from 16 October to 3 November 1965.

Great Northern Diver *Gavia immer*

Very scarce winter visitor.
This has been the most frequent of the divers to visit the county in the present century, with some 25 records, 15 of these occurring in the 1950s. The most recent records were in 1960; one was seen on Badshot Lea Pond on 6 February and a bird, possibly the same one stayed at Frensham Great Pond from 28 February to 27 March.

Over half the records have been in February and the rest in October, December, January and March.

The bird has been recorded on both large and small waters throughout the county, occasionally on the Thames and exceptionally, gale blown or stranded in an oiled con-

Red-throated Diver *Gavia stellatus*

dition away from water as at Chiddingfold on 20 February 1950.

Great Crested Grebe *Podiceps cristatus* Moderately common resident. Winter visitor. At the end of the last century this species was comparatively rare and was breeding only spasmodically in five localities: Frensham, Gatton, Richmond Park, Vachery and Windsor Park. There had been a marked decrease in the nineteenth century in the British Isles and the total population in mid-century was down to about 42 pairs. Recovery began before 1900 and continued well into the present century.

In Surrey the increase up to the mid-1930s was steady with new waters being colonized at the rate of about five or six per decade. It is characteristic of the species however that the population is subject to a good deal of shifting, with breeding birds moving from one water to another, old sites being deserted and new ones colonized at a fairly steady rate.

Since 1931 the status of the species has been closely studied both nationally and locally. National censuses were undertaken in 1931 and 1935 (*BB*, 26:62-92; *BB*, 44:361-9) and a sample census including Surrey was maintained over the years 1946-55 (Hollom, 1959) and a further national census organized by the BTO was made in 1965 (Prestt and Mills, 1966). In these last two censuses, counts were made in early June of all adult grebes on all suitable waters in the county. The results for Surrey were as follows:

1931: 47 breeding pairs on 24 waters, with a total of 123 adults on 28 groups of waters.

1935: 25 breeding pairs on 12 waters.

1946-55: average annual total 140 adults (minimum 94 in 1947, maximum 210 in 1950).

1965: 29 groups of waters held 108 to 115 adults.

The results reflect a fairly stable population in Surrey over the past three decades of the review period with something like fifteen breeding localities and a population of 20-30 breeding pairs, the more important breeding sites being Badshot Lea, the Frensham Ponds, Gatton Park and Papercourt and Thorpe GPs.

The species will nest on almost any large pool with some weed or emergent vegetation to provide anchorage for its nest. The minimum size tolerated is approximately five acres but narrow waters in steep valleys are avoided. All but the very largest breeding waters are usually vacated in winter and winter flocks congregate at the Thames Valley reservoirs at Walton, Island Barn and Barn Elms. This build up begins in some years as early as July. Some big counts have been as follows:

257 at Walton (Chelsea and Lambeth) on 13 November 1937, 120 at Island Barn on 23 September 1961 and 64 at Barn Elms on 28 July 1962.

The biggest ever flocks recorded in the county occurred in the severe weather of early 1963. There were 375 on Queen Elizabeth II Reservoir on 13 January, numbers rising to between 300 and 500 on 19 January but dropping to 10 on 26 January. At Walton (Knight) numbers rose to 305 on 3 March. Peak numbers on the Thames in the freeze-up were 110 at Teddington Lock on 27 January, 200 between Kingston Bridge and Richmond Bridge on 1 February and 400-500 between Putney and Kingston on 2 February. The largest concentration since 1963 has been 200 at Queen Elizabeth II Reservoir on 7 October 1967 and the maximum recorded number in the last three years of the review period was 150 at the Knight and Bessborough Reservoirs on 17 January 1970.

Birds begin to return to their breeding waters in February or March and nesting usually starts in April with territory adjustment continuing till May.

Only one bird ringed in the county has been recovered and that was ringed at Morden on 2 February 1965 and recovered in Wiltshire on 13 August 1966.

Scarce visitor.

Red-necked Grebe
Podiceps grisegena

The first county record of this species in the present century was at Barn Elms Reservoir in 1913 since when there have been ten further records from that locality. There have been four records from the Frensham Ponds: a 'pair' on 9 July 1925 and single birds on 23 January 1949, 3 December 1959 and 9 May 1968. Other localities where the species has been recorded have been Guildford SF (in 1944 and 1949) and the Walton Reservoirs while in April 1964 birds in summer plumage were reported from Holmethorpe GPS and Childown Hall, Chobham. There was an unusually large number of records in 1969; birds were reported from Walton in January with two present from 22 February to 14 April and in the latter part of the year there were single birds at Barn Elms Reservoir on 4 and 6 October, Island Barn Reservoir on 31 October 1969, Walton on 2 November (two being present in December) and Queen Elizabeth II Reservoir on 27 December. The Hersham Ringing Group operating at Walton in the winter of 1969/70 rescued two birds from the inlet tower of Knight Reservoir where they had been caught up whilst diving for food and they were released after ringing, apparently no worse for the experience. These were only the third and fourth birds of this species to be ringed in the whole of the British Isles.

The species has been reported in all months of the year except June. There is some concentration of records in December and again in March/April, the latter suggesting that passage birds are involved.

Slavonian Grebe
Podiceps auritus

Scarce winter visitor. Probable passage migrant.

This attractive species is seen in most winters as a lone visitor to the reservoirs, the Thames or the Frensham Ponds. The first record in the present century was of one on the Thames at Richmond on 16 February 1917. There were seven records from Barn Elms Reservoir over the period 1918-54 and at least 15 records from Frensham from 1923-67. Three birds were recorded at Mitcham 15-20 February 1937 following easterly gales in January (*BB*, 30:372) and there is one record of a bird on the R. Wandle at Carshalton from 28 January to 6 February 1963. The records span the months August to April with most occurring in February and November, this suggesting that passage birds may be involved.

Black-necked Grebe
Podiceps nigricollis

Uncommon visitor and passage migrant.

Prior to the 1920s this species was an extremely rare visitor to the county. In the period 1924-36 it was thought that one or two visited the county every year (*BB*, 32:69) and the records suggest that occurrences continued at this frequency till the early 1960s.

From the mid-1960s Island Barn Reservoir has been increasingly frequented by the species. Since the winter of 1966/67 between two and four birds have wintered there and in 1969 there was a marked autumn peak, clearly of passage birds, with ten (the highest number ever recorded in the county) on 19 October. In 1970 there were passage peaks both in the spring (eight, all in summer plumage, on 29 March) and in the autumn. The first autumn record was of one on 8 October and numbers rose to eight on 26 October and dropped to two by 8 November.

Records in the main are of ones or twos at the Frensham Ponds, Barn Elms, Island Barn and the Walton Reservoirs with occasional records from the Thames and smaller waters as at Boldermere (Wisley), Enton and Gatton. It has been recorded in all months but most records occur in the period September to March.

There are no ringing returns to suggest the source of

17 (top) *Gatton Park Lake, Reigate.* A quiet, private water where the shooting interest is the only major disturbance to the birds (*D. Washington*)

18 (bottom) *Woodland pool near Abinger.* Typical of many, this small water has Moorhen, Coot, Little Grebe, Mallard and Mandarin Duck nesting most years on and near it (*D. M. T. Ettlinger*)

these birds although it seems likely that they come from central/eastern Europe. The species no longer breeds in Ireland and is declining in Scotland and the small population there is unlikely to be the source of birds wintering or migrating through south-east England.

Moderately common resident. **Little**
This species is widely distributed over the county, breeding **Grebe**
on small ponds, gravel pits and lakes that provide sufficient *Podiceps*
surface vegetation on which it can anchor its nest. It also *ruficollis*
breeds on the river courses of the Mole and Wey as for
instance between Leatherhead and Cobham on the R. Mole
(which stretch usually holds three or four pairs) and on the
R. Wey near Stoke water meadows at Guildford.

It is difficult to assess any changes in numbers of breeding pairs in the county since the turn of the century because of the lack of precise figures but the indications are that the species is now less common than formerly. Autumn concentrations of 60-100 were recorded at Frensham in the late 1940s and early 1950s, whereas in the 1960s they seldom exceeded ten birds.

One of the largest breeding concentrations in the county was reported from Fetcham Mill Pond where 12 pairs bred in 1931 and 1932 and autumn flocks of c. 50 occurred in October and November. The good numbers ceased to breed at this site in 1934 when the pond was disturbed during the creation of nearby watercress beds. The largest breeding concentration in the 1960s was reported from the Ash Vale GPS in 1967 when six pairs were present and at least 15 young were raised.

The species disperses to larger waters and rivers during the harder weather of mid-winter and it is possible that some shift of population takes place, with resident birds moving south and visitors from the north or the Continent moving into the area.

Extremely scarce vagrant. **Leach's**
There are only two recorded occurrences for the first half of **Petrel**
the century of this essentially pelagic species. One was of *Oceanodroma*
a bird seen by W. A. Shaw on Frensham Great Pond on *leucorrhoa*
30 December 1911 and the other reported by D. Seth-
Smith, was of a bird captured in a snow drift at Dorking
on 27 December 1927 and identified after it had died two
days later (*BB*, 21:236).

The remaining records relate to the remarkable wreck in Britain in 1952 involving an estimated 6,700 birds. Four were found in Surrey: one alive at Cranleigh on 31 October, one

19 (top) *The River Mole*, from the Canadian Bridge, Leatherhead (*D. M. T. Ettlinger*)
20 (bottom) *The River Wey*. A quiet backwater near Guildford (*D. M. T. Ettlinger*)

82

dead at Haslemere on 1 November, one dead at Richmond on 2 November and the fourth, also dead, at Kingston Hill on 14 November (*BB*, 47:137-63). Eric Parker also reported one from Unstead SF on 28 September 1952; supporting details are lacking although circumstantial evidence suggests that this bird was in the wreck.

Storm Extremely scarce vagrant.
Petrel This status was also indicated for the species by Bucknill
Hydrobates and for the latter part of the nineteenth century there is
pelagicus only the record of one bird killed by flying into glass at Nork Park, Banstead in 1896. A male bird was caught alive at a street lamp in Guildford on 28 December 1901 (*Zool.*, 1902). A bird which was not storm driven (as there had been no recent gale) was seen swimming and flying at Frensham Great Pond on 5 October 1932 by L. S. Venables (*BB*, 27:27). A storm driven bird which did not survive reported by Eric Parker from Hambledon on 26 August 1951 is the last recorded occurrence of the species in Surrey.

Manx Extremely scarce vagrant.
Shearwater All the reports of this species in the present century have
Procellaria come from the London area. One was reported from Clap-
puffinus ham in 1946, one from Barn Elms Reservoir on 8 September 1953, and another, badly oiled, was found on a pond on Mitcham Common at about the same time. Single birds were picked up exhausted in gardens in South Norwood on 9 September 1968 and 6 October 1969; both were rehabilitated and released, apparently in good condition, at Brighton.

The county can also claim a link with R. M. Lockley's homing experiments with this species in June 1937. Two birds taken from their burrows on Skokholm were released at Frensham and were back in their burrows 24 hours later. The distance from Frensham to Skokholm is 200 miles direct or 390 miles by the shortest sea route from the nearest coastal point (*BB*, 31:244).

Fulmar The inclusion of this species rests on one record, that of a
Fulmarus dead bird picked up by Lt W. P. G. Taylor in a wood on
glacialis Whitmoor Common on 20 April 1941 (*BB*, 35:40).

Gannet Extremely scarce vagrant.
Sula bassana There have been at least seven records of this species in the county in the present century. One, evidently wounded, was seen on the Wey near Godalming on 17 February 1906 (*Zool.*, 1906), one was reported in the *Daily Mirror* on 12 November 1927 as being found in a cottage garden at Kenley,

one was recorded at Wandsworth in May 1930 and one was seen in flight at Waterloo Bridge on 28 January 1941. An adult was picked up at Barnes Railway Bridge on 31 January 1956 and later released in the Thames Estuary by the RSPCA. A single bird was seen flying west at Tolworth on 25 November 1958 and finally a sick sub-adult bird that first appeared on Frensham Little Pond on 27 August 1963 subsequently died.

Regular visitor.

Cormorant
Phalacrocorax carbo

This species occurs in good numbers on the Thames and associated reservoirs in winter but it has been recorded in all months of the year.

Prior to the 1940s the bird was a very rare straggler to Surrey, the odd records being mainly of single birds at Frensham Great Pond but after 1946 the species was increasingly reported from the Thames above Kew Bridge and from the Walton Reservoirs. The first substantial gathering recorded was of 30 at Walton Reservoirs in March 1954. These reservoirs seem to be particularly suited to its needs and the bird can be seen regularly in the winter months on the causeway separating the Knight and Bessborough Reservoirs. When the Queen Elizabeth II Reservoir was opened in 1962 the species immediately found the platform towers in the centre of the reservoir particularly attractive for resting and roosting. The biggest counts at these reservoirs are recorded from November to March and total numbers increased in the late 1960s. There were 104 on 28 January 1968 at Walton and 130 at dusk at Queen Elizabeth II on 12 January 1969. As the Walton and Queen Elizabeth II Reservoirs are adjacent there is probably a regular interchange of birds between them and also with Island Barn Reservoir to the east. Numbers from May to August are usually very small.

In the severe weather of January 1963 large numbers were reported from the Thames with c. 60 between Kew and Richmond on 26 January.

In the last decade of the review period the species was regularly reported in ones and twos from the ponds of outer Surrey including Enton, Frensham, Hedgecourt and Vachery and the gravel pits at Holmethorpe, Papercourt and Thorpe. Occasionally birds are reported in flight well away from an aquatic environment, as for instance one flying south at Caterham on 26 July 1966 and one flying east over Thursley Common on 5 November 1967. Eleven were recorded flying SSE over Ewell on 26 November 1969.

Shag Irregular winter visitor.
Phalacrocorax There were only six records for the first half of the present
aristotelis century, two of which were of three birds on the Thames
at Barnes in April and May 1937 and Chiswick in February
1938. Since 1958 however it was recorded annually in the
county excepting only 1964 and 1970. The occurrences have
been between the months of December and March although
there have been single records in August and October and
the three birds seen at Barnes on the Thames in February
1937 stayed there throughout April and May and one remained till 28 June. The records usually concern only one
to three birds but occasionally larger numbers are involved.
Nine were recorded in the county in February 1958 (*BB*,
51:131). In the second week of March 1962 in very cold
weather with strong NE winds a wreck of birds occurred in
southern England. Up to a dozen immature Shags were
reported from various parts of the county and in addition,
six were seen in flight over South Croydon on 28 March
(PCGS).

Surprisingly a number of the records over the review
period have been of birds found in back gardens, namely at
Worplesdon Hill, Childown (Chertsey), Hindhead and In-
val (Haslemere).

A bird found at Morden on 17 February 1953 had been
ringed as a young bird on the Farne Islands in 1952.

Heron Moderately common resident.
Ardea cinerea There is little doubt that the Heron has lost ground in the
county since 1900. Of the four heronries in use then, three
have been abandoned while three new ones have been
started, one of which has not survived. A series of national
Heron censuses was started in 1920 and reported at ten year
intervals until in the 1960s they became an annual event.
The total number of nests counted in Surrey in selected
years has been as follows:

1928: 66, 1938: 113, 1954: 93, 1959: 66, 1960: 60 and
1970: c. 50.

The following is a brief summary of individual heronries
compiled from the census figures and other published
material:

Waverley (near Farnham): This site was of ancient origin.
It had 18 nests in 1892 and 15 in 1913. At least part of it
was destroyed by tree-felling in 1920 but there were still
four occupied nests in 1941; it finally succumbed before the
end of the war when all the trees were cut down.

Peperharow: There was a small colony here in Bucknill's

time and it was still present in 1907. It was subject to persecution and was deserted in 1910.

Richmond Park: This colony started with a single pair in 1880 in the Sidmouth and Pond Plantation and by 1909 had grown to 30-40 pairs. It reached its maximum in 1939 with 61 pairs. In 1941 it was bombed and in the following years was disturbed by tree-felling which caused some desertion and in 1947 it was down to ten pairs. It recovered to 23 pairs in 1953 but by 1960 only seven pairs were present; there was no breeding success and breeding has not occurred there since.

Burwood Park, Walton: Fifteen to 20 pairs nested here from at least 1925. This heronry is thought to have originated from nearby Ashley Park where a heronry had thrived in the nineteenth century. There are no records of breeding at Burwood after 1942.

Virginia Water, Windsor Great Park: This colony is of ancient origin. There were about ten nests in 1910 all in Berkshire. In 1948 the heronry moved into the area it still occupies at Fort Belvedere on the Surrey side of the border. There were 48 nests in 1949, numbers rising to a maximum of 70 in 1954 after which there was a gradual decline to 18-20 in the early 1960s but there was some recovery towards the end of the decade and about 40 nests were occupied in 1970.

Gatton Park: This heronry started in 1930 with one pair and by 1943 had increased to seven pairs. There was then some fluctuation with numbers of pairs not rising above 12 until 1961 and 1962 when peak numbers of 18 were reached. There was a reduction to eight in 1964 and numbers since then have continued on the low side with no more than four or five pairs nesting 1967-70.

Chilworth: This heronry in trees overlooking Waterloo Ponds was first recorded in 1964 with two or three nests. It grew slowly to eight pairs in 1967 and then up to 1970 numbers fluctuated between three and five pairs.

A small heronry of two to three nests was discovered in 1969 at Pirbright although no evidence of successful breeding was obtained and the site was deserted in 1970.

There have been a number of single nests recorded viz: one at Albury for a few years prior to 1907 (*Zool.*, 1907) (possibly a forerunner of the Chilworth colony), one in the unlikely position on the base of a fountain in a pond near the Palm House of Kew Gardens in 1907 (*BOC Bull.*); a pair nested at Broadwater, Godalming from 1948 to 1950 and in 1970 a pair successfully raised a brood of three in a nest 30 feet high in an Alder tree at Ockley Court.

National figures show the total Heron population to be fairly static in the south of England with hard winters having an immediate adverse effect on numbers but with the population quickly recovering to normal levels (Parslow, 1967). Generally speaking in Surrey with annual breeding numbers in the range 30-50 in the late 1960s numbers compare unfavourably with the numbers recorded in the first half of the century.

In the autumn and winter months the birds disperse to reservoirs, gravel pits, river courses, lakes and wet boggy areas (such as that on Thursley Common) where they are able to find suitable food. Numbers at reservoirs where the birds often resort to rest, are sometimes high; 38 were counted at Walton on 8 July 1962 and 15 at Barn Elms Reservoir on 19 November 1967.

Ringing returns do not show any very pronounced movements. Three birds of the year ringed at Virginia Water in 1947 were recovered in Buckinghamshire or Berkshire in the same year and a bird from Walton in 1935 reached Ardingley, Sussex, in its first winter. Another bird ringed at Walton in 1930 was recovered where ringed in 1938.

Purple Heron
Ardea
purpurea

Bucknill referred to the one specimen, originating from Stafford, reputed to have been shot at Frensham but he was unable to obtain any details and the record is open to some doubt. There is one record in the present century—an immature bird was present at Frensham Little Pond from 18 to 25 September 1955 and was seen by many observers.

Night Heron
Ardea
nycticorax

Extremely scarce vagrant.

Although two or three records for the county were known in 1900 the species was not recorded again until the 1960s. One was present in Battersea Park in November and December 1967 and an adult was present in and around a small chicken-run adjoining Berrylands SF from December 1966 till at least 15 June 1967. Both these birds were however subsequently thought to have escaped from London Zoo (*BB*, 61:334). An immature bird was present in a riverside garden at Farnham from 1 December 1968 till the end of the year and although the record was accepted by the Rarities Committee of *British Birds* it was pointed out that an average of eight or nine disperse each year from a free flying colony at Edinburgh Zoo Park and any record of this species must be accepted with a *caveat* as to the possibility of the bird not being genuinely wild.

Little Bittern
Ixobrychus minutus

Extremely scarce vagrant.
Three or four previous records were known for the county in 1900 and there has been a similar number since then. An immature bird was identified at Pen Ponds, Richmond Park, on 20 August 1954 and was still present there on 24 August and on 27 and 29 August an immature, presumably the same bird, was seen at a muddy pool at Beddington SF. In 1956 a very noisy but shy pair frequented some heavily overgrown sludge lagoons at Beddington SF from 18 June to 14 July and single birds were seen there on 6 and 14 August. There was no evidence of breeding. The latest record in the period under review is of a decomposing bird found at West Byfleet on 22 August 1961 and identified by an official of the RSPB.

Bittern
Botaurus stellaris

Very scarce vagrant.
There have been 15 published records of this species in the present century; eight of the records occurred prior to 1950 and seven between 1956 and 1965. All except one occurred in the months December to March, the exception being one bird at Frensham on 26 July 1959. The records are widely scattered throughout the county and include four from the Frensham area, two from Peperharow and others from small, reed-fringed streams as at Abinger, Brook and South Munstead. The effect of extremely hard weather has sometimes clearly been the cause of the birds' appearance and in 1947 during and after a prolonged cold spell birds were reported from Peperharow in January, Beddington SF on 1 February and a suburban garden at Carshalton on 18 March.

White Stork
Ciconia ciconia

Extremely scarce vagrant.
Bucknill included this species in his *Birds of Surrey* on the strength of two records for which details were no longer available. One bird was seen on the ground in Richmond Park on 11 May 1930 (*The Field*, 155:773) but was thought to be an escape. In 1967 a remarkable and unprecedented series of records occurred in England and Scotland starting in mid-April and involving 13 or more birds, one of which, soaring over Abinger, was seen by W. Ruttledge on 3 June. These were clearly genuinely wild birds that had been displaced during their normal spring migration (*BB*, 61:335).

In 1939 some breeding birds were brought from their nests in Poland in an experiment to see whether they could find their way back to their nests. They were released after marking at Haslemere Museum and were traced as far as the east coast, after which unfortunately no further reports of them were received.

Spoonbill
Platalea
leucorodia
No records of this species have occurred in the county since a female was shot at Clandon Park on 26 November 1901 (*Zool.*, 1902).

Flamingo
Phoenicopterus
ruber
In a letter to the *Daily Telegraph* dated 29 March 1968 J. Wentworth Day cited from his records from Hampshire a Flamingo seen on Frensham Great Pond in 1909. Possibly the same bird is referred to by the *Haslemere List* (1921) under *Phoenicopterus ruber*, the bird having been seen by O. H. Latter and H. Bentham. Neither record is supported by any further details, nor is it clear if the bird was seen in the Surrey part of the pond, so the record must be regarded as unacceptable for the purpose of this review.

Many birds of this species seen at large in the present century have been under suspicion as probable escapes. One such, recorded on Pen Ponds, Richmond Park on 9 December 1932 stayed in the vicinity till the middle of January 1933 (Collenette, 1937).

Mandarin
Duck
Aix
galericulata
Moderately common resident, locally distributed.
This attractive, introduced species has now firmly established itself in the county and present indications are that it is extending its range and increasing in numbers.

The species is popular in private, ornamental wildfowl collections and there is no doubt that the present wild stock originated from this source. The first authentic record of the species seen in the free flying state was in 1929 when D. Goodwin noted birds on the R. Bourne. At about this time Alfred Ezra put some pinioned birds down on a small private pond near Cobham and the young reared were left unpinioned. The population here built up to about 150 birds and some birds spread to the surrounding countryside. This stock is thought to be the origin of a breeding colony which had established itself around Virginia Water in Windsor Great Park by 1933 and which by 1939 was quite large. This area has continued to be one of its main strongholds. The species bred (unsuccessfully) at Thorpe in 1946 and in 1953 a duck was seen on the Surrey side of the Thames at Runnymede with seven small young. In 1951 the estimated population in southern England was over 500, 400 of which were resident in Surrey and East Berkshire (Savage, 1952). From the late 1950s regular breeding has been reported from numerous areas centred on Cobham and in 1967 D. Washington found an old established colony on the Mole at Leigh; up to 28 were seen that year in this locality but previous totals were said to have exceeded 100 at times. In 1969 I. R. Beames located 55-60 pairs in the middle reaches of the Mole from Cobham to Esher and in the surrounding areas and in that year, came evidence of its spread to the outer areas of the county as at Thursley in the west and Vann Lake in the south.

The species is particularly suited to the Surrey countryside and especially the woods and fields in the Mole and Wey Valleys and does in fact adapt to woods containing only very small ponds well away from the river systems. It nests in trees, holes in old oaks being particularly favoured and is frequently seen feeding on acorns and on freshly growing cereal crops in spring. It appears to be largely sedentary and rarely resorts to the reservoirs but in winter flocks of 50 or more do build up on the larger lakes and ponds, as for instance at Painshill Lake (Cobham) and Virginia Water.

Wood Duck
Aix sponsa

Escape, feral birds occasionally breeding.
The Wood Duck, or Carolina Duck, is a close relative of the Mandarin, its preferred habitat being a similar one. As with the Mandarin, it has long been kept in British wildfowl collections (including several in Surrey) on account of its attractive plumage. In its native North America it frequents small lakes, rivers and marshy areas in deciduous woodland feeding more on land (on nuts, berries, etc.) than on water. It nests in holes in trees, sometimes a long way from water. It will breed in captivity and it is not surprising that escaped birds, finding themselves in a suitable habitat, have also sometimes bred. Escapes have been seen from time to time but usually go unrecorded although Bucknill mentioned a pair shot apparently in a wild state near Dorking prior to 1835. Occurrences towards the end of the review period include a drake at Norbury Park on 3 May 1959, two drakes and a duck on the R. Wandle at Hackbridge 13-27 October 1969 and a fully winged pair on Cutt Mill and adjacent ponds during 1969 when a duck was seen with four medium-sized young on 9 July. The Cutt Mill birds are known to have been of local origin. A pair was present here in the breeding season in the following year. At Guildford SF one was seen on 13 April 1967 and on 13 September 1970 a party of eight—a male and a female in eclipse and six birds of the year—was seen on one of the shallow lagoons by some trees. They were resting, some on water and some

on logs emerging from the water and had presumably bred not far away. Guildford SF, perhaps unlikely in itself to have provided the nest site, is bounded by the R. Wey and a belt of mature timber and pollarded willows. In December 1970 five drakes and three ducks were seen several miles further down the R. Wey at Wisley. There were also reports of several pairs on the Surrey/Berkshire border in the north-west of the county in 1969.

In view of the successful colonisation by the Mandarin it seems likely that at least sporadic breeding by escaped birds of this species will continue and that the Wood Duck may establish itself in a feral state in the county.

Mallard
Anas
platyrhynchos

Very common resident. Winter visitor.
This is a common and widespread species breeding in all parts of the county, including built up areas where rivers, ponds, lakes, reservoirs, sewage farms or gravel pits provide sufficient cover for nesting. Its most usual nesting situation is on the ground in vegetation adjoining water but it will readily take to trees as for instance pollarded willows and even larger trees when ground cover is scarce or insufficient and it will nest well away from water. Broods of ducklings are a common sight on lakes, reservoirs and ponds but many of them fall victim to predators. At Barn Elms Reservoir in 1969 no less than 31 or 32 broods were counted; in the same year 12 broods of 66 ducklings were reported from Thorpe GPs. Smaller waters will carry proportionately smaller numbers as for instance on Milton Court Pond, Dorking, where five and six broods were counted in 1960 and 1961 respectively.

The species congregates in the winter resorting to the rivers and larger lakes and reservoirs and this process starts in July. Winter numbers are considerably increased by visitors, mainly from the Low Countries. The average winter population on the Thames Valley reservoirs over the years 1957-67 was approximately 2,200 (Hammond, 1968) of which a third would probably be present on Surrey waters, principally Queen Elizabeth II and Barn Elms Reservoirs. Much higher numbers resort to the Thames and at the peak period in December and January well over 1,000 might be counted in the stretch from Putney to Teddington. The average winter population in the whole county is probably around 5,000. Some of the largest concentrations were counted in the hard weather of January 1963 when numbers of normally wintering birds were swollen by immigrants driven in from the Continent. A total of 3,552 was reported in that month on the stretch of the Thames from Putney to Teddington.

Winter numbers on the outer Surrey lakes as at Frensham, Gatton and Hedgecourt are usually of the order 100-200. A record of 3,000 at Vachery Lake on 26 September 1965 is exceptional.

It is difficult to assess whether the status of the bird has changed since the turn of the century but it seems likely that, with reservoir surface area increased at least fivefold, winter numbers are much higher than formerly. National Wildfowl Count numbers show little change in the wintering population from 1949-64.

Except where it relies on feeding by the public as in the parks and parts of the Thames, the species regularly flights at dusk, usually in small parties, to feeding areas at sewage farms, water meadows and similar aquatic habitats that provide the food plants it requires.

Teal
Anas crecca

Scarce resident. Common passage migrant and winter visitor. The breeding status of this duck appears to have changed very little in the present century. In the 1900s a few pairs were recorded breeding, especially on the western heaths as at Frensham, Pudmore and Thursley and occasionally at Hedgecourt Pond in the south-east. Breeding has been reported spasmodically over the years with occasional colonization of suitable habitats as provided by sewage farms at Epsom, Guildford and Unstead. Breeding was suspected in at least three areas in 1969 and in 1970 was proved in one area in west Surrey where two or three pairs were present.

As a winter visitor the species is numerous and widespread. Flocks of 30-40 are frequently recorded from reed-fringed waters, riverside marshes and sewage farms and these are recorded at any time from October to April. The largest gatherings have been as follows: c. 170 at Send on 18 February 1945, up to 200 at Enton in the winter of 1953, 100 at Unstead on 13 February 1954 and 600 at Guildford on 13 February 1954. The only very large gathering away from the reservoirs in the 1960s occurred during the hard weather of 1963 when 400 were recorded on the Thames from Putney to Barnes on 20 January and up to 100 were counted at Beddington sf, also in January.

Regular winter flocks build up at three principal sites: Barn Elms, Island Barn and Queen Elizabeth II Reservoirs. There is an early record of c. 300 at Island Barn on 27 March 1937 but regular counts did not begin there till 1954. Birds begin to appear in August but peak numbers are not recorded till January or February. The largest counts at these reservoirs have been 273 at Queen Elizabeth II on 16 December 1962, 500 at Barn Elms on 11 February 1968 and 500 on Island Barn on 28 December 1969. Figures of Wildfowl Counts analysed over the period of 1957-67 show that the average wintering number on the Thames Valley reservoirs was about 900 of which about a half shared Island Barn and Queen Elizabeth II Reservoirs. Only King George VI Reservoir in Middlesex was shown to hold more than either (but less than both) of these reservoirs (Hammond, 1968). Numbers at the reservoirs drop away quickly in April and the species is seldom recorded from May to July.

The reservoirs of Island Barn and Queen Elizabeth II appear to be particularly suitable for this duck as the gently shelving banks allow the birds to rest and preen undisturbed during the day. At dusk the birds flight on to the nearby river systems and sewage farms to feed, returning at or before dawn to the safety of the reservoirs. The species is rarely recorded from the steep-sided reservoirs of the Walton Group.

Very few Teal have been ringed in Surrey but nationally, ringing has shown that British visitors and passage birds come from Iceland, the Low Countries, Scandinavia and the Russian Baltic republics and even as far east as the White Sea and beyond the Urals.

Garganey
Anas
querquedula

Extremely scarce summer visitor and scarce passage migrant. Bucknill classed this species as a rare summer visitor in 1900 and suspected that ornamental wildfowl collections were the source of the few Surrey records then known. The first recorded occurrence in the present century was at Richmond Park on 17 March 1927. Two were recorded at Brooklands SF in the spring of 1937. An increase in spring passage records (March and April) in the 1940s included four at Frensham on 27 April 1947 and ten at Barn Elms Reservoir on 18 March 1947 which latter record appears to represent the biggest concentration recorded in the county.

Records for both spring (March to May) and autumn (July to September) became almost annual in the late 1950s but occurrences in the 1960s were variable, with for instance, only one spring record in 1964 and 1965 and several spring and four-five autumn records in 1968 and 1969. The records are scattered over the whole county and are not confined to the reservoirs but include the lakes, ponds, sewage farms, marshes and river courses.

Surrey lies on the western fringe of this species' breeding range and there have been a few breeding or suspected breeding records in the middle years of the present century. With increasing disturbance and restriction of suitable habitats breeding is now less likely. Douglas (1951) recorded it as breeding in the Leatherhead area some time between 1939 and 1951. A pair was present at Guildford SF in 1945 and may have attempted breeding. Two pairs were present on flooded land at the Walton GPS in 1951 and breeding was suspected. A duck, with two small young, was seen on the R. Wey at Weybridge in 1952 and a pair was again present at Guildford SF throughout the breeding season in 1959.

Gadwall
Anas strepera

Very scarce resident and scarce winter visitor.
Prior to the 1930s this species was but a very scarce vagrant in the county. Since 1936 however, a small breeding colony centred on Barn Elms Reservoir has been in existence. It is thought that this population originated from captive birds breeding in St James's Park. Numbers have varied between one and three pairs and in recent years not more than one pair has been successful. Away from Barn Elms the species nests only intermittently. Breeding was noted at Beddington SF in 1938 and 1939, a pair with two young was seen at Leigh Place, Godstone on 24 July 1967 and breeding occurred at Godstone again, this time on Bay Pond, in 1969 when a brood of five was seen on 22 June.

Apart from supporting a regular breeding stock Barn Elms Reservoir and the adjoining stretch of river is the only location in the county where the species can reliably be seen throughout the year. The small breeding population is swollen in autumn and winter by immigrants and from the early 1940s the wintering flock has varied between 20 and 40. Numbers in the late 1960s and in 1970 however have been higher. Up to 50 were recorded in the winters of 1968/68 and 1969/70 and in December 1970 the total rose to 91, the highest number ever recorded in the county.

Away from Barn Elms the species is comparatively scarce. There is a series of autumn and winter records from Richmond Park from about the mid-1950s involving numbers of up to ten birds. In outer Surrey it is recorded only very infrequently and as a singleton or in very small numbers.

Wigeon
Anas penelope

Winter visitor.
As a regular winter visitor, this species is now commoner than previously. There are comparatively few records for the first decade of the present century although Bentham reported wintering parties of up to 30 birds from such localities as Frensham, Hedgecourt Pond and Godstone and

there is one early record of 200 seen at Barn Elms Reservoir after hard weather (*Zool.*, 1909). In the 1940s numbers began to increase in various parts of the county and by the 1950s a flock of between 50 and 80 birds was regularly to be seen each winter at the Walton Reservoirs where the birds were able to feed on the grass growing on the causeways separating the reservoirs. Over the years 1957-67 the average mid-winter population on the Thames Valley reservoirs was 252 of which about a third was present on the Surrey reservoirs of Barn Elms, Walton and Queen Elizabeth ii (Hammond, 1968). Away from these three strongholds the bird is irregular, small parties being seen on the outer lakes, marshes and on flooded meadows as at Shalford (50 in December 1969) and occasionally on the Thames. Numbers in the last few years of the review period were lower than in mid-century and flocks rarely exceeded 40 birds.

Wintering birds usually depart in March (but small numbers may be present in early April) and returning birds are not usually seen in any numbers till November or December although odd birds have been recorded as early as July (e.g. one at Barn Elms Reservoir on 17 July 1965). It is, of course, possible that some birds recorded in the spring and autumn are on passage but it is impossible generally to separate passage from wintering birds.

Pintail Scarce winter visitor and passage migrant.
Anas acuta There are only two records for the first two decades of the present century, being of a pair in Richmond Park on 23 March 1907 and a drake at Frensham Great Pond on 8 February 1908. Four were recorded at Barnes on 22 February 1924 and one or two were recorded every winter in Richmond Park from 1926 to 1930. From about the mid-1930s records have been made almost annually usually of ones or twos and concentrated on the R. Thames and reservoirs in the Barnes district with irregular occurrences in outer Surrey. Twenty-five at Cutt Mill Pond in January 1939 is the largest number ever recorded in the county. The species is reported exceptionally in August and in May (two at Brooklands on 7 May and 14 August 1936 and one at Barn Elms on 2 May 1966) but most records are concentrated in the period October to March. Numbers over two are now exceptional, 14 at Barn Elms on 12 January 1963 and 12 in Richmond Park on 7 November 1964 being the biggest counts in the last decade of the review period.

Regular visitor and passage migrant. Occasionally breeds. **Shoveler**
There is no doubt that this species is now appreciably com- *Spatula*
moner than at the turn of the century. Bucknill considered *clypeata*
it to be a rare winter visitor but it experienced a large increase and spread in the early part of the century in Britain
(Parslow, 1967) and it is now a regular winter visitor to the
county in numbers of over 100. Its increase is chronicled
largely from the reservoirs and in particular those of the
Walton Group. Numbers up to the early 1930s were low
and in twos and threes occurring during the winter and on
spring and autumn passage. A record number of 88 in a
flock was counted on Island Barn Reservoir in the winter of
1937/38 and flocks between 20 and 30 were being regularly
reported at the Walton Reservoirs by the mid-1940s. Following the opening of Queen Elizabeth II Reservoir in 1962
this site was increasingly favoured by the species. In the
period 1957-67 the average number wintering on the Thames
Valley reservoirs was 137 of which approximately a third
could be found on the Queen Elizabeth II Reservoir and a
considerably smaller fraction at Walton and Island Barn
(Hammond, 1968). Since then wintering Surrey birds have
concentrated even more on Queen Elizabeth II Reservoir
and peak numbers (usually in October) have fluctuated
between 100 and 120. Outside this main wintering area the
species is still irregular except possibly at Barn Elms, occurring in small numbers in all parts of the county on ponds,
lakes, sewage farms and marshes. Post-breeding birds appear
on the reservoirs as early as July, numbers building up to a
peak in autumn. Spring dispersal takes place in early March.
   Breeding has occurred or been suspected at irregular
intervals but with the loss and restriction of suitable habitats
is becoming less likely to occur. In 1932 a young bird was
shot at Beddington where adults had been present during
the breeding season. In the 1930s circumstantial evidence of
breeding was noted from Brooklands SF and in the early
1940s breeding of up to three or four pairs was proved in
at least two years (1943 and 1944) in the Wey Valley around
Send (*SEBR*). A pair nested near the Moat Pond at Elstead
in 1950 and L. J. Raynsford saw a brood of six on Sweet-
water at Witley in 1954, this record being the last recorded
breeding in the review period.

Scarce winter visitor. **Red-crested**
All Surrey records of this species must be considered in the **Pochard**
knowledge that breeding pairs have been kept in the Royal *Netta rufina*
Parks' collections in London for many years. However, the

Red-crested Pochard has been spreading on the Continent in recent times and it now breeds in Germany, Denmark and Holland. Large winter flocks have been reported and as long ago as 1952, 500 were seen on the Yssl Meer (*BB*, 14:105).

Numbers of this order so near to the East Anglian coast suggest that some of the birds which have been seen in this part of the country during the last ten years were genuinely wild. Ringing recoveries from this species would be particularly helpful but unfortunately very few birds are ever handled.

The *Haslemere List* (1955) gave the first Surrey record at Frensham Great Pond where a bird was seen on several occasions between 19 November 1931 and 29 January 1932. The next sighting did not take place till 23 November 1940 when another appeared at Beddington SF and the third record during this period, before several pairs were introduced into Regent's Park as well as St James's, was at Barn Elms Reservoir on 2 May 1946.

There were only two more records during the 1950s—of single birds at Barn Elms Reservoir between 27 November and 1 December 1955 and Enton Ponds near Godalming on 5 August 1959. From 1961 onwards at least one has been seen in each year with the exception of 1965. Significantly perhaps, Barn Elms Reservoir has been by far the most favoured locality. Up to four birds were seen there from 27 January to 10 February 1970. The only other localities where they have been seen have been Frensham, Gatton Park, Holmethorpe and Papercourt GPS and on the R. Thames.

Scaup
Aythya marila

Regular winter visitor in small numbers.

In 1900 the Scaup was an exceptional winter visitor but after 1923 records became more frequent. P. A. D. Hollom (*BB*, 32:66) gave its status as 'one or two birds almost every year' between 1924 and 1936 in Surrey.

Since the Second World War the number of sightings each winter has increased but this may well be due to the larger number of people visiting the reservoirs. Although records have come from the larger waters in several parts of the county at one time or another, most of the birds have appeared at Lonsdale Road, Barn Elms, Island Barn and the Walton Reservoirs.

The largest number reported was seven in March 1956 at the end of the hard weather and in February 1962 at Barn Elms. At the Walton Reservoirs the 1963 frosts brought in another small party which was present from January to

21 *Great Crested Grebe.* An incubating hen makes a threat display to a passing Moorhen. This species is now common on suitable waters (*D. M. T. Ettlinger*)

March. The usual number was four but six birds were seen on 20 January.

In hard weather Scaup have been seen in some unlikely places; notably there were single birds at South Norwood Lake in the London suburbs in March 1956 and on the R. Wandle at Carshalton from 8 to 12 February 1963.

The only ringing recovery is of a bird of the year marked in North Iceland on 6 August 1947 which was reported from Barnes on 5 March 1950. This may be a significant pointer to the origin of the birds which winter in this area as a high proportion of the birds ringed abroad and recovered in the British Isles have come from that country.

Moderately common resident on suitable waters. Abundant autumn and winter visitor.

Tufted Duck *Aythya fuligula*

There has been a marked and dramatic change in the status of this species in the present century. In 1900 breeding had not been proved and there were only a few winter occurrences. Then in 1922 Bentham noted in *British Birds* (6:158) that the species had become a regular winter visitor to the east of the county in the previous two or three years. Numbers in wintering flocks prior to that year rarely exceeded 20-30 and 50 was exceptional. In the next few decades the position changed rapidly, no doubt largely due to the building of new reservoirs in the Thames Valley. The maximum number occurring over the period 1924-36 was 514 on 24 October 1931 at Chelsea and Lambeth and 730 on 30 January 1935 at Barn Elms and Lonsdale Road Reservoirs (*BB*, 32:65). An increase was noted in the number of birds wintering on Virginia Water in 1936 (*SEBR*). By the 1950s the species had become one of the most abundant winter visitors. The average number of regular wintering birds on the London reservoirs 1957-67 was approximately 3,500 of which about half frequented the Surrey reservoirs of Barn Elms and Walton (Hammond, 1968).

The place of the Walton Reservoirs in the birds' annual rhythm has become particularly significant. In late July and early August the number of birds at Walton begins to build up until in some years over 500 have gathered. These birds then moult. This locality is in fact the only one in the London area where large scale moulting flocks assemble regularly. After moulting the birds disperse or migrate and the number of birds falls off in September and October only to increase again in November as the first winter visitors arrive. Cold weather in December or the

22 (top) *Pair of Mandarin Duck*. Now a dynamic and spreading species in Surrey (*I. R. Beames*)

23 (bottom) *Group of Canada Geese on Mytchett Lake*—a well established species now (*D. M. T. Ettlinger*)

New Year usually causes a big influx which shows first at Barn Elms Reservoir where upwards of 1,000 birds have arrived over the space of a few days in some winters. There are small influxes at the other reservoirs and on the waters of outer Surrey. There is then a gradual falling off of numbers throughout the county until by the end of March most of the birds have dispersed.

P. F. Bunyard reported what he believed to be the first authentic breeding record for Surrey when he saw a pair of Tufted Duck with nine ducklings on 'a large pond' in 1912. Since then there has been a steady and continuing expansion till by the end of the review period the species was breeding on almost any suitable water every year throughout the county including the London suburbs. When mowing operations allow the vegetation on the tops of the embankments at Barn Elms Reservoir and at Walton to become sufficiently rank, birds will breed successfully in spite of disturbance from anglers. An unusually successful year at the former was 1963 when 37 young were hatched from eight broods. On outer Surrey waters the largest number of broods has been seven—at Frensham in 1953. The largest clutch on record for the county was in 1934 when a nest containing 17 eggs was found on a moor adjoining a marsh in west Surrey.

When the Knight and Bessborough Reservoirs at Walton are in full use a number of wildfowl of several diving species are trapped in the intake towers and these birds have frequently been ringed. Of four Tufted Duck ringed in September and October during the 1930s two were recovered the following January in Oxfordshire and Ulster and a third near Birmingham during the March of a later spring. The fourth was recovered at Walton again in the January of the third winter after. Two ringed in February 1958 (one at Island Barn Reservoir) were both shot in Finland in April 1959, presumably on their way back to their breeding grounds.

During the 1960s a number of reports were received of single birds resembling the Lesser Scaup (*Aythya affinis*)— a North American species. These are now thought to have been hybrids of Tufted Duck/Scaup.

Pochard Common winter visitor. Occasionally breeds.
Aythya ferina Bucknill considered this species as 'rather scarce' and reported it to be much less numerous in the 1890s than it had been 60 years earlier but it was nevertheless still commoner than the Tufted Duck.

Bentham's records show that flocks of up to several hundred occurred in the winter months at Frensham Little Pond in the first decade of this century and his count of 400 on 14 February 1909 still remains the highest ever recorded concentration in the county away from the reservoirs. Bentham also noted flocks of up to 50 at Hedgecourt Pond in the second decade of the century and he recorded 140 there on 10 January 1915. The species was recorded as occurring on the Surrey portion of Virginia Water since the early 1930s and it was reported as increasing there in 1936 (*SEBR*).

The Birds of the London Area (1957) state that in 1905 the Pochard frequented Richmond Park and 121 were present in February 1906. In November 1909 a flock of over 100 at Barn Elms Reservoir was noteworthy. After the First World War numbers of Pochard wintering on the reservoirs gradually rose. There was an unprecedented total of 500 at Barn Elms Reservoir on 3 December 1925 but the usual winter peak at this reservoir stayed at between 200 and 300 until 1933 when further increases were noted. By 1939 the usual peak had exceeded 500. The first mention of the species at Walton Reservoirs in Bentham's diaries does not occur before 1930 when seven on the Chelsea and Lambeth section on 12 January and 40 on 14 December were recorded.

The Thames Valley reservoirs had an average wintering number of 1,200 over the period 1957-67 of which c. 500 were recorded at Barn Elms Reservoir and less than 100 at Walton (Hammond, 1968). There were exceptional numbers at Barn Elms Reservoir in the winter of 1970/71 and c. 1,500 were recorded there on 19 December 1970.

Annual movements of the Pochard differ in some respects from those of the Tufted Duck. Although a few birds return in June in some years, the Pochard does not appear to have any regular moulting place and normally none is seen till some weeks later but by September, 100 are often present at Barn Elms Reservoir. As with the Tufted Duck, numbers fall away till November. Small and medium-sized flocks also arrive on some of the country waters including, from the late 1960s, Broadwater at Godalming, Fetcham Ponds, Papercourt GPs and at times Winkworth, as well as Gatton Park and its older haunts at Frensham and Hedgecourt.

The authors of *The Birds of the London Area* (1957) pointed out that this species 'tends to be fickle' in its choice of locality but apart from showing that the Pochard preferred the shallower reservoirs which are 10-20 feet deep and areas of about 20 acres, they could throw little light on the reasons for these preferences. Food requirements must obviously play a considerable part but little is known of the way in which these differ from those of other diving duck.

As with other species of duck, hard weather movements are frequently noted but these are usually smaller than those recorded for the Tufted Duck. One of the largest however was in the winter of 1946/47 when there were 1,160 at Barn Elms Reservoir on 24 December and upwards of 2,000 in the following March at Walton.

The *Haslemere List* (1921) referred to pairs seen in that locality in May but it was not till 1927 that breeding was proved in the county and that at Barn Elms Reservoir. There was further breeding at this site in 1929 and 1933 with a suspected attempt in 1930. From 1931 to 1933 young were reared at Beddington and in Richmond Park in 1931 and 1932 but not again at this latter site till 1969. A brood was reared in Battersea Park in 1954 but the birds may have originated from pinioned stock that had recently bred in some of the central London parks. In 1953 and 1954 summering pairs were noted at Hammer Pond, Thursley and though attempts at breeding were suspected no proof could be obtained. The only other breeding records for the county are for Thorpe GPs where there was successful breeding in the years 1966-68.

Ferruginous Duck *Aythya nyroca* Very scarce winter visitor.

The Ferruginous Duck, or White-eyed Pochard, which breeds in Eastern Europe and certain Mediterranean regions, is also frequently kept in captivity and the origin of birds seen in the wild in the county must therefore always be subject to the usual *caveat*. The species was introduced into St James's Park in 1912 and again in the 1930s when birds bred successfully for several years.

Bucknill knew of only one record and that was undated and otherwise unsatisfactory. The first record in the present century was in 1920; the *Haslemere List* (1921) referred to one at Frensham on 8 October that year. There were no further records till 22 December 1932 when one was reported from Virginia Water (*BB*, 26:279).

Since the Second World War there have been up to ten accepted records, all of single birds, from Barn Elms and the Walton Reservoirs, Gatton Park Lake, Godstone and Hedgecourt Ponds, all in the period December to March.

Winter visitor in small numbers. **Goldeneye**
The building of the reservoirs changed the status of this *Bucephala*
species completely in the last 50 years of the review period. *clangula*

For the nineteenth century there are seven records and
the only birds which escaped being shot were a pair which
'visited some ornamental water near Kew in the spring of
1898' for some days.

After 1900 the number of sightings rose slowly and from
1909 onwards the Goldeneye was recorded almost every year
in ones or twos either on the reservoirs or on country
waters such as Frensham and Hedgecourt. The authors of
The Birds of the London Area (1957) showed that the
Staines Reservoirs (Middlesex) were the most frequented at
first and that by 1921/22 as many as 25 birds were present
there. From 1925 onwards Barn Elms Reservoir was visited
regularly and small parties began to winter at the Walton
Reservoirs. Bentham reported 12 birds at this latter site on
12 January and 14 December 1930; 33 were seen on 13
January 1934. During the 1950s and 1960s numbers wintering at the Walton Reservoirs rose gradually and the concentration on the centre part of the Chelsea and Lambeth
section had reached double figures in the early part of
1955. In severe weather this water and the others for which
the species shows a preference, may freeze over within a
week or ten days and the Goldeneye take to nearby rivers.
In 1963 the total number on the Thames between Richmond and Kew rose as high as 40 by the second week in
January. The average wintering flock on the London reservoirs 1957-67 was 63 of which about a third occurred at the
Walton Group (Hammond, 1968).

In some seasons the first Goldeneye arrive before the end
of October but as a rule they do not appear until November.
Numbers are high from January until March. Stragglers,
often 'brown heads' which have not paired, remain until
April. Reports after the middle of this month are rare. A
pair was recorded at Frensham on 13 May 1907 (*Zool.*,
1907), another at Hedgecourt on 24 April 1910 and a female
remained at Barn Elms Reservoir until 2 May in 1958.
After the hard winter of 1962/63 an immature bird stayed
at Barn Elms Reservoir from 23 April 'until at least 15
July' and a 'brown head', possibly the same bird, was seen
at Richmond Park on 13 August. The same summer a
duck made a long stay on Frensham Great Pond. It was
first noticed on 21 July and it remained to moult, being
flightless for a time in August and September. It was joined

in November by two other birds and remained till the pond froze over on 15 December.

During the last decade of the review period, records from outside the London area became more frequent and the only places from which there are fewer records than formerly are in the south-east of the county where coverage was less good than in the earlier years of the century.

Drakes may begin to display late in February in some years and most of them pair before leaving for their northern breeding grounds.

Long-tailed Duck
Clangula hyemalis

Scarce winter visitor.

This northern pelagic species was not noted in Surrey till 1928 (the first time in the London area) when an immature drake stayed at Barn Elms Reservoir from 13 November till 17 December. The second record was at Walton on 27 January 1938 and the bird remained till 2 April at which time it appears to have moved to Island Barn Reservoir and stayed till the 19th. Since the 1940s however, its appearances have become more regular and the species has favoured the Walton Reservoirs rather than Barn Elms Reservoir and unlike some of the other scarce visitors it has usually remained for some time in the winters during which it has appeared, staying, more than once, from late autumn to early spring.

In contrast with the London area, there have been only three reports from outer Surrey, the first not till 15 December 1957 when a duck was seen at Enton Ponds. There was an immature bird at Frensham on 9 and 10 November 1961. There were two at Frensham on 28 October and 18 November 1967 with three on the 5th. It seems probable that the birds at Send GPs the following day and on 12 November were the same trio. During this period one or two birds were seen on different dates at Barn Elms, Island Barn and Walton Reservoirs. An immature drake remained at Barn Elms from 6 November till 18 February 1968 and one, probably a duck, which was first seen on 17 March 1968 stayed till 10 May, which was a later date than normal. The autumn of 1967 was, in fact, a period during which there was 'a notable influx' of this species throughout Britain and Ireland (*BB*, 61:47 and 133).

Velvet Scoter
Melanitta fusca

Very scarce winter visitor.

This northern maritime species was not recorded in the London area before 1927 and there were no Surrey records till 1948 when there was a surprising total of over 20 on the reservoirs in adjoining Middlesex on 30 October. One was reported at Walton Reservoirs on this date and another at Barn Elms Reservoir on 14 November.

There were no more sightings till 10 February 1952 when an immature bird was reported from Barn Elms. However, the cold spell early in 1956 produced the largest influx into the county to date. On 30 January one bird was reported at Pen Ponds, Richmond Park. On 23 February there was one at Walton Reservoirs, numbers rising to six on 25 February when there was also one at Island Barn Reservoir. From 26 February till 25 March, four were seen at Walton Reservoirs on many occasions and a straggler remained till 31 March. The following autumn an immature bird stayed at Frensham Great Pond from 4 to 24 November. The only other record from outside London was also from Frensham, a single bird on 26 March 1961.

The remaining reports were of a drake at Barn Elms Reservoir on 29 November 1958, a duck on the Thames at Teddington Weir on 26 and 27 January 1963 and an immature bird at Walton Reservoirs on 9 and 10 February the same year. The last report in the review period was of a pair at Barn Elms Reservoir during the third week of October 1969.

Common Scoter
Melanitta nigra

Winter visitor in small numbers.

Bucknill mentioned three nineteenth-century records with a degree of reserve. The first record after 1900 did not occur till 16 April 1924, when a bird was reported at Flashes Pond, Churt. *The Birds of the London Area* (1957) did not refer to the species as an annual visitor to the London area before 1926.

Since that time sightings in Surrey have become regular and since the Second World War, at least one bird has been seen each winter. Barn Elms Reservoir and the R. Thames nearby are visited most often, with the Walton Reservoirs also attracting a small number.

In outer Surrey the Frensham Ponds have the most records, the first on 24 October 1931 and the next on 28 September 1933. The largest number in Surrey up to the end of the review period was a party of eight on Frensham Little Pond on 18 November 1959.

In hard weather birds have been seen in such unlikely places as Beddington sf, on the Beverley Brook by the playing fields, on Wimbledon Common and the R. Wandle at Carshalton. The hard frosts of 1963, as well as those of 1956, produced more records than usual but the records in normal years show that autumn migration brings in more birds than the spring.

A very late spring record was of three pairs at Barn Elms Reservoir on 16 and 17 June 1963.

Ruddy Duck
Oxyura
jamaicensis

Very scarce visitor.

This North American species is now accepted as an addition to the British List (*The Ibis*, 113 : 421) and a feral population originating from escapes maintains itself in the West Country. As the species was known to originate from captive collections full documentation of occurrences in the county is almost certainly lacking. However, it has been reported from Island Barn and the Walton Reservoirs on a number of occasions. At Island Barn Reservoir a duck or immature bird was recorded in February 1958 and 1959 and again on 23 January 1965 (D. Parr). At Walton a duck was recorded on 13 December 1964, in January 1965, on various dates from 25 September 1965 to 13 February 1966 and again on 15 January and 12 August 1967. There was a drake at this reservoir on 14 December 1969 (C. Ogston).

Eider
Somateria
mollissima

Extremely scarce vagrant.

There has been only one record of this species in the review period. A single drake in partial eclipse was seen by P. G. Davis on the Great Pond at Frensham on 10 July 1965.

Red-breasted Merganser
Mergus
serrator

Scarce winter visitor.

The Red-breasted Merganser is largely a maritime species outside the breeding season and for this reason does not visit the main waters in the county to the same extent as the Goosander. Bucknill could trace only one record in the second half of the nineteenth century while the first quarter of the twentieth century produced only three records. Two birds were seen at Frensham Little Pond on 28 December 1913, (*BB*, 7 : 300), four in Richmond Park on 20 February 1916 and there was a single bird at Frensham on 11 May 1921.

The species was reported from Barn Elms and Walton Reservoirs in the winter of 1928/29 and from this time have been seen almost annually on one or other of the London reservoirs (*The Birds of the London Area*, 1957). Five were seen at Dorking on 20 January 1937 (*BB*, 30 : 374) and four were at the Walton Reservoirs on 28 December 1938 (*BB*, 32 : 307). Twenty-five birds including three drakes were recorded at Frensham Little Pond on 13 January 1939. In the immediate post-war years, singles were seen on Hedgecourt Pond on 9 January 1947 and Frensham on 2 April 1949.

The Walton Reservoirs have had numerous records and the species has also been reported from Barn Elms Reservoir, Beddington SF, Frensham Ponds and Island Barn Reservoir. In 1956 exceptional numbers were recorded; birds were present at Barn Elms Reservoir from 25 February—4 March (maximum nine), at Walton from 25 February—19 March (maximum 13) and at Island Barn Reservoir from 12 February—15 March (maximum four). This period corresponded with the extension of the breeding range in north west England (1950) and Wales (1953) an extension which did not appear to continue beyond 1960 (Atkinson-Willes 1963).

In the last decade of the review period records were less frequent and in five of these years there was none at all. Single birds were recorded at Enton, Frensham and the Walton Group of Reservoirs. Five were seen on the Thames in the severe winter of 1962/63 and four visited Frensham Little Pond on 1 December 1968.

Goosander
Mergus merganser

Regular winter visitor.

In the first two decades of the century the Goosander was a rare straggler to Surrey. There are records from Frensham Great Pond of one on 14 February 1909, a pair on 2 December 1911, 13 on 13 March 1920 and one on 20 March 1921. From 1924 it became an annual visitor in increasing numbers to Surrey and especially to the Walton Reservoirs. A hundred were recorded there in January 1929 and maximum numbers at these reservoirs continued to rise with 180 on 28 December 1938, 320 on 2 February 1945 and 550 in February 1947. These peak numbers usually reflected increases due to hard weather movements, numbers during milder winters being lower. The highest counts of all occurred during the severe weather in the early part of 1963. A large influx occurred on 5 January and on 27 January more than 850 were counted flying in to roost on the new Queen Elizabeth II Reservoir. Numbers at the adjoining Walton Reservoirs reached c. 500 on 3 February when the same number was also counted on Queen Elizabeth II Reservoir. Numbers at Island Barn Reservoir reached a maximum of 190 on 10 March. Birds on the Thames also increased dramatically during the freeze-up and 139 were counted on 12 February between Walton and Chertsey. These numbers represent the highest ever recorded for this species in the county and although the Walton Reservoirs still attract the largest flocks, numbers in the second half of the 1960s rarely exceeded 50.

On the comparatively small waters of outer Surrey a few birds are recorded in most winters usually in the period November to March. The birds usually appear in late October or early November, although since the mid-1960s they are now rarely recorded before December. Peak numbers occur from January to March. May records are exceptional, although there is a record of three immature birds summering in 1936 on Mount Pond, Clapham Common.

These visitors to Surrey are probably all of foreign origin and there is no evidence that Scottish birds fly south to winter on the Thames Valley reservoirs. Of seven birds ringed at Walton in the winter period (November—February) one was recovered from West Finland in September, three from Sweden in April, one from the Netherlands in December and one from Archangel, Russia, also in April.

Smew Scarce but regular winter visitor.
Mergus The status of this species has shown a remarkable change
albellus in the period under review. Bucknill's records were confined to four occurrences and only two further occurrences were recorded before 1920. These were of single birds at Frensham on 30 April 1907 and 10 January 1915. Harting (1910) mentioned that 'the rarest duck seen in the Weybridge area was a Smew shot near Sunbury in December 1908'; although doubt remains as to whether the record could be accepted as being for Surrey it sheds light on the status of the species at that time. By the middle of the 1920s the Smew had already gained the status of an annual visitor and at the Walton Reservoirs 'large numbers' were reported in 1925, 24 in 1930, 38 in 1931 and 51 in 1934, while in a period of severe weather at the end of 1938, 117 were reported at the same location (*The Birds of the London Area*, 1957). During this period of expansion at the reservoirs, sightings were also made at Enton, Frensham, Hedgecourt and Wire Mill Ponds. Little counting was possible during the Second World War due to restrictions on access to the reservoirs but in the severe winter of 1946/47, 78 were at Barn Elms and 125 at Walton. There was evidence at this time that the Walton Reservoirs were less favoured than hitherto and the main wintering concentration in Surrey became centred upon Barn Elms Reservoir. At this water the maxima ranged between 35 and 75 birds in the years 1954-60. The corresponding period at the Walton Reservoirs saw a fall from 30 in 1954 to four in 1960. The species also occurred with some regularity at Frensham Ponds, Island Barn Reservoir, Lonsdale Road Reservoir

and Walton GPs. Occasional records were also received from Virginia Water, Richmond Park, Enton and the Thames.

After 1960 there was a downward trend in winter maxima although in the very severe winter of 1962/63 there was a temporary return to the numbers of the mid-1950s. Many of the waters in the county including stretches of the Thames were icebound during this severe spell which probably accounted for the unusual sight of 23 birds on the Thames at Kingston, three at Ockham Mill, one on the R. Wey at Elstead and one on the R. Wandle at Carshalton.

The decline continued to such an extent that in the final three years of the review period the maximum counts were seven and five at Barn Elms (1968 and 1969) and nine at Walton (1970).

The species usually begins to arrive in November. Numbers increase in December and maximum counts are usually made in January or February. By mid-March the main concentrations have gone but occasionally single birds can be seen into April.

Scarce winter visitor and irregular summer visitor. **Shelduck** *Tadorna tadorna*

The Shelduck was seldom recorded in the early years of the century and only five records are given before 1930. Six birds were at Hedgecourt Pond on 6 March 1914 and a dead bird was found at Godstone in the same year. Two birds were at Godstone Pond on 19 December 1920 (*BB*, 15:90), eight at Barn Elms Reservoir on 13 September 1926 and 12 were recorded there on 26 August 1929.

In the next decade there were several records for Brooklands SF. Birds were seen on seven occasions involving a total of 18 (*BB*, 28:342 and 30:346). An interesting feature of these records is that a pair of birds was involved in April 1933, May and June 1934 and May 1936, the other records being of a single bird on 22 March 1931 and seven on 7 May 1936. Elsewhere in the county winter records were received of single birds at Beddington SF, Frensham Ponds and on floodwater at Pyrford.

There was little apparent change in status until the species began to be recorded annually in the early 1950s. At the end of the review period it could be regarded as a regular visitor in small numbers and one which had been recorded in all months. Most records relate to the October—April period and concern up to four birds. The largest counts have been 16 on 13 April 1957 and 13 on 28 September 1958 at Island Barn Reservoir parties of 12 and 22 in flight at Barn Elms Reservoir on 24 February 1965. Birds are seen which are almost certainly escapes and these often remain in the same locality and become very tame. Normally however, the birds do not stay for any length of time and this supports the view that the species returning from its annual moult in north-west Germany disperses through south-eastern counties when returning to breeding grounds in the north and west of Britain between late autumn and early spring (Atkinson-Willes, 1963).

In addition to the reservoirs the Shelduck has been recorded on most of the large waters in the county and has been seen with some regularity at Beddington and Guildford SFS.

Ruddy Shelduck
Casarca ferruginea

There are three records of this species in the present century. Single birds were reported from Beddington SF 12-19 December 1929 (H. Bentham), Guildford SF on 23 May 1945 (*SEBR*) and at Hersham SF in 1968 (*SBCQB*, 47, *September 1968*).

It is doubtful whether any of these records refer to truly wild birds since the species is widely kept in captivity in ornamental collections and in zoological gardens. Bucknill was of the same opinion concerning earlier records for Surrey and it is therefore open to question whether the Ruddy Shelduck can legitimately be included in the systematic list for the county.

Geese

There is very little habitat in Surrey where wintering geese could sustain themselves and consequently many records are of geese in flight and classified as 'grey geese' through lack of specific identification. Records normally refer to the period between November and March and sightings range from single birds to skeins of up to 100. The two largest sightings in the 'grey geese' category were of c. 100 flying NNE over East Horsley on 18 March 1956 and a similar number travelling northwards over Leatherhead on 30 December 1962.

Grey Lag Goose
Anser anser

Irregular visitor.

There are very few records of this species in Surrey. The normal wintering grounds are in Scotland with a small population in north west England. It is therefore possible that with the exception of birds occurring in seemingly hard weather movements, records of the species relate to birds escaping from fully winged collections of which there are an increasing number in the south of England.

There were no records in the present century before 1947

the year in which a single adult bird was present at Hedge-court Pond on 9 April; its extreme wariness pointed to its being of truly wild stock. Two adults and an immature bird flew into Barn Elms Reservoir in an extremely exhausted condition on 5 January 1963 and stayed in the area until 9 February. In both these years exceptionally hard weather had been experienced during the winter and the appearance of these birds may have been a consequence of hard weather movements.

In 1967 five were seen in flight at Holmethorpe SPS on 1 April and six were present at Barrow Green SP on 19 July. Both these records and that of two birds seen on flooded meadows at Unstead SF on 25 March 1969 were thought to refer to feral stock rather than birds of a truly wild origin.

White-fronted Goose *Anser albifrons*

Irregular passage migrant.
The White-fronted Goose is the most frequently identified of the grey geese in Surrey. Records usually refer to birds in flight although occasionally there are reports of birds on the reservoirs. The earliest record in the review period was of a flock of 12 (one of which was shot) over Caterham on 25 February 1927 (*The Birds of the London Area*, 1957). Two were present at Beddington SF on 16 January 1943 (*BB*, 36:203). Records became more frequent in the last two decades of the review period, due probably more to the increase in observers than to change in status. On 1 February 1954, 64 were seen over Sutton and on 5 February 1961, 67 flew NE over Epsom. The largest number recorded was 180 flying NE over Ewell on 4 March 1968. There are also records of several smaller movements in this period. November/December records are generally of a southerly movement while February/March movement tends to be in a northerly direction.

Bean Goose *Anser arvensis arvensis*

Extremely scarce winter visitor.
In the country as a whole this is one of the rarer wintering geese. It is regular in East Anglia so there is a possibility that the records in Surrey could be of stragglers from this wintering population, particularly in times of very hard weather. The first Surrey record was of a single bird at Frensham on 8 December 1945. In 1963 during the severe weather of that year seven were present on 21 January and fed for a number of subsequent days on the banks of the new Queen Elizabeth II Reservoir and a single bird was at Walton Reservoirs on 2 March 1963.

Pink-footed Irregular winter visitor.
Goose As in the case of other geese it is difficult to distinguish
Anser between truly wild stock and free-flying escapes from orna-
arvensis mental collections. In the present century the earliest record
brachy- was of ten at Beddington SF on 23 December 1938 (*BB*,
rhynchus 32:307). Three were observed at Barn Elms Reservoir a
week later and in view of the severe weather at the time
both these records were thought to refer to genuinely wild
birds (*The Birds of the London Area*, 1957). In 1956, c. 80
birds were seen flying north over Old Coulsdon on 26
February. Four of the remaining five records relate to
single birds, two of which were certainly escapes. The fifth
record was of four birds flying NE at Brockwell Park on
28 March 1968.

Brent Goose Extremely scarce vagrant.
Branta This is the most maritime of the wintering geese and visits
bernicla the south and east coasts in good numbers. Records of
genuinely wild stock can therefore be expected particularly
in times of hard weather. On the other hand the Brent
like other geese, is often kept in wildfowl collections and
records of single birds must inevitably be suspect for this
reason.

There are three records which fall into the first category
and which were made during periods of severe weather.
Eight were at Island Barn Reservoir on 17 December 1938
(*BB*, 43:307), two at Chiswick Eyot on the Thames on
14-16 February 1940 (*BB*, 33:315) and a party of six at
Frensham in severe weather early in 1940 (Vesey-Fitzgerald,
1949).

Other records concern two birds at Frensham on 23
April 1923 (*Haslemere List*, 1955) and a tame bird which
stayed at Frensham Little Pond from 22 March to 2 April
1953. A single bird was at Beddington in 1942. Three
visited the lake at Gatton Park on 12 December 1951. The
most recent records are of single birds in Richmond Park
and at the Walton Reservoirs both on 23 January 1966 and
one in flight over Bookham Common on 22 February 1970.

Barnacle Extremely scarce vagrant.
Goose This species winters in the Solway Firth and on certain of
Branta the Hebridean Islands. The Surrey records in the review
leucopsis period are few and are given subject to a more than usually
strong *caveat* that records might well refer to escaped birds
as this species is very widely kept in ornamental collections.

Two were seen in Witley Park in February 1919 (*Haslemere List*, 1921). Four at Beddington SF on 5 April 1959

flew in from the SE and departed in a NNW direction without settling. One was seen grazing with Wigeon at Walton Reservoirs on 29 January 1967 and a single bird was recorded throughout 1970 from the Ash/Frimley/Camberley area where it consorted with Canada Geese.

Resident, locally common.
This species was introduced into the country over 200 years ago. At the beginning of the century it was fairly common in the county but confined to private ornamental collections of wildfowl. Occasionally free-flying birds were shot and assumed to be escapes.

Canada Goose *Branta canadensis*

It was first recorded breeding in the free state at Godstone in 1905 and by 1930 it had established itself as a resident at nearby Gatton Park. It was reported breeding again at Godstone (two pairs on Bay Pond) and also on Elstead Common in the west in 1932. The colony at Gatton thrived and the resident flock had built up to 200 birds by 1936. It is thought that birds spread from here to other suitable waters in the district but precise documentation is lacking. Control measures were taken at Gatton starting in 1936; in 1938 only one pair bred there and during the war years when the military authorities took over the park, breeding ceased entirely.

Although records are lacking it seems probable that breeding continued in small numbers especially in the northeast of the county in the 1940s and early 1950s. Definite breeding was reported from Painshill Park, Cobham, in 1956 and in the next decade breeding was increasingly reported from all parts of the county. In 1967 breeding occurred in at least 12 areas and many of these held more than one pair. In this particular year five pairs raised 23 goslings in Battersea Park and there were at least three pairs at Cobham.

This species readily takes to small waters especially where small (wooded or open) islands provide the sort of nesting site the bird likes and the abundance of this kind of water in Surrey, together with an increasing tolerance by landowners and the public, probably accounts for its success.

There is no evidence that locally raised birds do not remain in the county throughout the year. In the late summer the birds congregate, flocks move about freely and can often be seen flying well away from water. Flocks of 50 or more are regularly reported from such localities as Enton, the Ash Vale and North Camp GPS, Cobham, Wisley and Holmethorpe. Two hundred were counted in three skeins over Ewhurst on 17 September 1970. Return to breeding sites usually takes place in March and nesting begins in April.

Mute Swan
Cygnus olor

Moderately common resident and winter visitor. This species is widely distributed throughout the county, breeding or attempting to breed on suitable waters such as ponds, lakes and on the quieter stretches of the Thames and its tributaries.

There is very little information on the breeding distribution in the early years of the century. In 1920 it was known to be breeding regularly at Fetcham Mill Pond, Beddington, Weybridge and Godstone and in the 1930s breeding numbers in the London area had increased; localities included Pen Ponds, Richmond Park, where breeding had lapsed for over 20 years. A breeding census of Mute Swans was organized in the London area in 1955, 1956 and 1961 and the population was judged to be fairly static over these years. The number of birds reported for the Surrey portion of the area in these censuses was as follows: 1955: 21, 1956: 34, 1961: 38. Most of the nests found were along the rivers, on lakes and ponds in parks, on commons and at other public places while a smaller number of records came from private waters, gravel pits, reservoirs, canals and sewage farms. In 1961 a total of 30 nests was found along the Thames (all upstream from Hammersmith) and three along the R. Mole (Cramp, 1957 and 1963). In the 1960s breeding localities reported to the Surrey Bird Club increased from four in the first few years, to between 11 and 16 by the end of the decade, with records widely scattered throughout the county. This increase no doubt represents a greater effort by observers to submit records rather than an actual increase in breeding numbers.

During the late summer, autumn and winter the birds form quite large herds. In the first decade of the century Bentham regularly reported up to 60 birds from Hedgecourt Pond in August and fairly high numbers were recorded there on other occasions up to the 1940s. Reports of the largest concentrations however have come consistently from the lower reaches of the Thames. Records from the Dyers' Company of the City of London relating to the swan-upping ceremony that takes place on the river in July, show that in the stretch from Battersea to Staines Bridge, numbers stayed around 150 in the period 1900 to 1920. There was a steady increase in the 1930s and in 1938, 418 birds including 60 cygnets were marked. There was a substantial drop in

24 *Sparrow Hawk*. Almost extinct in the county a decade ago, this species is recolonizing old haunts and showing signs of expansion (*F. V. Blackburn*)

numbers during and after the Second World War and in
1951 only 112 were recorded in the stretch from Putney to
Staines. Large numbers of birds were attracted to the
Thames during and after the Festival of Britain in 1951
and a count in 1954 recorded 479 in the Putney to Staines
stretch (*The Birds of the London Area*, 1957). In December
1956, two oil barges sank in the river and no less than 800
birds had to be treated and at least 243 died (*LBR*, 21:15).
Numbers in the 1960s show a continuing decline from
previous years' levels and in 1968 the peak number on the
stretch Putney to Barnes was 66 on 14 January. Fairly high
numbers are known to occur in the vicinity of Kingston
Bridge although details are lacking. Winter concentrations
from other parts of the county were around 20 at the end
of the review period, this number having been reported
from Enton in November 1968 and Shalford on 19 January
1969. There were, however, 48 at Frimley GP on 13
December 1970.

Ringing returns suggest that the county's resident population is augmented in the winter by birds from other areas.
A bird ringed at Kew on 28 December 1957 was recovered
on 9 September 1959 at Ludham in Norfolk, a bird recovered
on 23 February 1963 at Dorking had been ringed at Hythe,
Kent in December 1961 and a bird ringed at Putney on 1
January 1965 was caught at Barrow-in-Furness, Lancashire
on 1 July in the same year.

Whooper Swan *Cygnus cygnus*

Scarce winter visitor. Probable passage migrant.
There is only one record of this species in the first half
of the present century, that of two birds at Frensham with
Mute Swans on 22 February 1920. Frensham again provided a record in 1953 with a family party of two adults
and two immature birds on 8 March. There was an unprecedented series of records in 1956 with ten birds divided
between three different areas (Barnes, Old Coulsdon and
Island Barn Reservoir) on 5 February, one in flight at
Epsom SF on 13 March and finally two adults and an
immature bird at the Enton Ponds on 6 October. There
were odd records in 1960 and 1962 and during and following the hard weather of early 1963 there were several
influxes into and through the county. The first influx was
on 6 January with three birds in the Walton area followed
by six on 20 January. The second wave arrived on 4 February when four were seen at Tilford and one appeared at
Sutton Place with numbers rising there to nine on various
dates up to 12 March. Up to 12 were present in the Shalford

25 *Hobby*. Surrey is one of the strongholds of this species in southern England.
(*J. A. W. Jones*)

area from 8-23 March and on 22 March a herd of c. 50 flew low over built-up Chessington at 1130 hours travelling ENE. Two birds present in the Bletchingly area from 1-8 April provided the last record for the year. Since then the specific records have been confined to 1967, the year in which there were two at Badshot Lea Pond and Barn Elms Reservoir on 7 January and 10 December respectively and two at Frensham on 23-24 April while one was present there on 10 December.

Bewick's Scarce winter visitor. Probable passage migrant.
Swan In 1900 Bucknill knew of no certain records and the first
Cygnus record for the county was of two on Frensham Little Pond
columbianus in very hard weather in January 1929. By the mid-point of the century the species had been recorded six times, 29 birds being involved; the largest number at one time was 16 at Barn Elms Reservoir on 5 March 1946. There were as many records in the 1950s as in the previous half century, all but one of the records being for outer Surrey (Shalford, Frensham and Enton). In the 1960s the species was recorded in all but four of the years, the largest numbers occurring in the hard weather of early 1963 when there were records of up to 17 at Barn Elms and on the Thames at Barnes in January, 24 at Queen Elizabeth II Reservoir with Whooper Swans on 20 January, one in flight over Richmond Park on 1 March and 12 at Shalford on 17 March.

The species has been recorded in all months from November to April with the bulk of the records occurring in the three months January to March.

Buzzard Very scarce resident. Passage migrant and winter visitor.
Buteo buteo This species was not thought to be resident in the county in 1900 though it was regularly reported from (and shot in) various parts especially in the west and in winter. In 1939 Edgar P. Chance persuaded Sir John Leigh, the then owner of the Witley Park Estate, to try an experiment in an attempt to introduce the species. Nine birds were released over the period August 1939 to April 1940. The experiment was a success and a fair proportion of the birds stayed in the area. None bred in 1940 but three pairs did so in 1941 and one or more pairs have probably bred in the area ever since although full documentation is lacking. The species may well have attempted breeding in other parts of the county. A pair was established at Oxted in the breeding season in 1937 but unfortunately the birds were shot by keepers. In 1955 a pair was present in the Thursley area

during the summer although no evidence of breeding was obtained.

Passage birds are reported from various localities with most records occurring in the period March—April and August—October. A smaller number of winter records occur in various parts of the county.

Rough-Legged Buzzard *Buteo lagopus*

Extremely scarce winter visitor. There have been only three records of this species in the present century. One was shot at Wonersh Park on 24 November 1909 (*Zool.*, 1909), one was seen at Croydon on 21 April 1912 (*BOC Bull.*, 32:179) and one was identified at Guildford SF on 9 May 1953.

Sparrow Hawk *Accipiter nisus*

Scarce and local resident. Over the period under review this species has been subject to considerable fluctuations in numbers as a resident bird in the county. At the beginning of the century it was widely distributed but much less common than the Kestrel; it was much persecuted by game keepers and thought to be decreasing but there were areas where it was not uncommon and Bentham reported that three or four bred annually on Limpsfield Chart. An increase generally was noted by 1940 when game preservation slackened in intensity due to the distractions of the Second World War. This increase continued through the 1940s and the species probably reached peak numbers as a resident bird in the early 1950s. Some idea of its success might be gained from records from the Oxted and Limpsfield area where the local sporting interests did not look on it at all with favour. Seven pairs bred in 1946 and not less than 18 were located in 1948 of which 11 were found within a radius of four miles of Limpsfield. In the 1950s the species bred in Dulwich and occasionally in Richmond Park and on Wimbledon Common.

A decline began nationally in 1954 and became catastrophic by 1960 especially in the south-east of England. It was thought that the resumption of game keepering in the early 1950s initiated a gradual decline which was overshadowed 1957-60 by a sudden drop due to the effects of toxic chemicals and in particular persistent organochlorine pesticides (Prestt, 1965). In 1963 the status of the species in Surrey was regarded as local/sparse (*opus cit.*).

Fortunately the bird was just able to maintain its resident status in the county and generally at least two breeding pairs were recorded. The worst effects of pesticides seems to have been passed by the mid-1960s following the voluntary ban on dieldrin on spring-sown wheat and in the last few years of the decade there was a hopeful increase in sightings and breeding records. In 1969 there were four definite and one suspected breeding recorded. In 1970 the species was present in the breeding season in 11 localities, although a worrying fact was the low success rate; three pairs in the Thursley area were reported as producing only one young each.

Goshawk Extremely scarce vagrant.
Accipiter The records of this species in the present century have all
gentilis been within the last two decades of the period under review. A pair was seen by Guy Mountfort 'at play' on 8 August 1959 at Woldingham. A juvenile was observed on 15 September 1960 at Beddington SF and the bird was not seen to be carrying jesses although one viewed at Kew Gardens on 29 and 30 September 1960 was carrying a bell and was obviously a falconer's bird. One was seen soaring over Frensham Common on 13 May 1961 and again on the following day.

Kite Extremely scarce vagrant.
Milvus There is only one record of this species in the present
milvus century; R. S. Brown saw an immature bird at Beddington SF on 15 August 1966.

White- The only county record of this bird in the present century
tailed is of an immature male shot by a keeper at Cheverills, near
Eagle Titsey Park, on 12 November 1906. The identity of the
Haliaëtus bird was confirmed by the British Museum (Pycroft, 1907).
albicilla

Honey Extremely scarce vagrant.
Buzzard Bucknill considered that this species may have bred formerly
Pernis in the county. There are no records for the first half of
apivorus the present century. There is a record of one on Box Hill on 27 July 1954 and satisfactory details were submitted of one in flight over Esher Common on 22 August 1959 and of one at Tilford on 7 June 1965.

Marsh Scarce passage migrant.
Harrier This bird has been recorded on ten occasions in the county
Circus in the present century and four of these records were in the
aeruginosus 1960s, the most recent being on 25 May 1966 on Ockley Common. The records, six in May and one each in the months of July to November, suggest that they refer to passage or post-breeding dispersal. The sightings have all been on the west Surrey commons with the exception of one at Beddington SF on 5 September 1954.

Scarce passage migrant and winter visitor. **Hen Harrier**
There are records of this species in every decade of the *Circus*
present century, usually of ones and occasionally twos, *cyaneus*
generally in the period September to April and concentrated
on the west Surrey heaths. There was an increase in reports
of the species in the 1960s and birds have spent the whole
or part of the winter on the Thursley/Ockley/Royal complex of commons in at least five of the past ten winters.
At least three were present in the Thursley area (one adult
male and two 'ringtails') in December 1969. Other records
in recent years have been of one on Epsom Common on 4
November 1965, one adult male on Ash Ranges on 6 April
1969 and a 'ringtail' at Cobham on 6 December 1969.

There is one record of a pair nesting in an undisclosed
area of the county in 1932 when D. Nethersole-Thompson
found a nest containing a clutch of five eggs from which
four young were hatched (*BB*, 26:279).

Scarce passage migrant. **Montagu's**
At the turn of the century the Montagu's Harrier was a **Harrier**
rare visitor; a number had been shot in the county and *Circus*
adorned various collections. In 1906 a pair was located on *pygarus*
Ockley Common and breeding was suspected. In the following year the birds returned to the same area and Bentham
discovered the nest on 21 May. There was at first some
doubt about the identity of the birds and it was not until
one of the two young raised was shot that the identity was
firmly established (*BB*, 1:237-42, 351-4). A pair returned to
Hankley Common in 1908 and although eggs were laid and
the nest guarded by an RSPB warden, the eggs did not hatch.
The only other breeding record is of circumstantial evidence
in 1917 when a young bird was nearly run over by a cyclist
in the same general area (*Haslemere List*, 1921).

Specific identification of harriers is not always possible
because of the close similarity of the female immature Hen
Harrier and female and immature Montagu's. However
there have been a few Montagu's Harriers satisfactorily
identified in the county from the mid-1930s and there was
an increase in the records in the late 1960s. There were
three records of 'ringtails' in the Thursley/Hankley area
in May of 1967, a sooty grey melanistic male on Chobham
Common on 24 August 1968 and an immature bird in
Richmond Park on 11 October 1969.

Scarce passage migrant. **Osprey**
There are half a dozen records of this species from various *Pandion*
lakes in outer Surrey during the first half of this century, *haliaetus*

two records in the 1950s and at least five records in the 1960s. In spring the birds do not linger and records are of single sightings over the period April to May but the records in autumn often involve birds which remain for some weeks in the same area, as for instance one which spent three weeks in October 1956 at Waterloo Ponds, Chilworth and one that lingered at a small lake at Wonersh throughout September and October 1968.

Hobby
Falco
subbuteo

Scarce summer visitor. Passage migrant.
In 1900 Bucknill classed this bird as a rare summer visitor but he knew of no breeding records although the bird was not infrequently shot during the summer months. It was first suspected of breeding in the south-west of the county in 1906 and in 1907 Bentham obtained confirmation of breeding on Ockley Common. In 1914 Bentham located three pairs on Thursley Common and one pair on Hankley Common. It seems likely that breeding in small numbers has continued in this area during the whole of the present century although there are many gaps in the records. The bird however is easily overlooked and its nest often difficult to locate. In 1935 at least six pairs were located in north west Surrey, another stronghold of the species. It was estimated that the breeding population of the county over the years 1962-64 was 12 pairs (Parslow, 1967). It is probable, however, that the number of breeding pairs at the end of the review period was in excess of 12. Breeding in 1969 was confirmed in four areas and suspected in three others, involving in all nine to ten pairs. Unfortunately the species still attracts excessive attention from bird-watchers and those with ulterior motives, resulting in disturbance and sometimes loss of eggs or young.

The most favoured nesting situation is in a disused crow's nest in a Scots Pine, generally in a small clump of trees or a single tree with a good vantage point.

The main influx of birds takes place in early May but there are occasional reports of birds in late April. Young are not usually on the wing till August and can be very noisy and conspicuous when just out of the nest. Late passage birds occur up till early October while the latest record is one of a bird seen by Bentham on the North Downs near Oxted on 12 November 1911.

Peregrine
Falco
peregrinus

Scarce winter visitor and passage migrant.
There has been no discernible change in the status of this species in the present century. In the last decade of the

review period there were ten records in seven years. It has been recorded in all months except January and May, the records being concentrated in the periods February to April and September to December. The localities where sightings have been made are scattered throughout the whole county, with the exception of the inner London urban areas.

Merlin
Falco
columbarius

Scarce winter visitor and passage migrant.
This species has been recorded on nine occasions in five of the years of the last decade of the review period and this incidence is probably indicative of its status in the present century. It has been recorded in all months of the year, most frequently in November and December. Some of the records in spring and autumn are no doubt of passage birds.

Red-footed Falcon
Falco
vespertinus

Extremely scarce vagrant.
W. A. Shaw referred to two occurrences, one of a bird shot in Witley Park in the early years of the century and a male seen by him on 11 July 1915 (*Haslemere List*, 1921). These records must be regarded with some reservations. The only recent record is of an adult male seen by R. M. Fry on Ockley Common on 13 May 1961 (*BB*, 55:571).

Kestrel
Falco
tinnunculus

Moderately common resident. Passage migrant.
In the first half of the century this species was apparently thinly distributed over the county with breeding occasionally reported from the outer areas, as for example the Thursley group of commons, Limpsfield and Haslemere and outer London suburbs such as Banstead, Coulsdon and Epsom. Nowhere was it thought to be common and in Richmond Park before the Second World War there was only one authenticated record of breeding. By the 1950s however, the species had established itself in such urbanized areas as Battersea and Lambeth, though the records as a whole were quite insufficient to indicate its true status in the county. In a national survey Prestt (1965) found the Kestrel to be sparsely distributed in the county and that, as with other areas of south-east England, there had been a moderate decrease in breeding pairs over the period 1953-63. In a further review Parslow (1967) noted a decided recovery in some southern counties, including Surrey, starting in 1964 and this is suggested too by the breeding records submitted to the Surrey Bird Club which showed an increase from eight definite and 14 possible breeding pairs in 1964 (total 22) to 18 definite and 16 possible pairs (total 34) in 1965. In 1967 an attempt was made to assess the total breeding population of the county (Parr, 1969) and 58 pairs were proved to be breeding, there being a further 32 suspected of breed-

ing. The total breeding population was estimated to be in the range of 130-60 pairs. In the survey, some very high breeding densities were located, most notably in Richmond Park where there were no less than 20 pairs (all except one having been proved to breed) giving a breeding density of one pair per 150 acres. Breeding in the park was almost without exception, in holes in oak trees.

The species is no doubt also a passage migrant through the area and records are received in spring and autumn of birds moving purposefully as though on migration. There is also a record of ten to 20 birds flying south in ones or twos over a period of 20 minutes in the morning of 28 March 1947 at Dulwich.

Ringing returns have shown a widespread and apparently random dispersal of Kestrels raised in Surrey. Of seven birds ringed as nestlings in Richmond Park over the years 1947-57, one was recovered at Walton two years later in June and two siblings were recovered, after three winters, in Gloucestershire in May and Acton (London) in September. Birds ringed as nestlings at Ewhurst and Walton have been recovered in the following year in Boston (Lincolnshire) in January and in Cambridge in February while two such ringed at Walton in June 1970 were recovered within two days of each other at Princes Risborough, Buckinghamshire and North Weald, Essex, in November of the same year. There is one foreign recovery, that of a bird ringed at Thursley in June 1940 and recovered at Cortes (Navarra) Spain in December of the same year.

Black Grouse Extinct.
Lyrurus tetrix Although Parslow (1967) implied that the species was extinct in Surrey before 1900, two pairs were recorded as breeding in a certain tract of wild country near Thursley in 1905. The last record in the decade was of one greyhen in 1906 although it is not clear whether this was in the same area.

There is a report in the *Surrey Bird Report* (2:12) of 'some seen in recent years ... probably introduced. At Runnymede, Egham, a Blackcock was feeding on the edge of a patch of boggy ground on 17 December 1954' (J. O. Owens).

The exact status of the species prior to 1900 is not clear due to conflicting reports and lack of information regarding the boosting of stock by introductions. However it is probable that the species was fairly common in suitable habitats, notably in the Bagshot and Haslemere areas, up to the last two decades of the nineteenth century when conditions apparently inimical to the species began to prevail. These would appear to include urban development and the presence of the military on large tracts of commonland.

However, suitable habitats have been preserved and in the absence of sufficient knowledge an exact appraisal of the species' extinction in Surrey cannot be given.

Red-legged Partridge
Alectoris rufa

Scarce resident.

In 1900 this species was considered to be a common resident, rapidly becoming abundant. In 1907 Bentham regarded it as abundant in the Oxted area as the Partridge (*Perdix perdix*). Since then lack of published records makes it difficult to give any accurate assessment of its real status in the county through the review period but the indications are that it has declined seriously in numbers but possibly not as dramatically as the Partridge.

In 1934 several pairs were nesting on the greensand commons around Haslemere (*SEBR*) but there were no reports of this kind from that area in the last few years of the review period. The species was recorded as breeding in the Leatherhead area prior to 1939 but it had disappeared from there by 1950 (Douglas, 1951). Records submitted to the Surrey Bird Club in the first half of the 1960s showed a declining trend; 20 localities were given in the *SBR* for 1960 but only nine for 1965; however since the middle of the decade the species appears to have been holding its own and definite breeding was reported from 11 of the ten kilometre grid squares of the *BTO* Atlas over the years 1968 to 1971.

The species is generally confined to the more rural areas and is dependent in the main on farmland (including rough pasture) for its nesting requirements although it resorts on occasions, for shelter and breeding, to gravel/sand pits or sewage farms.

National statistics show that the Red-legged Partridge has generally increased in recent years and is now a more successful species than the Partridge, probably due to a combination of factors—later nesting and different food preferences. However, county records in the 1960s do not exactly reflect the national trend and on the strength of these records there does not appear to be any marked difference in status or distribution between the two species in Surrey. It is probable that both species are equally under-recorded and deserving of a higher status than the one accorded to them.

Partridge
Perdix perdix

Scarce resident.

As with the Red-legged Partridge (*Alectoris rufa*) there is no doubt that the species has declined in numbers during the present century. Bucknill classed it as a very common resident, Eric Parker considered it as still very common around Hambledon in 1910, Bentham regarded it as plentiful on the North Downs in the 1920s and Beadell regarded it as still plentiful in the same general area in the 1930s. Precise documentation of its status and distribution has been however sadly lacking.

The species will nest close to built-up areas although its general requirements are open agricultural country. In 1947 a pair bred at Kew where it had not been recorded since 1909. During the nineteenth century it had been common in Richmond Park but by 1936 no more than five or six coveys were recorded there; however, in the 1950s, following a period when a large area of the park had been used for war-time agriculture, 113 birds were counted in one part of the park. Breeding was also recorded in Kew in 1950 (*The Birds of the London Area*, 1957).

During the 1960s records submitted to the Surrey Bird Club varied but in no year did the localities where the species was sighted exceed 13. Parslow (1967) describing the national status of the species referred to a steady long-term decrease in the present century, accelerated since 1940. Records from the county are in line with this trend but the reasons for the decline have not been clearly established. There is strong evidence that it has been associated with changes in insect population and in particular with a decline in arthropods, on the larvae of which the chicks of the species feed (Potts, 1970).

Quail
Coturnix
coturnix
Extremely scarce summer visitor. Scarce passage migrant. In the first half of the present century there was a very marked and widespread decline in the distribution of this species throughout England but since 1942 records have increased somewhat (Parslow, 1967). The records from the county are in line with this general position. The species was suspected of breeding at Old Oxted in 1909 and in Richmond Park in 1913. It was heard calling at Tilford on a number of occasions in May 1954 but it was not till 1964 that proof of breeding was obtained for the county in the present century; a female with six young was flushed at Chertsey on 8 August at a spot where a maximum of seven birds had been heard calling in July and a bird was flushed from two eggs in that area on 29 August. In the last decade of the review period the Quail was reported from at least one locality in every year except in 1969. In 1970 it was reported calling at Compton, a male was seen and heard

on several occasions at Horley and up to four birds were heard calling from meadowland at Thorpe during June although no evidence of breeding was obtained.

There is one remarkable ringing recovery of the species from the county. On 3 May 1965 L. G. Weller trapped and ringed a bird on his farm at Ewhurst and it was subsequently shot in north west Spain on 15 September of the same year. This was the first foreign recovery of a British-ringed Quail.

Pheasant
Phasianus colchicus

Common resident.
This species is widely distributed throughout the rural and suburban areas of the county. It is probably less numerous now than in the first half of the century and its fluctuations and distribution are clearly influenced by artificial rearing and game protection. Detailed information on its true status is difficult to come by because few observers take the trouble to record the species. About 100 were seen in Kew Gardens in 1936 and the species was still common there in 1950. Following wartime cultivation of Richmond Park the species increased there appreciably and c. 190 were counted during April 1952. It is unlikely that these numbers could be found in any comparable area in the county at the present time. Records from 96 acres of grassland with scrub on Bookham Common show that in 1969 there were seven territories, compared with two or three territories in the previous five years (G. Beven).

Crane
Megalornis grus

Very scarce vagrant.
This species has been reliably recorded in Surrey on only two occasions. A single bird was seen flying south over Frensham Little Pond on 16 June 1966. (In that year 11 records were accepted by the Rarities Committee of *British Birds*—the highest total for a number of years except when there was an exceptional influx in autumn 1963.) The second record was of two seen by Mr and Mrs C. K. Dunkley at Newlands Corner on 22 October 1968 (*BB*, 62:466).

Water Rail
Rallus aquaticus

Very scarce resident and locally distributed winter visitor.
The skulking nature of this species makes quantitative assessment difficult and it is likely that it is frequently overlooked. The records available indicate that its status has not greatly changed since the beginning of the century. There has been considerable pressure on the habitat favoured in Bucknill's days—the swampy thickets and bramble-covered stream edges. The Water Rail is fortunately a species which

readily adapts to new habitats—the sewage farm, overgrown sandpit and watercress bed.

The species is recorded in the breeding season most frequently at Frensham where a nest with nine eggs was found on the Little Pond on 30 May 1939. Breeding was also proved at Beddington SF in 1955 and it possibly occurred at Epsom SF in 1956. Juvenile birds were seen at Unstead SF in 1956 and Guildford SF in 1957. On 11 June 1959 G. Douglas reported watching an adult bird with five or six young crossing a road at Ockham Common. Summer records have also been made at Pudmore, Fetcham watercress beds, the Devil's Punchbowl, Cutt Mill, Ockley and in recent years at Thorpe GPs.

From August/September there is a marked increase in numbers and generally records are received from up to 20 localities. Winter visitors leave by the end of March.

Two birds were ringed at Leatherhead in February 1959; one was recovered locally in March of the following year while the other was found at Pfaffenhaffen (Bas Rhin), France in March 1960.

Spotted Crake
Porzana
porzana

Extremely scarce passage migrant and summer resident. It is probable that in common with other members of the rail family the Spotted Crake is overlooked. There are only eight records for this century, all of which are given below.

A single bird was seen at Brook on 1 May 1906 and two birds were present at the same location at a later date (*Zool.*, 1907). A pair remained in a marsh near Witley from April to July 1930. On 31 December 1944 a single bird was seen on the site of Frensham Great Pond which was drained at the time (*SEBR*) and in December 1955 a good description was obtained of a bird seen on two occasions at Epsom SF.

The remains of a dead bird were found on 7 November 1959 at Fetcham watercress beds where a sighting was made earlier on 3 October. In the same year birds were seen at Guildford SF on 5 August and during the period 6-11 September.

Both in 1964 and 1965 up to four birds were heard calling in June and July at Beddington SF and although no evidence was obtained the circumstances suggested that breeding occurred or was attempted (*LBR*, 34:86-8). In his review of the national status of this species Parslow (1967) reported an increase in records in the 1960s and considered that the Spotted Crake might have become an annual breeder in the British Isles.

Bucknill quoted two authenticated records. The first, of a **Baillon's Crake** bird which was in the Charterhouse Collection, was taken *Porzana* at a spring in Church Street, Godalming in 1837. The *pusilla* second bird was caught alive in a meadow between Mitcham and Carshalton at the end of May 1874 and was kept in captivity for some time by being fed on minced meat and bread.

In the present century there has been no positive record although a small crake flushed from an overgrown dyke at Beddington SF on 13 November 1955 was either of this species or a Little Crake (*Porzana parva*).

Bucknill described a bird in the Charterhouse Collection **Little Crake** that was shot at Bramley in 1860. In the present century a *Porzana parva* single bird is recorded in the *Haslemere List* (1921) as seen on one of the ponds on a common (probably Haslemere) on 17 September 1910 by W. A. Shaw. No supporting evidence is quoted so the record cannot be accepted without reservation.

Very scarce visitor, formerly bred. **Corncrake**
In 1900 Bucknill was still able to describe the Corncrake as *Crex crex* a fairly abundant summer visitor which was subject to fluctuations in numbers from year to year. The year 1896 is mentioned particularly as a year in which the bird was plentiful.

The turn of the century marked the beginnings of a rapid decline. A report on the ten years up to 1913 could only refer to occasional pairs in the county. There were in fact only two published breeding records in this period, both from Caterham, in the years 1911 and 1912 (*Country Life*, 33:651). Breeding was reported from Beddington SF in 1918 and was thought to have occurred in the Limpsfield area up to 1928. In 1934 four pairs bred on the south side of Epsom Downs and pre-1939 breeding was known in the Leatherhead area (Douglas, 1951). The last recorded breeding attempt in the county was in the Wey Valley below Farncombe where a nest with two eggs was found on 14 June 1946; the nest was subsequently robbed (*SEBR*).

Subsequent records have been almost all of single birds flushed during the migration season and these are concentrated in the early 1950s.

The pattern of the Corncrake's decline in Surrey mirrors the rapid reduction in numbers in southern England and the Midlands with the advent of more sophisticated farming techniques and machinery. Only one record was made in the period 1960-70 (at Ockley during the last week of May

1966) which does not give any grounds for optimism on the future of the species.

Moorhen
Gallinula
chloropus
Common resident and winter visitor.

There has been probably little change in status of the Moorhen since the beginning of the century. The species breeds commonly on ponds, lakes, sewage farms, watercress beds, gravel pits, streams, rivers and even on quite small reed-fringed bogs on open commonland whenever its two essential requirements of water and adequate cover can be met. Nesting commonly starts in March with repeat or replacement clutches occurring throughout the summer.

In autumn and winter the main concentrations appear at such places as Godstone Pond, Guildford sf and Unstead. It occurs only exceptionally and in small numbers on the reservoirs which have insufficient cover for its liking. Autumn concentrations appear to be mainly of juvenile birds, as for instance c. 120 recorded at Guildford sf in October 1970. These were probably locally bred birds exploiting a favourable food supply. Most of the winter concentrations undoubtedly originate from the smaller waters which are more readily frozen in winter but some birds originate also from outside the county.

Where there are concentrations, numbers of Moorhen are difficult to count and it is only exceptionally that gatherings of over 100 birds are recorded. Two hundred were however recorded at Guildford sf in the winter of 1956 and an even larger congregation of 500 birds was reported from the same locality in 1959.

Some evidence of the origin of the wintering birds is given by the recovery of a bird ringed at Amager in Denmark on 9 August 1962 at Godalming on 15 November in the same year.

Coot
Fulica atra
Common resident and abundant winter visitor.

Bucknill was of the opinion that at the turn of the century the Coot population was going through a period of low numbers and forecast a subsequent increase. What evidence there is suggests that Bucknill's forecast has proved right. At Englefield Green for instance Coot were first seen about 1928 and by 1934 numbers were increasing rapidly; numbers at Virginia Water were said to be increasing in 1935/36. Described as a local bird in the Busbridge area in 1922, it was recorded as common in 1958. Breeding in parks and lakes in suburban Surrey has certainly increased in recent years; for instance Battersea Park was colonized in the early 1950s.

As a breeding species the Coot requires a larger area of water than the Moorhen and is therefore more restricted in its distribution, preferring the larger lakes, ponds and gravel pits but it will tolerate fairly small water surfaces if sufficient cover is present. In the early 1960s it bred for a number of years on the comparatively small effluent beds at Hersham SF. It seldom attempts breeding at the reservoirs because of the lack of cover.

In 1957 a breeding survey carried out in the London area (within 20 miles from St Paul's) disclosed a total of 90 nests in the part in Surrey; 89 of these were on lakes and ponds and one on a reservoir. The waters with the largest totals were: Waddon Ponds: 30 pairs, Fetcham Mill Ponds: 18 pairs and Gatton Park: 11 pairs. The survey also disclosed a fairly high non-breeding population and 82 such birds were counted on Island Barn Reservoir on 22 June (Homes, Sage and Spencer, 1960).

Nesting usually begins in late March or early April and continues through the summer. There is one very late record from Frensham where a bird was seen on eggs on 15 October 1958 and a juvenile was seen there on 1 January 1959.

In winter the birds congregate on the larger waters and numbers are greatly augmented by visitors from the Continent particularly so on the Thames Valley reservoirs. In the earlier years of the century winter concentrations reported from Frensham and Hedgecourt numbered 150-200 birds and reached 250 only exceptionally. Coot-shoots occasionally took place during the 1930s particularly at Frensham and these may have played a part in keeping numbers down. After the Second World War wintering populations reached new peaks and 900 were counted at Frensham in February 1951 and c. 1,000 were counted at Walton Reservoirs in November 1959. Numbers however vary a good deal from winter to winter and are probably dependent on the total winter influx from the Continent but, in general, numbers have been lower in the last few years of the 1960s.

One ringing recovery suggests the source of our winter visitors; a bird ringed near Redhill on 27 January 1963 was recovered at Stadil Fjord, Denmark on 17 March 1963.

Oystercatcher
Haematopus
ostralegus

Scarce visitor.
This species was seldom recorded before 1900 and the first record this century was not until 1922 when on 10 March there was a single bird at Frensham Little Pond. On 30 August 1927 one was seen flying over Barn Elms Reservoir

but there are few other records before 1950. From 1953 to the end of the review period, however, it was seen annually and upwards of 45 occurrences have been distributed between various localities in all months except October and November.

Barn Elms Reservoir and Frensham Ponds account for about half the total. Most of these records refer to single birds and the largest party was nine at Barn Elms Reservoir on 19 March 1953. Birds on nocturnal passage have been heard on a number of occasions at localities including Crystal Palace, Merstham and Streatham.

Lapwing
Vanellus
vanellus
Locally common resident, passage migrant and winter visitor. As a breeding bird the Lapwing has declined in numbers since the beginning of the century. Bucknill had noted a decline earlier, which he ascribed partly to egg collection and land drainage but it was still numerous enough for him to say that it usually nested in 'colonies'. Bentham found the Lapwing plentiful in some areas where it no longer is today; for instance, large numbers were nesting near Frensham Ponds in 1908 and on Ockley Common in 1909 and 1913. However, Bentham too recorded a decline in numbers and could find no evidence of breeding on Walton Common in 1913 'where it formerly did so in considerable numbers'. Referring to the Ockley Common breeding population he wrote that 'the eggs were much sought after by the villagers, a man boasting that he had in one season taken twelve dozen clutches'. It is not surprising that not many years passed before the breeding stocks were reduced to vanishing point. Egg collection is not now a limiting factor of such importance and there has been no significant land drainage at Frensham or Ockley but there has been no subsequent recovery to former numbers, only a few pairs remaining. The much greater accessibility of those areas with improved roads and means of transport and the greater use made of them for recreational purposes has probably inhibited recovery, since as a ground nesting species with conspicuous behaviour, the Lapwing is particularly vulnerable where there is casual interference. Encroachment by birch and pine may also have been a factor.

If not as abundant as formerly the Lapwing is still a common breeding bird, thinly scattered over the whole county apart from the inner metropolitan area. There are no really large breeding colonies but at least 60 different breeding localities have been noted in recent years. Water meadows and damp pastures along the valleys of the Wey

and the Mole still presented a relatively undisturbed habitat
at the end of the review period and in 1969 there were about
30 pairs between Leatherhead and Stoke D'Abernon alone
and good numbers along the Wey between Broadford and
Burpham.

There have at times been substantial colonies on some of
the sewage farms. An estimated 60 pairs bred at Unstead
in 1951 (but numbers were much reduced at the end of the
review period). A few pairs used to nest at Epsom SF in the
1950s until the farm was closed down and the breeding
populations at Beddington and Guildford SFs declined following modernization of the farms. Intermittent breeding
has also been recorded at Hersham SF and has no doubt
occurred on most of the farms when they were in a suitable
condition but modern methods of sewage disposal are
greatly reducing the importance of sewage farms as breeding sites. The other wetland habitat is damp commonland
such as is found in west Surrey and at Bookham. Only a
pair or two nest in most such places.

On farmland, particularly freshly ploughed arable soil (in
all parts of the county) breeding is frequently attempted.
Loss of clutches due to agricultural operations has not been
quantitatively measured but is thought to be high. Even so
the Lapwing will lay a second time and it seems likely
overall, that arable farmland is of great importance in maintaining population numbers. The preference of the species
for bare soil as a nest site is well demonstrated by the re-
colonization of Richmond Park in 1943 when part of it was
brought under cultivation. Breeding success was poor and
the colony died out in the 1950s when cultivation ceased.

Birds are often present throughout the year in breeding
localities and the breeding stock is probably largely resident
in the county except in times of hard weather. Flocking
begins in June and from July onwards the population is
much increased by immigrants. Flocks of 600 or more are
not uncommon on farm fields and sewage farms in August.
Many of these birds pass on and then, with the onset of
hard weather in November or December there are further
waves of immigrants from the east and north-east. The birds
may pass over the county in a succession of small flocks
moving by day, totalling 1,000 birds or more, or they may
stay, at least temporarily and large concentrations, e.g. 3,000
at Beddington SF on 15 January 1956, 2,000 on 1 February
1956 and 1,200 at Epsom SF on 1 February 1956 have sometimes been reported. The recovery of a bird at Smolensk in
the autumn of 1968 which had been ringed as an adult at

Ewhurst on 9 September 1961 shows encouraging longevity and illustrates migration. Return passage has been observed in March and this too may be upset by contrary weather. On 4 March 1970, 10,500 Lapwings, possibly representing the largest movement ever recorded in the county, were seen moving SE over Kingston just before and during an ENE blizzard and smaller numbers moving in the same direction were widely reported from many parts of the county. Two days later a return movement of c. 2,000 birds flying NNE in two and a half hours was seen at Worcester Park.

Ringed Plover Passage migrant and winter visitor.
Charadrius On 30 May 1909 Bentham found a nest with four eggs on
hiaticula sparsely covered ground 300 yards from Frensham Great Pond. He did not visit the site again until July and it is not known whether a brood was reared. Heavy recreational use of the area makes any current attempt at Frensham highly improbable but in 1961 when the Queen Elizabeth II Reservoir was under construction, at least one pair summered; breeding was suspected but could not be confirmed. The species has nested at a number of sites in the London area since 1957, including Stanwell Moor GP (in political Surrey but outside the vice-county) in 1967. One of the Thames Valley gravel pits or sewage farms may therefore provide a nesting site before long.

The Ringed Plover is mainly an annual passage migrant with peak numbers in April/May and August/September but it has occurred in every month of the year since 1955. Records for January are scarce, though there have been a few, e.g. one at Guildford SF on 31 January 1958 and one at Beddington SF on 4 and 11 January 1959. February and March birds are not much more common but it has occurred in recent years at Abinger watercress beds, Barn Elms Reservoir, Beddington SF, Epsom SF, Frensham, Guildford SF, Holmethorpe GPS and Queen Elizabeth II Reservoir. The bird at Abinger was seen during the severe weather of February 1963 when the unfrozen water there attracted waders of several species. There were up to four at Beddington SF on various dates from 17 February to 5 March 1963. The species occurs widely in April and May. The numbers seen at any one time are not large—usually not more than three—but occasionally there are parties of six or more. There are only occasional sightings in June and the first three weeks of July. The return passage then gets under way, numbers reaching a peak in August and continues into early September. Though not large, the autumn passage is more considerable than that in spring and it has been recorded on most of the sewage farms, at gravel pits such as Thorpe and Send and in Richmond Park. There are a few stragglers later in September and in October. November and December occurrences are very exceptional but there was one at Walton GP on 9 November 1957 and one at Queen Elizabeth II Reservoir on 4 December 1964.

Before the 1950s the species was infrequently seen and probably overlooked, though there are a few nineteenth-century records and Bentham found it at Hedgecourt Pond in 1911. It was also among the waders reported by P. A. D. Hollom as a double passage migrant at Brooklands SF in 1936.

Little Ringed Plover
Charadrius dubius

Scarce summer visitor. Passage migrant.
This species first bred in Britain in 1938 and its first known breeding attempt in Surrey was at Guildford SF in 1948. A pair stayed for a week in the vicinity of an area of rough stony ground which was flooded shortly after. Breeding definitely occurred near Richmond in 1950, the nest being found on top of clinker which was being dumped in an old pit and in subsequent years there has been at least one nesting attempt in the county with a maximum of 13 pairs reported present in 1962. Although it is probably fair to assume that the presence of a pair indicates nesting, actual proof of breeding is sometimes difficult to obtain from casual records. The indications are that in the county as a whole, following the initial colonization, the breeding population settled at a level of about ten pairs, this level being reached in the late 1950s. Numbers recorded at the end of the 1960s were however lower and breeding was recorded at only four sites in 1969 and 1970.

Consolidation or further increase seems dependent on an extension of habitat provided in the main by gravel pits and, while new pits continue to be opened, this to an extent balances the losses. Old pits become overgrown and unsuitable while others are filled. The sites have all tended to be short-lived and are in optimal condition when being actively worked. This has resulted in many clutches and young being lost. The huge gravel floor of the Queen Elizabeth II Reservoir, when under construction, was essentially temporary. The species also bred for several years in the early 1950s at Guildford SF but this terminated with the modernization of the farm. Guildford SF has provided the only ringing recovery to date—a juvenile ringed there on 6

June 1954 and recovered at Lot-et-Garonne, France, 480 miles south, on 29 March 1955.

Passage birds have been seen at many places in the county, mainly gravel pits and sewage farms, the earliest being 26 March (Frensham, 1967) and the latest 19 October (Guildford SF, 1969).

Kentish Plover
Charadrius alexandrinus

The only record in this century is of an exhausted bird found at Ewhurst Green on 8 October 1960. This record was accepted by the Records Committee of the Surrey Bird Club but not by the Rarities Committee of *British Birds*. Bucknill mentioned one said to have been shot near East Molesey in the spring of 1878.

Grey Plover
Charadrius squatarola

Scarce passage migrant and winter visitor.

The Grey Plover has always been a scarce bird in Surrey. Bucknill had only a few undated references and the first record for this century was of two in flight over Barn Elms Reservoir on 23 November 1932. Since then there have been upwards of eighteen occurrences—the increases probably reflecting an increase in observers rather than a change in status. There have been four occurrences in May and the other records are spread over all months except June, September and December.

The largest number seen at one time was four flying south over Thursley on 1 October 1938. Several of the birds seen, e.g. at Brooklands SF 26-27 May 1936, two at Guildford SF on 22 August 1944 and two at Queen Elizabeth II Reservoir on 12 May 1961, have been in full or almost full summer plumage.

Golden Plover
Charadrius apricarius

Winter visitor and passage migrant.

Although Bucknill mentioned a decline prior to 1900 there is no real evidence of any change of status since. Bentham found flocks of up to 50 fairly frequently in east Surrey in the early years of the century and also saw the species at Beddington SF, Ockley Common and other localities. At the end of the review period it was an annual visitor to the county and had been seen in every month of the year. From January to March the numbers seen are sometimes substantial, the largest being a flock of 100 at Beddington SF on 24 January 1958. Occurrences in April and May are rare but there was one bird in Richmond Park on 4 April 1958 and 30 were seen at Hersham SF flying north on 21 May 1959. One was also heard flying over Ockley Common on the night of 8 May 1961. In 1969 a bird summered at Brooklands Airfield—a very exceptional occurrence. The species is seen occasionally in August and September and flocks of up to 60 have been seen on many occasions from October to the end of the year.

The Golden Plover often associates with Lapwings on stubbles, the short grass of playing fields or airfields or on arable farmland. A high proportion of records relate to birds seen or heard flying over.

The bird seen in Richmond Park on 4 April 1958 was a male in almost complete summer plumage and had characteristics of the Northern race (*C.a.altifrons*).

Turnstone
Arenaria
interpres

Scarce winter visitor and passage migrant.

The earliest record in this century is of one at Frensham Ponds on 20 May 1921 (*Haslemere Review*, 1968) at which time there were only two previous records, the most recent in 1893. The next record was of a bird seen at Barn Elms Reservoir on 16 May 1933. P. A. D. Hollom saw one at Brooklands sf on 30 May 1934 and there was another at Barn Elms Reservoir on 4 May 1937. More intensive watching in recent years has shown that a very small number occurs almost annually, the species having been seen in every year except one, from 1954 to 1969, usually in ones and twos and with the largest party being eight at Beddington sf on 13 January 1955. There have been some thirty-four records in the review period with winter occurrences being exceptional and over half the birds seen in well marked passage periods from 1 May to 20 May (13 times) and 19 to 29 August (seven times).

Snipe
Capella
gallinago

Scarce breeding species, locally distributed. Common passage migrant and winter visitor.

In the breeding season small numbers of Snipe are found on the wetter parts of the west Surrey heaths, such as Pudmore, on the marshy parts of commons elsewhere, as at Bookham, Wisley and in the Limpsfield area, on water meadows and marshes of the Wey Valley below Guildford and the Mole Valley below Leatherhead and on at least one sewage farm (Beddington). There has been a certain amount of habitat loss during the century from land drainage and the modernization of sewage farms but overall the range is still similar to that described by Bucknill. Proof of attempted breeding has been obtained on a number of occasions but in most cases it is not known whether the birds present have actually succeeded; this prevents a real assessment of population changes from being made.

There does, nevertheless, seem to have been a decline in

the number of breeding pairs since 1900. Bentham, writing of the early years of this century, was still able to say that it nested in large numbers on Pudmore and Hankley Common but this could not be said of any part of the county at the end of the review period. What seems to have happened is that there has been some contraction of range due to loss of habitat, while such large breeding concentrations as might have existed have been reduced to a few pairs each, perhaps in part because of disturbance following the increasing use of these areas for recreational purposes. There has however been a marked decrease in southern counties generally, from the late 1940s onwards (Parslow, 1967). The species appears to be present in its suspected breeding localities throughout the year apart from temporary absences due to weather conditions (e.g. water meadows drying out in late summer or freezing up in severe winter weather). A nestling ringed at Elstead on 13 May 1914 was recovered at Steyning, Sussex on 11 January 1916.

Large numbers of Snipe pass through the county in spring and autumn and many winter. N. J. Westwood (*SBR*, 7:22-6) in a seven-year study of the pattern of Snipe migration at Guildford sf from 1954 to 1960 showed how there was a gradual build-up of numbers from late August to an autumn peak averaging 430 birds in November, with numbers falling off in mid-winter to about 100 and rising again to a smaller peak of c. 140 in March followed by a rapid fall off in April. The pattern is similar at other sewage farms. The largest concentrations have been at Beddington sf where up to 1,000 have often been seen in the winter months in the 1960s with a maximum of an estimated 5,000 in December 1962 and over 1,000 on 27 December 1968. The numbers wintering at some other sewage farms, notably Earlswood, Hersham, Ripley, Unstead and (before its closure) Epsom, have also been considerable, though falling short of the numbers recorded at Beddington and Guildford.

Away from these areas large numbers are seldom recorded, though over 50 have on occasions been counted at a number of gravel pits, water meadows and damp commons and small numbers can be found in suitable localities in many parts of the county.

From an analysis of the ten Snipe ringed in Surrey and subsequently recovered outside the county, a rather irregular pattern emerges. Two of them were recovered in the breeding season further east (ringed Epsom sf 7 December 1957: recovered at Smolensk, ussr, 17 May 1959—ringed Guildford sf, 12 August 1958: recovered near Ottersberg, Germany, 23 April 1962). Two others (ringed Ripley, 25 October 1964: recovered Jutland, Denmark, 20 August 1965—ringed Earlswood, 20 December 1963: recovered Murmansk, USSR, 21 August 1965) also suggest breeding populations well to the east as the origin of autumn immigrants. Another bird ringed at Leiden, Holland on 2 September 1962 and recovered at Hersham on 6 October 1962 also showed westerly movement in the autumn.

Of Snipe ringed in Surrey in the autumn and early winter and recovered outside the county in the winter months some recoveries might be put down to hard weather movements of resident or immigrant birds which would normally have wintered. For example four ringed in November and December 1962 before the advent of the severe weather, were recovered at Torpoint (Cornwall), Irum (Spain), Oistreham (France) and Tavistock (Devon) in January 1963. Another was ringed at Hersham on 25 November 1967, controlled at Hersham 17 December 1967 and recovered Santander, Spain on 16 January 1968. Other recoveries demonstrate westerly movements in the autumn-winter period or the use of different wintering areas in different seasons.

Several Snipe have been ringed on sewage farms in the winter and recovered on the same or other sewage farms in Surrey in subsequent years. One ringed at Hersham on 4 November 1961, was controlled at Hersham in October 1962 and November 1964.

Winter visitor in small numbers.

Jack Snipe
Lymnocryptes
minimus

The Jack Snipe is a regular visitor to sewage farms and is also seen rather infrequently on water meadows, damp heaths and commons and in other suitable habitats; it is probably often overlooked because of its reluctance to be flushed. Autumn arrivals have been noted from 14 August (Beddington SF, 1954) onwards but more usually in the latter half of September and the species is not normally present in any numbers until towards the end of October, the numbers then remaining fairly steady until March. Most birds have left by the end of the month but some remain in April and exceptionally it has been recorded in May—at Beddington SF in 1954 and Epsom SF in 1956. At most sites only a few birds have been seen at a time but there have been some fairly large counts—42 at Beddington SF on 31 January 1954 in a cold spell and 64 there on 20 November 1955, up to 73 at Epsom SF January-February 1956. One ringed at Epsom on 7 December 1957 was recovered on 3 January 1958 at St Augustine, France, c. 400 miles WSW, so that possibly some Jack Snipe leave the county as a result of hard weather well before the end of the season.

It has been recorded regularly from the sewage farms at Beddington, Camberley, Epsom (before closure), Guildford, Hersham and Unstead and occasionally from many other localities including Bookham Common, Fetcham Mill Pond, Frensham, the Holmethorpe/Limpsfield area, Pudmore, Richmond Park, South Norwood Lake and Walton GP.

Woodcock
Scolopax
rusticola
Moderately common but local resident. Winter visitor. This species is often overlooked and consequently under-recorded but it has probably not suffered such a drastic decline as feared by Bucknill 'through the increase of building and reclamation of low-lying grounds'.

The Woodcock is widely distributed in the county but the majority of breeding and roding records are for the more rural areas in the centre and south-west; it prefers mixed woods or young plantations with wet or boggy ground at hand where food can be obtained.

Some areas recur time and again in the records and include habitats evidently well suited to the requirements of the species. Such areas include Limpsfield, Esher, Bookham, Horsley, Thursley and Haslemere. In the 1930s the breeding density was estimated to average two pairs per square mile in the Haslemere district (Alexander, 1945). Twelve pairs were estimated to be present around East Horsley in 1967. Breeding was suspected in Richmond Park in 1969. There are probably fluctuations in the population level but in recent years reports of breeding or roding have regularly come from 15-25 localities.

In winter there appears to be an influx into the county but the origin of such birds is not known. During the winter period, especially November to February, the species is recorded in a number of additional localities including birch woods with Bracken undergrowth and sewage farms as at Beddington and Guildford. When the weather is severe birds are occasionally to be found in urban areas. Winter records are usually of odd birds but there are several records of up to six and one of 12 at Chertsey on 8 March 1969. Generally numbers are such that the shooting bags recorded in the 1930s when several estates of almost 2,000 acres could each produce a bag of 20 birds on the 'best' days (Alexander, 1945) would not now be equalled.

Very scarce summer resident. Passage migrant and winter **Curlew**
visitor. *Numenius*
It had been established that the species was breeding in the *arquata*
county at the end of the nineteenth century and it was
apparently breeding in the early years of the present century.
Since 1913 there has been a fairly continuous record of
breeding especially in the general area of Thursley in the
south-west of the county and from areas north of the Hog's
Back, as for instance on Chobham, Bisley and Whitmoor
Commons. At Thursley numbers fluctuated between one
and five pairs during the last decade of the review period
and it is probable that the number of pairs which bred in
the county during this decade was less than the twelve pairs
estimated for 1940-41. The birds arrive at their breeding
grounds in the second half of March and eggs are laid in
April.

The species is usually recorded in every month of the year,
though there are few records in May except at the breeding
grounds and there is a dearth of records following the
autumn passage in October. The largest flocks are recorded
in December and January when there are hard weather
movements. There are records of 30 birds at Ewhurst on
6 December 1962, c. 20 at Beddington sf on 26 January 1963
and c. 54 at Beddington on 31 January 1956. At other times
of the year parties are usually less than ten and the majority
of records are of ones and twos but there is one record of 50
birds seen on 16 July 1929 (*BB*, 32:75). The species has
been seen regularly throughout the year in small numbers
at Beddington sf.

Regular spring and autumn passage migrant, usually in **Whimbrel**
small numbers. *Numenius*
There are two fairly clearly defined periods of passage in *phaeopus*
Surrey. The spring movement begins soon after mid-April
and ends in about the third week of May. But numbers in
May compared with the autumn no longer justify the description of the Whimbrel at the 'May-bird' in Surrey.

There is one record for June. A bird was seen heading
sw at Lyne sf on 24 June 1967. From mid-July the autumn
passage builds up and August has double the number of
records of any other month. Numbers fall off again and no
records have been received after 18 September.

Many of the records refer to birds flying over and calling,
often at night when it is difficult to know what numbers
are involved. However when it is possible to assess numbers, singles and small groups are usual although excep-

tionally there are larger concentrations. For example, c. 50 were heard calling as they flew south over Colley Hill, Reigate on 24 August 1948, 22 flew NE in heavy rain at Enton on 25 April 1961 and 35 flew south at 2000 hours at Guildford SF on 29 July 1966.

Black-tailed Godwit
Limosa limosa

Scarce passage migrant, mainly in the autumn. Bucknill recorded three occurrences in the county, the last of which was in 1895 and there were no further records until that of a party of seven at the Surrey Docks in 1917 (*BB*, 22:241). The next record was of one at Brooklands SF in August 1932. Since then there have been records of 70-80 birds, over half the records being in August. The remainder are scattered mainly over April-May and September there being odd records in March, June, July and November. Nearly all have been from sewage farms and gravel pits; Guildford and Beddington SFS have been the most regular. Numbers have never exceeded eight birds in one group and stays of more than one week are exceptional.

Bar-tailed Godwit
Limosa lapponica

Extremely scarce spring passage migrant and winter visitor. Bucknill regarded this species as a very rare straggler in Surrey and no records before 1936 have been discovered for this century.

The species has been recorded in the review period as follows: One was found dead near Pen Ponds, Richmond Park on 21 February 1936; a male in summer plumage was seen at Brooklands SF on 4 May 1936; single birds were at Beddington SF from 2 to 8 February 1956 and at Barn Elms Reservoir from 26 April to 1 May 1957; one in winter plumage was seen at Beddington SF on 16 April 1966; one was recorded at Barn Elms Reservoir on 17 and 29 January 1970.

Green Sandpiper
Tringa ochropus

Common passage migrant. Scarce winter visitor. Most records of this species are from sewage farms and gravel pits but it is sometimes recorded from comparatively small ditches and streams throughout the county and it could be flushed from any sort of aquatic habitat providing sufficient cover. Peak numbers occur during autumn passage but it has been recorded in all months of the year and small numbers are recorded every winter. The year 1962 was a particularly good one with 158 records in all, covering every month and from 20 different localities; the highest monthly number of birds was 57 in August.

In the early months of the year records are scattered and there are rarely more than a few birds in one locality. Spring passage takes place in April but in some years is barely detectable and by the first days of May most birds have gone from the county. There are very few records between 5 May and 15 June. The period of autumn passage varies from year to year though it is always in the three months July—September and it is at this time that most of the larger numbers have been recorded. The largest concentrations in the review period were all at Guildford SF—c. 15 on 12 August 1939, 17 on 3 September 1954 numbers rising to 20 on 31 October and 14 on 22 August and 17 September 1956. Numbers generally fall in September although the species is regularly recorded in the remaining months of the year.

There are no indications of any major change in the pattern of records since 1900 and the increase in records is probably due to there being more observers.

Wood Sandpiper *Tringa glareola*

Very scarce passage migrant, mainly in autumn.
It is strange that no records have come to light for this century prior to 15-16 August 1934, when one was seen at Brooklands SF, for the species had been seen on a number of occasions in the nineteenth century. However after 1934 records steadily increased and the species is now known as a regular annual visitor although always in small numbers. Guildford and Beddington SFS are the most regularly visited although it has occurred in a number of other suitable localities.

There was a period between 1956 and 1960 when spring records were almost as numerous as autumn records but outside this period there have been only two records in spring: in 1942 (30 April-1 May) and in 1965 (21-22 May). There was an unusually early bird on 9 April 1960 at Barn Elms Reservoir but otherwise spring records have been confined to the very end of April and to May.

In 1957 there were several records in June and in 1959 one on 1 July but generally there is a gap in records between the end of May and the middle of July.

Autumn passage is heaviest in August, fading away in September. The largest parties recorded in the autumn passage were eight at Guildford SF on 27 August 1952 and 12 at Guildford on 23 July 1957. The latest record is of one at Guildford SF on 17 September (1963).

Common Sandpiper *Tringa hypoleucos*

Occasional summer resident, common passage migrant and scarce winter visitor.
There are a few records of the species breeding before 1900. In the early years of this century probable breeding was recorded at Peperharow in 1910 and a family party of six

was seen at Witley Pond in 1911 (W. A. Shaw). There appear to be no breeding records after that time until 1969 and 1970 when pairs were present in two localities (1969) and in one locality (1970) during the breeding season (May to August) and display activity including song-flights and distraction display were observed.

The Common Sandpiper has always been fairly common near aquatic habitats such as river banks, reservoirs, sewage farms and gravel pits in Surrey on both spring and autumn migration. On the open edges of reservoirs it is seen regularly and more often than the Green and Wood Sandpipers.

Birds seen in March may have over-wintered or be early passage birds but the spring passage usually extends over April and May, the pattern being ones and twos in scattered localities, with occasionally double figures as in 1948 when there were 12 at Barn Elms on 29 April and 18 at Guildford SF on 20 May.

During June the species is generally scarce but numbers begin to build up again from about 10 July. The heaviest passage is always in August though there are usually appreciable numbers remaining in September. It is in these two months that the largest parties are seen. There are several reports of 20-30 birds and the highest number recorded was 30-35 at Barn Elms Reservoir on 14 August 1968.

The last of the passage birds depart in October but there has been an increasing number of birds over-wintering during the last years of the review period. Six birds at Unstead SF on 24 January 1956 were exceptional.

The only foreign ringing recovery from the county was of one ringed at Guildford on 27 April 1960 and shot near Arroyo de San Servan, Badajoz, Spain on 20 August of the same year.

Redshank
Tringa
totanus
Scarce summer resident. Passage migrant and winter visitor. Bucknill knew of no evidence that the Redshank had ever bred in the county although, following the species' dramatic decline as a breeding bird at the beginning of the nineteenth century, its recovery had begun elsewhere in southern England as early as 1865.

The species was first recorded breeding in Surrey at Beddington SF about 1910 and breeding continued there until the late 1960s. The first recorded breeding in outer Surrey was at Itchingwood Common where Bentham found a nest in 1915. From this date there appears to have been a steady increase throughout the 1920s with nine pairs recorded from Elstead in 1921 and in 1925 Bentham reported that it was so numerous in the Thursley area (near Pudmore) that numbers were difficult to estimate. Expansion seems to have maintained its momentum in the 1930s, 1940s and 1950s and new breeding stations were reported from Brooklands SF (20-30 birds on most visits in 1936— P. A. D. Hollom), Leatherhead, Wisley and Guildford, also Epsom and Unstead SFS. The year 1956 was a particularly good one with breeding reported from Beddington SF (nine pairs), Epsom SF, R. Wey, Guildford (up to 15 pairs), Thursley Common and Unstead SF (three pairs).

A slight decline was detected in south east England from 1940 (Parslow, 1967) but this was not reflected in Surrey until the 1960s when a fairly rapid decline set in. In 1961 the only recorded breeding was from the site of the Queen Elizabeth II Reservoir under construction at Walton. A new colony was discovered at Milford in 1962 (six pairs) but this had disappeared by 1964. The only breeding pairs reported in 1967 and 1968 were two and four respectively from the water meadows in the Mole Valley at Stoke d'Abernon.

During its heyday the bird was recorded in large numbers during passage particularly in March/April and August/September. The largest number was 100 recorded at Send Marsh on 3 April 1943. There are however numerous winter records as for example 15-16 which spent January and February 1963 at Beddington SF (in severe weather). It is commonly recorded in small numbers from many suitable habitats throughout the county in all months particularly during passage periods.

Spotted Redshank *Tringa erythropus*

Scarce passage migrant, mainly in autumn. Bucknill cited only one record of a bird shot in 1855 near Godalming. There were no records in this century before 1924 the year in which a bird was seen at Frensham on 5 May. There were five more records between 1924-53. Since 1953 the species has occurred almost annually and the majority of records have been in August and September.

Although exceptionally the species has been recorded in January, October and December, most birds occur in the passage periods March to May and late July to September. Autumn records outnumber those in spring by almost four to one. As might be expected, the records are concentrated on the sewage farms and gravel pits. The largest concentrations were six birds at Beddington SF 26-30 August 1965 (three of these stayed until 1 September and one to 6 September) and six at Hersham SF 6-10 September 1966 (three stayed until 12 September).

Yellowlegs sp. Vagrant from North America.

Tringa
melanoleuca/
flavipes
A yellowlegs was recorded at Unstead SF 29 January-13 February 1954 (CNHS) but specific identity was not established beyond doubt. In the autumn of 1953 when a number of American waders were reported in this county, two Lesser Yellowlegs (*T. flavipes*) appeared at Perry Oaks SF and the one remaining there until 9 December might conceivably be the bird recorded at Unstead.

Greenshank Regular passage migrant, mainly in autumn.

Tringa
nebularia
In most years there are some spring records mainly in the period from the end of March to mid-May, though in some recent years as in 1961 and 1966 there was none for this period. Usually only single birds are reported on the spring passage. There are scattered records of Greenshank in June but the autumn passage does not usually commence until mid-July.

The autumn passage reaches its peak in August when numbers of up to nine are regularly reported, though the total number of birds during the month in the county rarely exceeds 20. Numbers decline in September and usually the last records occur in mid-September. However there are three or four records for October and one for November while one bird wintered at Unstead SF in 1955/56 (*SEBR*), and two were seen at Thorpe GPS on 13 January 1968.

The species was recorded much more regularly later in the review period than in the early years of the century when it was considered rare. The increase in records in the last two decades may be the result of more concentrated watching at the gravel pits and sewage farms.

Knot Scarce passage migrant and winter visitor.

Calidris
canutus
Bucknill described this species as 'an occasional straggler' to the county and this description could be regarded as still appropriate in 1970.

In the period 1900-70 the species was recorded in 13 years, eight of them after 1954. The records are usually of single birds and occasionally of up to four but there were two exceptional records: a flock of 23 at Beddington SF on 2 February 1956 and the other a flock of c. 50 observed flying fairly low, calling over Wisley Village after sunset on 23 August 1968. The species has also been recorded from the Barn Elms and Walton Reservoirs, the R. Thames, the sewage farms at Epsom, Guildford, Unstead and Worcester Park, the ponds at Enton and Frensham, Henley Park and Send GP.

Most records of the species are for January and February

although there are records in all months except June and July. The birds are usually recorded as being in winter or first autumn plumage although partial and full summer plumage birds have been reported and one bird was observed in summer plumage at Guildford SF on 14 April in 1957.

Purple Sandpiper
Calidris maritima

Extremely scarce visitor.
There are only three records of Purple Sandpiper in Surrey in the period under review. D. Gunn saw one at Barn Elms Reservoir on 2 November 1933 (*BB*, 27:208), B. S. Milne observed one at Beddington SF on 2 February 1956 and the third was recorded at Thorpe GPS by M. J. Cowlard on 30 November 1970.
Bucknill cited only two definite occurrences of the species prior to 1900.

Little Stint
Calidris minuta

Scarce autumn migrant.
The Little Stint is an irregular autumn migrant occurring in very small numbers and most often only singly.
Bucknill mentioned a bird killed at Battersea in 1869 but considered that the species was often overlooked. The first record in the present century was made by Bentham at Frensham Ponds on 22 July 1919. From 1930-69 the species was recorded in 15 years, the records involving approximately 50 birds. The largest concentration recorded was ten at the site of Queen Elizabeth II Reservoir on 1 October 1960.
With the exception of the 1919 record mentioned above all birds have been recorded in the period 15 August to 12 October, the main movement occurring in September. There have been no records of the species passing through the county on spring passage.
Little Stints have been recorded at the sewage farms at Beddington, Brooklands, Esher, Guildford and Molesey, at Barn Elms, Island Barn and Walton Reservoirs, Thorpe GPS and the ponds at Frensham.

Temminck's Stint
Calidris temminckii

Extremely scarce passage migrant.
Bucknill did not refer to this species and in the present century it has been satisfactorily identified only five times in Surrey. P. A. D. Hollom saw one at Brooklands SF on 29 May 1936 (*BB*, 30:347) and a single bird was seen in company with Common Sandpipers at Guildford SF 23-26 August 1944 by J. G. Harrison and D. Seth-Smith (*BB*, 38:138). One was observed at Barn Elms Reservoir on 12-13 May 1951 by B. A. Richards and A. G. G. Thompson and

one was identified at Holmethorpe sps on 4 June 1961 by R. L. Rolfe. The last record was of a bird seen and photographed at Barn Elms Reservoir on 5 and 7 September 1965 (*LBR*, 30:32).

It is interesting to note that the 1961 and 1965 records mentioned coincide with peak occurrences of the species in Britain and Ireland during the period 1958-67 (Sharrock, 1970).

Pectoral Extremely scarce vagrant.
Sandpiper The first recorded occurrence of this North American species
Calidris in Surrey was of a single bird which frequented a rubbish
melanotos tip pool at Epsom from 30 August to 8 September 1952. This bird was trapped and ringed by I. C. T. Nisbet. One was seen by K. D. Edwards at Epsom sf on 19 and 20 September 1956 and presumably the same bird was seen there on 24 September by Bentham. R. M. Fry identified one at Pudmore, Ockley Common on 30 August 1964.

Dunlin Passage migrant and winter visitor.
Calidris At the end of the review period this species was the
alpina commonest shore wader occurring in the county. Records in the first three decades of the present century were however very few. P. A. D. Hollom in 1936 in amplification of its status at Brooklands sf reported that there were never more than three at a time seen on spring or autumn passage. From about the middle of the 1940s however, an increasing number of records was received and by the 1950s the species was being reported annually.

It might be reported in any month of the year although June records are exceptional. Spring passage birds are usually noted in April and May. Autumn passage which starts in July is heavier than that in spring and odd birds or small numbers are regularly recorded in the winter period. The species is certainly subject to hard weather movements and winter records are often associated with severe weather. Generally records are of single birds or small parties but larger concentrations are occasionally reported as for instance 20 on the shore of the R. Thames opposite Chiswick in December 1938, numbers up to 25 at Broad Mead (Send) and Unstead sf in the periods January—March and November—December 1946. The largest concentration ever recorded in the county was of c. 70 at Queen Elizabeth II Reservoir on 16 September 1962.

The species has been recorded from most of the Surrey sewage farms particularly Beddington, Guildford and Unstead, from all the reservoirs, the larger ponds and the river systems and gravel pits, anywhere in fact that offers a congenial shore line.

Very scarce passage migrant, mainly in autumn. The Curlew Sandpiper occurs irregularly in Surrey and there are records of only 29 birds in the review period. Usually single birds are recorded although occasionally small parties are seen, the largest being six at Guildford SF on 29 August 1960. The main period of passage is August-September although there are records of single birds in July, October and November. Spring passage has only been recorded twice in the review period; a single bird was at Frensham on 13 April 1906 and a party of four at Brooklands SF on 2 June 1939. The only winter record is of a single bird at Unstead SF on 16 January 1946 (*SEBR*).

    The species has been recorded at the sewage farms at Beddington, Brooklands, Godalming, Guildford, Hersham and Unstead, Barn Elms Reservoir, the ponds at Frensham and the Lower Pen Pond in Richmond Park.

Curlew Sandpiper *Calidris testacea*

Scarce passage migrant and winter visitor. There were less than half a dozen records of this species in the county in the first half of the present century but after 1954 it was recorded in every year up to 1970 with the exception of 1965. Usually only single birds are recorded although small parties have been observed, the largest being eight at Frensham Great Pond on 11 May 1969.

    Spring passage is recorded in late April and May and autumn passage less regularly, in July, August and September. There have been a number of records in the early months of the year (January to March) probably due to hard weather movements.

    Most of the records have come from Barn Elms Reservoir, Guildford SF and Frensham Great Pond although there are records from other sewage farms and reservoirs and Gatton Park Lake.

    Bucknill stated that the species had been shot not infrequently on Frensham Pond and near Putney Bridge on the Thames, both localities where it was most frequently recorded at the end of the review period.

    There is one remarkable recovery; a bird ringed by P. G. Davis at Frensham on 13 August 1966 was controlled at Heacham, Norfolk on 17 May 1969.

Sanderling *Crocethia alba*

Scarce passage migrant and winter visitor. The Ruff is now a regular passage migrant in Surrey in small numbers. Spring passage is recorded from March to

Ruff *Philomachus pugnax*

the middle of May and is very light in comparison with that in the autumn. Autumn passage through the county is first recorded in the middle of July and continues to the end of September. There is one record for October and the species is occasionally recorded in the county during the months November to February, the latest sightings probably being of early passage birds.

Numbers involved are usually ones and twos although occasionally up to nine have been recorded. (Exceptional records are of concentrations of 17 and 25 at Beddington SF on 2 February 1956 and 8 September 1968 respectively.)

Ruff have been recorded at most of the sewage farms, Beddington and Guildford being particularly favoured. Other records have been made at widely spread localities including Ash Vale GP, Barn Elms and Walton Reservoirs.

The species was seldom recorded in the county before the 1950s. When P. A. D. Hollom gave a record of one at Brooklands SF on 30 July 1934 (*BB*, 28:342) he commented that there were only three previous records.

Avocet
Recurvirostra avosetta

Extremely scarce spring migrant.
During the review period this species was recorded on four occasions. Two were seen at Frensham on 16 March 1929, there were single birds at Brooklands SF on 13-16 June 1932 (*BB*, 26:55-56) and at Beddington SF on 19 May 1955 and the last record was of 12 birds at Holmethorpe SPS on 16 March 1969 when they were mobbed by Great Black-backed Gulls and after circling and landing twice made off in a north easterly direction.

Black-winged Stilt
Himantopus himantopus

Extremely scarce vagrant.
There were no reports of this species in the first half of the present century. In 1955 there were two records—a bird seen at Beddington SF on 17 August and two seen at Epsom SF on 9 September. Bucknill found that it had occurred on a few occasions and quoted a letter from Gilbert White of Selborne describing the first occasion the species was recorded in Surrey; six birds came down on Frensham Great Pond in 1779, five were shot and one was left unmolested.

Grey Phalarope
Phalaropus fulicarius

Extremely scarce autumn passage migrant and winter visitor.
In the first half of the present century there were only three records of this species—one seen after gales on reservoirs 'near Hammersmith Bridge' on 21 September 1930 (*BB*, 24:166), one found dead at Barn Elms Reservoir on 9

November 1931 (*BB*, 25:203) and one at Cutt Mill Pond in 1940 reported to Eric Parker (*World of Birds*). In the period 1951 to 1970 there were 14 records all of single birds in the autumn or winter. All these records were of birds seen at ponds (Fetcham and Frensham), sewage farms (Epsom and Guildford) or reservoirs (Barn Elms and Island Barn) and, with the exception of one (at Frensham on 25 January 1953), occurred in September and October. In a number of cases the birds lingered for two or three days.

Bucknill classed the species as an irregular winter straggler and cited a large wreck that occurred in 1866 when there were several birds in the county.

Red-necked Phalarope
Phalaropus lobatus

Extremely scarce vagrant.
Although Bucknill included this species as a Surrey bird he admitted that the evidence for its inclusion was slender. It is curious that although the Grey Phalarope which does not breed in the British Isles as does the present species, has occurred on a number of occasions in the county in the present century, it was not until 1970 that the Red-necked Phalarope was satisfactorily identified. B. Bland saw one, possibly two, at Godstone SP on 16 August 1970.

Stone Curlew
Burhinus oedicnemus

Extremely scarce vagrant. Formerly bred.
Bucknill stated that this species was formerly a regular and common summer visitor, also very rarely occurring in the winter. It used to nest along the Hog's Back and was still seen regularly in one locality in 1898. By the turn of the century it was on the verge of extinction but the nesting of two pairs at Caterham in 1900 was reported in *The Zoologist*.

Following this breeding record there were no published records until 1944 when one was seen at Broadford Marsh in July (*SEBR*). Since 1950 there have been nine in the period up to 1970 occurring in seven different years and all of single birds with the exception of two seen at Beddington SF on 23 August 1955. The records were in the months of March, May, July—October and December.

Pratincole
Glareola pratincola

Mrs R. Brown watched a bird of this species for about an hour on 11 September 1948 at Barn Elms Reservoir. It was thought to be a bird of the year (*BB*, 42:221).

Arctic Skua
Stercorarius parasiticus

Extremely scarce vagrant.
The first recorded instance of this species in the county was in the winter of 1920/21 when one was seen frequenting the Surrey Docks in December and January (*BB*, 22:24). There have been five further records since that date all in

the autumn and presumably of birds on passage albeit away from their normal environment, the high seas. One, thought to be an immature bird, was seen on Wimbledon Common late in August 1922 and was there again on 8 September (*The Field*, 140:387, 476). An adult was seen at Barn Elms Reservoir on 9 September 1954 and one was found dead near Island Barn Reservoir on 22 October 1960. One flew west over Barn Elms Reservoir on 9 September 1964 and the last bird recorded in the review period was a dark-phased adult flying west along the edge of Hackhurst Downs on 31 August 1969.

Great Skua
Catharacta
skua

The only record for Surrey is of two seen chasing Black-headed Gulls at Waterloo Bridge on 14 April 1915 (*The Birds of the London Area*, 1957).

Pomarine
Skua
Stercorarius
pomarinus

Extremely scarce vagrant.
The first and only record of this species in the county is of one seen at Barn Elms Reservoir on 25 October 1970 by W. Y. N. Roberts.

Gulls

Since 1900 there has been a remarkable increase in the numbers of gulls wintering in the county. In the early years of the century records of all five common species of gull were generally confined to small numbers on or near to the Thames and elsewhere in the county records were irregular and few. The expansion began in the mid-1920s and has continued steadily since.

The increase appears to have been linked with developments following upon urbanization, man-made habitats such as sewage farms and rubbish dumps providing sources of food and the reservoirs safe roosting places.

In 1900 the total acreage of reservoir surface in the London area was little over 300 and in Surrey only the comparatively small reservoir complexes of Chelsea and Lambeth (two of the Walton Reservoirs) and Barn Elms/Lonsdale Road at Barnes were in use. By 1962 the acreage of surface water had increased over five fold and the acreage of Surrey reservoirs exceeded 700.

It is known that gulls were roosting at Barnes (Barn Elms/Lonsdale Road) from the end of the nineteenth century but the increase from those early days has been inadequately recorded and it was not until past the century's mid-point that any nationally organized systematic study was made.

The first national enquiry into the winter roosting of gulls on inland waters was sponsored by the BTO in 1952-53 and it was repeated again in 1963. Total roosting numbers in England rose during the intervening period from 330,000 to 504,000 (Hickling, 1967).

Numbers of wintering gulls have continued to rise and gulls are now a very conspicuous part of the winter scene in Surrey.

Winter visitor.

This species was nearing extinction in the British Isles at the end of the nineteenth century but since then it has experienced a remarkable increase and expansion (Parslow, 1967). In the first quarter of the present century it was seldom recorded. There were only six records in the London area up to 1921—mainly from the R. Thames. One was recorded on Limpsfield Common in 1904 (*Zool.*, 1907) and there was an immature bird at Frensham on 2 June 1906. From about 1926 it became a regular winter visitor to the Thames and in particular Barn Elms Reservoir, steadily increasing in numbers and by the early 1950s a roost of between 300 and 500 had been established at the Walton Reservoirs. The species was first recorded at Beddington SF in 1947 and 12 were seen at Epsom SF on 10 February 1948. With increasing exploitation of inland feeding areas provided by sewage farms and rubbish dumps the species was increasingly reported from a wider area away from the Thames and associated reservoirs. Records of a hundred or more occurred, as for instance at an Egham rubbish dump in December 1956 and Brooklands on 29 December 1966.

As a roosting bird the increase has been equally spectacular viz:

Great Black-backed Gull *Larus marinus*

Reservoir	1953 (January)	1963 (December)	1968 (December)
Barn Elms	—	100	10
Island Barn	—	—	100
Queen Elizabeth II	—	250	500
Walton	350	650	2,450

Counts of Great Black-backed Gulls roosting on Surrey reservoirs in winter (ex Sage, 1964 and Parr, 1970).

The largest numbers are reported at the end of December or early January and most records occur in the period September to March, but odd birds may be reported in any month.

Evidence of the sources of our winter visitors is provided by birds picked up dead bearing foreign rings. No less than five birds ringed as nestlings on the Great Ainov

Islands, USSR in 1961 and 1962 have been recovered in the period November—February from the Walton Reservoirs. One nestling from Stavanger, Norway has also been recovered there and another nestling from the Great Ainov Islands has been recovered at Barn Elms Reservoir in March of the year following ringing.

Lesser Black-backed Gull *Larus fuscus*

Winter visitor and passage migrant. From being an occasional visitor mainly confined to the Thames at the start of the century, this species has become a regular winter visitor several thousand strong and a very common passage migrant in even greater numbers. In the first two decades of the century Bentham recorded singletons or very small parties of passage birds in spring and autumn over the North Downs. A marked increase in records occurred from the mid-1920s with Barn Elms Reservoir providing the bulk of these. Largest numbers were seen in the late summer and early autumn and by the 1930s peak numbers were in the range 120—280. By the middle of the century fairly large flocks began to appear in localities away from the Thames as at Wimbledon Golf Course and Beddington SF. Bentham recorded 98 at Beddington SF on 30 October 1947 and by 1955, 400 had been recorded there in December. Up to this time the species had been largely a passage migrant with biggest numbers occurring in autumn. Six were recorded as wintering at Barn Elms in 1943 and thereafter there was a steady increase in numbers of wintering birds. None of this species was counted at the reservoir roosts in January 1953 but the following figures illustrate a rapid build-up in the 1960s.

Reservoir	1963 (December)	1968 (December)
Barn Elms	100	30
Island Barn	—	1,000
Queen Elizabeth II	250	1,000
Walton	200	100

Counts of Lesser Black-backed Gulls on Surrey reservoirs in December (ex. Sage, 1964 and Parr, 1970).

During the autumn migration large numbers congregate on undisturbed open spaces, as for instance at Sandown Park, Esher, where a peak of up to 1,500 was recorded on 6 October 1969 and on market garden land at Hersham where large numbers have congregated from July onwards in the last two decades of the review period. Numbers recorded in outer Surrey are less than in the Thames Valley and tributary areas, as for instance a maximum of 80 at Broadwater in the autumn/winter of 1968/69 and 16 at Frensham in the same period. Numbers roosting on the reservoirs build up to a peak in September/October; for example 4,000 were counted at Island Barn Reservoir on 5 October 1960.

The Scandinavian race (*L. f. fuscus*) was first recorded in Surrey at Barn Elms on 23 February 1929 (*BB*, 22:329) but some large concentrations of this race have been recorded in the 1960s on market garden land at Hersham during the autumn passage in August and September. Wintering birds however appear in the main to be of the British race (*L. f. graellsii*). At Beddington SF in the winter of 1959/60 not more than two birds per day were considered to be of the Scandinavian race (Barnes, 1961).

Winter visitor.
Records in the first quarter of the present century were of small numbers usually from the vicinity of the R. Thames and the first large flock reported was of 120 on the Crystal Palace Fields on 5 February 1925 (Bentham). Forty were recorded from Barn Elms Reservoir in December 1929 and 100 were roosting at Barnes in 1931. From about this point onwards there was a rapid increase as the species discovered and exploited new feeding sources at sewage farms and rubbish dumps. Bentham recorded 250 at Epsom SF on 8 January 1933 and numbers here and at Beddington SF occasionally exceeded 500 in the 1940s. The roosting population in the London area as a whole rose from 16,800 in 1952-53 to 28,812 in 1963-64 (Sage, 1964) and mid-winter counts at Surrey reservoirs in the three years 1953, 1963 and 1968 were as follows:

Herring Gull *Larus argentatus*

Reservoir	1953 (January)	1963 (December)	1968 (December)
Barn Elms	100	100	30
Island Barn	1,000	—	900
Queen Elizabeth II	—	7,000	1,000
Walton	4,000	200	—

Counts of Herring Gulls on Surrey reservoirs in winter (ex Sage, 1964 and Parr, 1970).

Birds are seen in smaller numbers in outer Surrey although occasionally large flocks are reported as for instance c.500 on the R. Blackwater in February 1954 in hard weather. There are no gull roosts in outer Surrey and a study of gull flight lines in the winter of 1968/69 showed that this species disperses from reservoir roosts to places as far away as Camberley, Aldershot, Godalming and Redhill (Parr, 1970).

The species may be reported in any month of the year although large numbers are confined to the period September to March with peak numbers occurring in January.

There is one report of the Scandinavian race (*L. f. omissus*) from Barn Elms Reservoir on 10 and 11 October 1968 but in view of the difficulty in separating this race from other yellow-legged forms it would be prudent not to accept this record without reservations.

Common Gull
Larus canus

Winter visitor and passage migrant.
As with the other 'common' gulls there has been a remarkable increase in the numbers of this species in the county since the early part of the century. It is now frequently seen, often in association with a larger number of Black-headed Gulls, on or around the Thames and reservoirs and at suitable feeding points as at sewage farms and rubbish tips throughout the county. In the first two decades of the century Bentham recorded the bird only three times —twice at Hedgecourt Pond in the autumn and once at Frensham (three birds on 4 August 1912). In 1926 however he recorded a flock of 60 on Epsom Downs on 31 January 1926 and from this time he had a series of records involving gatherings of up to 300 birds on the downs around Epsom often in January or in early spring. One record of 1,000 birds on 24 January 1943 was exceptional. Regular reports of birds seen on sewage farms as at Beddington, Epsom and Guildford began in the 1940s.

Numbers of birds roosting at London reservoirs increased dramatically over the period 1952/53 to 1963/64, from 6,150 to 18,580 (202 per cent increase) (Sage, 1964), although large spring roosts of over 40,000 had been recorded at Littleton Reservoir, Middlesex, as far back as the 1930s (*The Handbook*, v:50-1). Numbers on Surrey reservoirs in more recent times have fluctuated somewhat although an upward trend is still obvious, viz:

Reservoir	1953 (Jan.)	1963 (Dec.)	1968 (Dec.)
Barn Elms	100	100	30
Island Barn	200	—	3,000
Queen Elizabeth II	—	—	500
Walton	1,100	—	—

Counts of Common Gulls on Surrey reservoirs in winter

(ex Sage, 1964 and Parr, 1970).

Dispersal from these roosts to feeding points in outer Surrey was shown in 1968/69 to be a feature of this species' behaviour as with other gulls (Parr, 1970).

Sage (1960) considered that there is a pronounced increase in the winter population of this species in the London area starting in late January and augmented by passage birds. This increase lasts through March into April. The species may be recorded in any month but the main autumn influx begins in July and spring passage and dispersal is usually over by the end of April.

Recoveries of ringed birds points to the Baltic area as the source of our winter visitors. Two birds ringed as nestlings in Sweden have been recovered, one at Queen Elizabeth II Reservoir (14 years after ringing) and the other at Island Barn Reservoir (both in February). Another bird ringed in the nest in Schleswig-Holstein, Germany was found dead at the Walton Reservoirs in March of the following year.

Glaucous Gull
Larus hyperboreus

Extremely scarce winter visitor.
Bucknill cited one doubtful record from Newark Mill on the R. Wey. In the present century it was not until the 1950s that occasional winter records were received. An immature bird was reported from Barn Elms Reservoir on 3 April 1954 and there were single records from Beddington SF in each of the following two winters. There have been two records in the 1960s—one from Barn Elms on 20 April 1960 and a second (an immature bird) from Molesey SF on 13 January 1963.

The species has not been reported from outer Surrey.

Iceland Gull
Larus glaucoides

Extremely scarce winter visitor.
The first Surrey record of this species was of an adult at Barn Elms Reservoir on 15 April 1939 (*BB*, 33:28) and in the winter of 1941/42 three birds were reported from the Lonsdale Road Reservoir. These early records stimulated some correspondence in *British Birds* concerning the difficulties and pitfalls of separating certain individuals of this species from small specimens of the previous species (Glaucous Gull) and these early records must therefore not be accepted without reservations. Since 1947 there have been seven published records claiming definite specific identification all from the Barn Elms area, the R. Thames or Epsom SF. As with the previous species there are no outer Surrey records.

Mediterranean The inclusion of this species in the present Surrey list rests
Black-headed on one record, that of an immature bird at Barn Elms
Gull Reservoir on 19-20 September 1957.
Larus
melanocephalus

Little Scarce passage migrant.
Gull Bucknill classed this species as a rare visitor and cited speci-
Larus mens shot at Cobham, Frensham and the R. Thames.
minutus The first record published in the present century was of one
in winter plumage at Barn Elms Reservoir on 1 November
1937 (*BB*, 31:238-9) and the only other record in the 1930s
was again in winter—at Island Barn Reservoir on 31 December 1938 (*BB*, 32:307). The remains of an adult bird of
this species was found at Frensham on 4 May 1940 (*BB*, 34:22).
Since 1954 there have been almost annual occurrences of
the species usually of single birds on spring (April-May) or
autumn (July-September) passage, most often the records
coming from Barn Elms but occasionally from Guildford SF,
other reservoirs and the Frensham area.

Black- Abundant winter visitor, some present all the year.
headed At the turn of the century this species had already estab-
Gull lished itself as an abundant winter visitor to the lower
Larus reaches of the R. Thames but inland records were infrequent.
ridibundus In 1903 a large flock frequented the Thames and nearby
fields at Twickenham and by 1906 it was the commonest
gull along the Thames at Kew, also frequently seen on the
lakes of Kew Gardens. In the first two decades of the century the species was only rarely recorded away from the
Thames and then in very small numbers, seven at Esher on
22 January 1910 and 12 on Frensham Great Pond on 5
August 1912 (both Bentham records) being exceptional.
From the mid-1920s however records of large numbers became increasingly usual and Bentham reported 50 at Munstead Marsh, Wonersh on 26 December 1924, 100 at Crystal
Palace on 26 February 1925 and that in 1929 numbers at
Beddington SF on 19 January exceeded 3,000. This gradual
spread and increase continued and the species is now one
of the commonest birds in the winter scene. It is quick to
exploit such feeding sources as sewage farms, rubbish
dumps, suburban gardens and parks and is frequently
found in built-up areas.
The species is the most abundant roosting gull at the
Thames Valley reservoirs and the increase in numbers since
the 1950s has been dramatic and appears to be still continuing.
The construction of the Queen Elizabeth II Reservoir

made a significant contribution to the increase and numbers
roosting at the peak time in January are now approaching
200,000, viz:

Reservoir	1953 (Jan.)	1963 (Dec.)	1968 (Dec.)	1969 (Jan.)
Barn Elms	10,000	20,000	24,000	25,000
Island Barn	10,000	100	15,000	37,500
Queen Elizabeth II	—	92,500	50,000	100,000
Walton	1,000	1,100	4,050	2,300

Counts of Black-headed Gulls roosting on Surrey reservoirs in winter, (ex Sage, 1964 and Parr, 1970).

The birds disperse from these and the Middlesex reservoirs to feeding points throughout the county, through the Wey Gap to Godalming and beyond, through the Mole Gap to Dorking and by direct flights to rubbish tips and sewage farms at Camberley, Aldershot and Redhill (*The Handbook* v:50-1 and Parr, 1970).

In the first decade of the century the species was essentially a winter visitor arriving from September and dispersing by April. In 1909 single birds were seen at Kew and Richmond in the first week of August and in 1921 many were still at Barn Elms Reservoir on 4 May. By the 1930s some birds were reported throughout the year as at Brooklands SF in 1936 when numbers were lowest in April rising to 92 by 5 June and a maximum of 400 on 13 July (*BB*, 30: 129). There has been one recorded breeding attempt in Surrey; in 1956 a pair was seen in display at Guildford SF on 5 June and a nest was found a week later but regrettably it was subsequently deserted.

Ringing recoveries show that most of the Surrey wintering birds originate from the Low Countries and countries surrounding the Baltic Sea. Of 11 birds ringed as nestlings and recovered in Surrey (principally on the Thames Valley reservoirs and sewage farms) three originated from the Low Countries and Germany and eight from the Baltic including four from the USSR Republics of Latvia and Estonia.

Kittiwake
Rissa tridactyla

Scarce winter visitor and passage migrant.
Bucknill described this species at the turn of the century as a regular visitor to the Thames straying into outer Surrey more or less frequently. There is some evidence to suggest that at the end of the nineteenth century and the beginning of the twentieth Kittiwakes were indeed coming up the Thames in numbers not generally equalled before or since. However there is a dearth of published records from the

Thames in the first quarter of the present century and in the second quarter records were of four or five birds a year in slightly more than half of those years. The published records from outer Surrey in this latter period are from Frensham with single birds recorded on 11 November 1921, 22 October 1939 and 3 April 1948.

In 1954 there was an exceptional record of 15 moving west (singly and in two small parties) amongst other gulls on 24 December followed by a further five on 25 December at Barn Elms Reservoir but this movement was exceeded in 1959 by two parties of c. 50 and c. 60 flying west over Fetcham Mill Pond on 22 February. In the 1960s annual numbers have fluctuated between one and six, more than half the records coming from Barn Elms Reservoir and others mainly from the Walton Reservoirs and Beddington SF while there is only one from outer Surrey (Frensham on 16 May 1967).

Most records occur in January or February and some of these relate to storm driven birds. A smaller proportion are recorded in the March—June and August—September periods and probably are of passage birds.

Black Tern
Chlidonias niger

Fairly common passage migrant.

In the last century Black Terns occurred in spring and autumn on the Thames and sometimes on other waters in the county. Records are scanty for the early part of this century but by the end of the review period the species was regularly recorded on the reservoirs or larger lakes and gravel pits during the main passage periods in May and August—September.

It is seldom recorded earlier than the last ten days of April and in most years the first record is in early May. Birds often arrive at two or three localities almost on the same day and do not usually stay long. Most spring records involve single birds or small groups although there are exceptional years. For example in 1948 there was a peak on 21 May when there were up to 50 birds at Frensham Ponds, 30 at Barn Elms Reservoir and eight at Guildford SF. Again in 1950 there were 30 birds at Frensham on 13 May and 19 at Barn Elms on 18 May, during a passage which extended from 11 to 18 May. The distribution of records over the county suggests that the species migrates cross-country rather than following the Thames.

Spring passage does sometimes last to early June and autumn passage can occasionally start as early as mid-July. It is heavier and more extended than the spring passage, spanning the months August and September. There are occasional records for October and one or two for November, the latest being on 11 November 1967 at Frensham. In 1963 there were 77 records in August and 54 in September with a maximum of 38 birds at Barn Elms on 30 August but generally numbers are considerably lower.

Black Terns appear annually at Barn Elms Reservoir and almost annually at Frensham Ponds and Island Barn Reservoir. They have also been reported from all the larger Surrey waters that are regularly watched.

Common Tern
Sterna hirundo

Fairly common passage migrant.
There is very often difficulty in separating this species from the next especially when seen at a distance and because observers have become increasingly aware of this many records, in recent years particularly, do not include specific identification. Bucknill however regarded the present species as a 'very regular visitor' as compared with the 'much rarer' Arctic Tern and until 1947 all records this century were of 'Common Tern'.

Since 1947 most records have been Common/Arctic Tern. Of the rest there are almost as many records of Arctic as Common Tern. For the sake of convenience all records of Common/Arctic Tern are considered in this section along with Common Tern leaving specifically identified Arctic Terns to the next section. The summary which follows will therefore include a proportion of the following species.

There are two main passage periods, one in April-May and a rather heavier one in August-September. The earliest record in the review period was of a bird at Barn Elms Reservoir on 8 April 1961 but passage generally begins a week or two later. There was a notably heavy passage in April 1947 when there were up to 26 birds at Barn Elms on various dates between 26 April and 1 May as well as smaller concentrations of up to nine at Frensham and up to seven at Stoke (Guildford). Usually single birds or small numbers are involved in the spring passage.

There are scattered records for June and July during the last twenty years of the review period and when in 1969 two Common Terns stayed at Thorpe GPS from 8 to 15 June the observer thought that they might have been prospecting.

Common/Arctic Terns are most likely to be seen in August when autumn passage gets into full swing. It is at this time that larger numbers can be expected, although these have been nothing to compare with the 500 birds on the nearby Staines Reservoir on 23 August 1950. The largest number recorded in Surrey during the review period was c. 90 birds at Barn Elms Reservoir on 15 September 1968. Movement continues at a reduced level in October and there were reports of odd birds seen at Frensham up to 12 November in 1967. Records of two exhausted Common Terns with gulls on Tooting Bec Common on 16 December 1925 and a flock of about 12 flying over West Norwood on the following day (*BB*, 19:256) were exceptional.

Arctic Tern
Sterna
macrura

Scarce passage migrant.
This species is regularly associated with the preceding species and it is often not possible to make specific identification, particularly in the autumn. Readers are therefore referred to the preceding section for a general survey of Common/Arctic Tern movements.

It is probable that this species is rather less common than the Common Tern. It has been identified specifically on an almost equal number of occasions but it must be remembered that only a minority of records are specific. The seasonal pattern is apparently similar although specific identity has been established more frequently on the spring passage —from the end of April to early May. There were more records of Arctic Terns in spring 1947 than in any other year and movement was then concentrated in the period 23 April to 5 May; the largest number seen together was ten at Barn Elms on 30 April when Common Terns were also present. The only definite autumn records of Arctic Terns in the last two decades of the review period were in September 1956, 1960 and 1970 when one or two birds were recorded from the Frensham Ponds and the Walton Reservoirs.

Roseate Tern
Sterna
dougallii

Extremely scarce passage migrant.
It seems probable that the species was shot on a very few occasions in the nineteenth century in outer Surrey. Only two acceptable later records of this species have been discovered. Two birds were seen on 18 July 1961 at Barn Elms Reservoir and one bird was recorded there on 24 July 1963. The report in *Countryside* (June 1921) of a tern with a rich pink colour on the breast seen at Barn Elms Reservoir on 28 April 1921 must be regarded as unsatisfactory in the absence of further details.

Little Tern
Sterna
albifrons

Scarce passage migrant.
The species was considered a rare visitor to Surrey in the early years of the century. P. A. D. Hollom in 1936 gave it

as 'occasional' in the county. Little information is available for the 1940s.

However in the last two decades of the review period reports tended to be more regular, probably as a result of increased watching, although there were some years in which no birds were seen.

The total number of Little Terns recorded in Surrey in this century is about 50. The earliest record is of one at Frensham on 21 April 1968 but it is not usually recorded till the end of that month and birds are also seen in May. There have been several records in June including that of three birds at Guildford SF on 5 June 1948. Several times as many have been seen in autumn (July—October) as in spring. Most reports are of one or two birds but there were ten at Barn Elms on 21 September 1955. The majority of reports towards the end of the review period were from Barn Elms Reservoir and Frensham Great Pond.

Sandwich Tern
Sterna sandvicensis

Scarce passage migrant, mainly in autumn.
Bucknill knew of only two probable occurrences, both involving specimens reputedly shot in Surrey. In this century records were very scarce up to 1947 with occurrences only in 1914, 1926 and 1931—all in July/August.

In 1947/48 there were quite large numbers at Barn Elms Reservoir with 25 on 19 September 1948 and 20 on 21 May 1949. After then the species was recorded in ten years out of 22, mostly in autumn, records generally involving one or two birds. The only larger numbers were five at Chipstead on 30 June 1959 and exceptionally c. 90 at Barn Elms on 15 September 1968. In all there have been four records involving some 30 birds in the period April—June and 20 records involving some 140 birds in the period mid-July to early October.

Barn Elms Reservoir has been a favoured locality for this species and it is suspected that most of the birds seen there have followed the river from the estuary.

Razorbill
Alca torda

Extremely scarce vagrant.
The only definite record since 1900 is of one bird on the R. Thames at Chiswick on 2 September 1964 seen diving and swimming upstream. The species very occasionally appeared in Surrey after rough weather during the nineteenth century.

Little Auk
Plautus alle

Extremely scarce winter vagrant.
Bucknill regarded this species as 'one of the most common of our purely tempest-borne stragglers' and gave a number

160

of winter records. During this century the species has been much less regular and only four definite records have been discovered, viz: one picked up alive at Ford Manor Estate on 2 February 1912 in very good condition (*The Field*, 2 February 1912), one at Chelsea and Lambeth Reservoirs or. 1 January 1930 when birds also appeared at the Round Pond, Kensington and at Staines (*BB*, 23:276), one at Barn Elms Reservoir on 20 November 1967 and one at the Walton Reservoirs on 24 October 1970. This last bird was taken to Sheffield Park rehabilitation centre in Sussex but died subsequently. All these records refer to the period October—February.

Guillemot
Uria aalge Bucknill described the species as an accidental straggler. The only known record for Surrey this century is of a bird discovered in a garden at Limpsfield on 14 January 1934 after a night of severe storms. The bird was obviously exhausted and was easily captured. It was fed on sprats but died within a week (*SEBR*).

Puffin
Fratercula Extremely scarce vagrant.
arctica The species has been recorded in the county in eight years of this century. Most of the records are for the winter months after periods of strong winds. Many of the birds have been found dead or in an exhausted condition.

In 1909 there were records at Croydon and Banstead on 29 October and 1 November respectively; in 1934 one was picked up alive at Banstead on 20 October; one was picked up alive near Milford on 16 February 1938 and another at Addington on 19 February 1944; the next record was at Merrow on 5 October 1946. In 1955 an immature bird stayed at Barn Elms Reservoir from 23 September to 18 October. One was found exhausted at Shirley on 2 November 1961. In 1967 there were three records: one on the unusual date of 3 July at Ewell Court Park, one at Merstham on 19 October and one of a bird swimming on the Thames at Barnes on 22 October. In all cases single birds were involved.

Pallas's Sand-
grouse This Asiatic species was recorded in Surrey in the last century during the great invasion years 1863 and 1888 and also
Syrrhaptes in 1889.
paradoxus A considerable invasion took place in May 1908 and Surrey is mentioned in *The Handbook* (IV:149) as one of the counties where the species was recorded.

26 *Nightjar*. Now largely restricted to heathlands and cleared woodlands in outer Surrey. (*M. D. England*)

Moderately common resident. Probable winter visitor. **Stock Dove**
At the start of the present century this species was going *Columba*
through an expansionist phase and Bucknill was able to *oenas*
describe it as fairly abundant and considerably on the increase, breeding commonly in park or downland and in open
woods where old timber provided sufficient holes for its
nesting requirements. It seems to have been particularly
numerous in the west of the county and in 1913 Bentham
regarded it as probably more numerous than the Woodpigeon
in woods around Thursley. National figures suggest that
the species continued to prosper until the mid-1950s. It had
colonized Battersea Park by 1952 and spread rapidly to
many inner London parks in the period 1950 to 1957.

A marked decrease, linked with suspected poisoning
from agricultural chemicals used as seed dressings affected
all populations in southern England from the late 1950s and
early 1960s (Parslow, 1967) and this was clearly reflected in
the paucity of records submitted to the Surrey Bird Club.
The species had disappeared from the London parks by 1961
(Cramp and Tomlins, 1966). Records received in the county
from 1960 onwards however suggest that the decline had
halted by the end of the decade and that the species was
again reasonably widespread in suitable places throughout
the county. Typical localities are the deciduous woodland
fringing Stoke Park, Guildford, with one to three pairs
usually present and in parkland at Ashtead containing well-
spaced mature oak trees many with suitable nesting holes
where five to ten pairs may be found.

The species flocks in winter and often feeds in association
with the Woodpigeon. In the first half of the century
Bentham reported winter flocks from the North Downs of
up to 50 birds and exceptionally during the 1940s of 100 or
more, as on 27 December 1941 when 100 were counted on
Walton Heath and on 9 December 1945 when 300 were
counted on Epsom Downs. There is also a record from the
Haslemere area when 'hundreds' were seen in flight over
Weydown on 8 November 1943. The largest concentrations
reported in the 1960s were 250 birds at Wanborough on 8
November 1965 and at Sutton Place on 1 January 1970.

Although direct proof is lacking it seems likely that some
of the wintering flocks contain immigrants from the Continent. The species is occasionally recorded in association
with immigrant Woodpigeon flocks in the autumn and in
one such movement on 18 October 1958 six were identified
during the morning and three in the afternoon moving NW.

27 *Lesser Spotted Woodpecker.* The least common of our woodpeckers but widely distributed in the county (*A. N. H. Peach*)

Feral Pigeon Resident, locally abundant.

As far as Surrey is concerned, by Feral Pigeon is understood a pigeon living 'in the wild' in association with others of its kind and belonging to stock which was originally domestic (and which is normally being reinforced with freshly lost domestic stock, particularly homing pigeons). All domestic breeds have evolved from the (wild) Rock Dove (*Columba livia*). The typical Feral Pigeon is often a nondescript bird but most birds are intermediate in type between the Rock Dove and the homing pigeon resembling the latter rather than their ancestral stock.

There is very little information available on the Feral Pigeon in Surrey apart from some documentation at the end of the review period and the more general information on 'London's pigeons'.

Bucknill accorded the Rock Dove the status of 'straggler' by which he appears to mean 'extremely rare' and gave his opinion that the few supposed occurrences of the species in Surrey were in fact Feral Pigeons. He did not refer to Feral Pigeons in general nor to 'London's pigeons'.

In *The Birds of the London Area* (1957) direct reference to the early decades of the twentieth century is not made but the Feral Pigeon is given as 'extremely numerous in inner London, less so in the peripheral areas, but colonies are present in most towns and suburbs where ... suitable breeding sites coincide with possibilities of obtaining food'. The greatest concentration was in inner London to a large extent north of the Thames but extending south of the river to include a large portion of metropolitan Surrey.

However, it is relevant to note that there was a large increase in the breeding population of inner London over the period 1951-65 and by 1966 it was thought to be more numerous in that area than the House Sparrow (Cramp and Tomlins, 1966).

It is known that in the 1960s the Feral Pigeon was well established in Surrey in 'outer London' areas including Epsom, Esher, West Ewell, Leatherhead, Richmond and Tolworth and it was also present and thriving in such towns as Dorking, Farnham, Guildford and Hindhead, with small colonies in some of the villages such as Shere. Returns submitted in connection with the BTO Atlas Survey commencing in 1968 showed the Feral Pigeon to be widespread throughout the county.

These birds are generally confined to older buildings and superstructures such as town railway bridges that provide the ledges for shelter and nesting. However, new buildings are colonized when they offer a 'foothold' and at Tolworth Tower, built in the mid-1960s, a small resident population had become established before the end of 1969.

The species is probably mainly dependent on man for its food but it is fond of grain and seeds and resorts to stubble fields in autumn and winter and is commonly seen foraging on the shore-line of the R. Thames.

Woodpigeon
Columba palumbus

Abundant resident. Winter immigrant and passage migrant. This species was described as an abundant resident and widely distributed in the county in 1900 and its status since then has probably changed very little. It had already established itself as a breeding species in central London in Bucknill's time and a big increase was noted in the inner suburbs of Brixton and Dulwich in the first decade of the present century although comments on its scarcity on Wimbledon Common were made as late as 1912. Some reduction in numbers in the London area occurred through an organized shooting campaign during 1939-45 but after the war its numbers quickly recovered and the population of urban and suburban areas continued to expand up to the mid-1960s and nesting was recorded from parks, gardens, frequently in trees, in busy streets and occasionally in buildings (Cramp and Tomlins, 1966). An example of high breeding density in the suburbs is provided from Morden in 1964 where in a quarter mile stretch of road no less than 12 breeding pairs were present.

The Surrey countryside, being well wooded, is particularly suited to the species' needs and it is widely and abundantly distributed in all parts, nesting in trees, bushes, hedges and exceptionally on buildings. The main nesting season is in the late summer (July and August) although nests have been found as early as January. A young bird was reported as successfully fledged at East Horsley on 23 February 1969. V. E. Edwards recorded a nest built in a Godalming factory almost entirely of metal, only two twigs being used.

During the late autumn the species congregates in large flocks which resort to the woods to feed on acorns and to arable land under cereals, grasses and clover. Flocks are often in the range of 500-1,000 and in some years can reach prodigious proportions. L. G. Weller reported one such build-up of numbers from Ewhurst in 1969 when during the latter half of October there was a steady increase, until on 11 November a flock estimated at 20,000 was present. Numbers on this scale had not been reported in the country since 1887 when a similar sized flock was reported from Gatton Park

(Bucknill). In January 1963 up to 5,000 were counted feeding on *Brassicae* at Addlestone and the predation on garden vegetables by this species in the winter months is a serious problem for suburban gardeners.

Large movements of passage birds are recorded in late October and November and there is little doubt that many of these birds originate from the Continent. There is considerable variation in the directions recorded. Westerly movements predominate but the picture is no doubt confused by dispersal from and return to roosts.

Turtle Dove
Streptopelia
turtur

Common summer visitor and passage migrant.

This species is common and widespread throughout the more rural areas of the county. As a nesting species it avoids the inner suburbs but it is recorded during the breeding season in the outer suburbs from gardens of sufficient size and with enough cover, as at Ashtead and Esher. It is however mainly concentrated in the outer rural areas, nesting in high hedges on agricultural land, thorn bushes on downland and commonland, in woodland and particularly in conifer plantations as at Prince's Coverts (Oxshott) and Cobham Park where breeding densities can be quite high. In 1969 there were seven territories in 96 acres of grassland scrub on Bookham Common compared with three in 1968 and no more than five in the earlier 1960s.

Of 19 Common Birds Census areas in the county studied over the period 1960-69 the species was absent from only four areas (Banstead—downland, Frensham—heathland, Leatherhead—downland and Clapham Common) and the highest density was at Warlingham on 227 acres of arable land containing a large element of thick and high hedgerow. Seven and three territories were registered here in 1967 and 1968 (Griffin, 1970).

Lack of quantitative assessment of breeding densities in the early years of the century makes judgment of a status change difficult, although as a breeding bird it has almost certainly been pushed further out from central London. Bucknill recorded it breeding in Dulwich, Wandsworth and Wimbledon. It was known to breed in Richmond Park up to the Second World War but no breeding records have been reported from any of these areas since the end of the war and the inner nesting limit is now about 15 miles out, with agricultural land at Chessington probably the nearest breeding area to St Paul's Cathedral.

It is recorded in most years in April but the main influx takes place in the first half of May and departure begins

towards the end of August continuing through September
and October. Occasionally birds have been recorded in
November; one was seen at Enton on 9 and 10 November
1956 and an apparently injured bird at Beddington SF on
23 November 1969. Flocking occurs from the end of July
and the birds congregate in areas where food is plentiful as
on stubble fields and at sewage farms. Eric Parker (*World
of Birds*) referred to flocks of up to 234 seen in a garden
off the Hog's Back in the early years of the 1930s; however more usual numbers in later years have been around
100. Maximum numbers of up to 100 occurred at Epsom SF
in mid-August 1955 and 1956, over 100 were seen at dusk
in stubble on 7 August 1962 at Ockham and the maximum
number recorded in the late 1960s was 55 at Old Lyne SF on
21 July 1968.

Migrating birds are occasionally reported, as on 23 August
1964 when c. 60 birds were counted flying ssw on a narrow
front at Addlestone.

No foreign recoveries of birds ringed in Surrey have been
reported but one ringed at Holmwood on 6 June 1926 was
found injured at Billingshurst, Sussex on 26 September 1932.

Collared Dove
Streptopelia decaocto

Common resident although localized.
The spread of this species into western Europe is one of the
most dramatic ornithological success stories of the twentieth
century. The bird first colonized England (Norfolk) in 1955
and its spread to the rest of the country was rapid and spectacular.

The first breeding record for Surrey came from Shamley
Green in 1960. In 1961 it was seen in two localities including
Carshalton where a small flock of up to 12 established itself
in a somewhat overgrown area of smallholdings and chicken
runs. The spread into Surrey seems to have radiated from
this north-east corner and by 1965 it had been recorded
in 23 separate localities with largest numbers reported from
Chessington Zoo and Shamley Green (up to 150 during the
winter months). The spread continued into the late 1960s.
It was first recorded from the Haslemere area in 1964 but
numbers in the extreme south-west of the county have so
far been low.

The fact that the bird has been recorded nesting in February (in Banstead) and November/December (in Weybridge) may go some way to explain the success of its spread.
It is a species apparently well able to adapt itself and profit
by man's activities. It feeds readily at chicken runs and
artificial feeding points such as Chessington Zoo and regu-

larly nests in close proximity to habitations and along main roads.

One bird ringed at Ekeren, Belgium on 6 March 1967 was recovered at Reigate on 8 June in the same year.

Cuckoo Moderately common summer visitor and passage migrant. *Cuculus* The Cuckoo is widely distributed throughout the county *canorus* and present as a breeding bird in all areas except heavily built-up parts of inner London where it is recorded only as a passage migrant. C. Dixon regarded it as common in suburban London in the early years of the century. In 1900 it was fostered by Sedge Warblers on Chiswick Eyot on the Thames, bred at Dulwich in 1935 while in 1938 had a Reed Warbler host in willowherb at Mitcham GP (now under industrial development). It was present on Streatham Common in 1949 and a young bird was seen on the wing there in 1950. In recent years young birds have been reported from Richmond Park and this area is probably now the inner limit of its breeding distribution in the London area of the county.

It is difficult to be sure of its status in rural and suburban Surrey because of lack of quantitative assessments. In 1913 Bentham considered it extraordinarily abundant on the commons south of Elstead and reiterated this opinion in 1919. He also considered it very abundant in the Blackheath/Farley Green area in 1930. The BTO Atlas and Common Birds Census records of the late 1960s show it to be generally and widely distributed. Indications of continuing abundance in the west of the county came in 1968 when P. G. Davis found young in no less than six Meadow Pipits' nests on the Frensham Commons.

Bucknill listed 20 host species that had been recorded in the county. These are, in roughly descending order of frequency: Dunnock, Meadow Pipit, Robin, Reed Bunting, Reed Warbler, Tree Pipit, Pied Wagtail, Linnet, Yellow Wagtail, Skylark, Chiffchaff, Willow Warbler, Wood Warbler, Spotted Flycatcher, Yellowhammer, Chaffinch, Cirl Bunting, Blackbird, Swallow and Song Thrush. In the present century nine more host species recorded in the county have been added to this list namely: Blackcap, Greenfinch, Nightingale, Red-backed Shrike, Sedge Warbler, Stonechat, Starling, Whitethroat and Wren. The records suggest that Dunnock, Meadow Pipit and Robin still remain the commonest fosterers. One particularly interesting record is of two young Cuckoos raised by the same pair of Pied Wagtails in a shed at Virginia Water (*BB*, 24:84).

The usual earliest arrival date is 10 or 11 April but there
are occasional reports in some years in the first week of
April and in 1965 it was reported from both Haslemere and
Grayswood on 1 April. Departure begins in July and August
and continues into September, most September records being
of young birds. The latest record in the review period is
of a juvenile bird at Beddington SF on 26 September 1965.

National figures suggest a general decrease especially since
the early 1950s (Parslow, 1967). A number of observers have
reported a decline in the county during the 1960s but the
evidence is somewhat conflicting and impossible to quantify.
Common Birds Census figures for the county from 1962 are
reassuring and suggest that the species continues to be widely
distributed and holding its own.

Two birds ringed at Beddington in 1957 have been re-
covered; one ringed on 13 September was found in Vendée,
France, on 20 October 1959 and the other ringed on 5
August, at Stockport (Cheshire) on 27 June 1961.

Scarce resident. **Barn Owl**
This species is now comparatively scarce and is distributed *Tyto alba*
very thinly over the rural parts of the county. It has certainly decreased since 1900 when Bucknill described it as
a common resident. In the first two decades of the century
Bentham had several breeding records from the Oxted and
Caterham areas. J. E. Harting, in a lecture at Weybridge in
1910, put it on a par with the Kestrel and Tawny Owl as
the commonest predator in that area. It was known as
breeding regularly in the Banstead and Chipstead areas prior
to 1930, though Beadell writing in the early 1930s claimed
that it had more or less disappeared from the Warlingham
district. In the 1930s and 1940s the species was occasionally
reported from widely scattered areas (*SEBR*) but breeding
records were very few.

A national survey organized by the RSPB in 1932 showed
that the species had declined for a number of years previously and was still doing so and this was attributed to
interference, scarcity of food, loss of nesting sites and rat
poisoning. The density of breeding pairs in Surrey varied
between 6-10 per 100 square miles and 26-30 per 100 square
miles with a total population approximating to between 130
and 160 breeding pairs (Blaker, 1934). The decrease continued until the late 1940s when there was a more general
decrease, particularly after 1955. This decrease is thought
by Parslow (1967) to have been accelerated by the advent
of toxic chemicals. The effects of agricultural pesticides on

predators focussed attention on the status of birds of prey and two papers in the 1960s (Prestt, 1965 and Prestt and Bell, 1966) emphasized the continued decline of this and other species. Surrey along with other counties in the south-east had suffered a moderate decrease over the period 1953-63. A special appeal was made in 1967 to observers in an effort to determine the status of the Barn Owl in the county. A total of only five breeding pairs was located and there were reports of sightings from eleven other localities. An interesting concentration of records from the north of the county, around Esher, emerged (Parr, 1969). In the late 1960s breeding was also reported regularly from Richmond Park.

There is no evidence to suggest that the species is other than entirely sedentary and no ringed birds have been recovered at any distance from the localities in which they were ringed.

Hawk Owl
Surnia ulula
A bird seen by R. W. Heenan and W. Kay Robinson at West Molesey on 27 December 1926 was thought to be of this species but the record was accepted only as a 'probable' (*BB*, 20 : 226).

Little Owl
Athene noctua
Moderately common resident.
This species is not native to Britain. It was successfully introduced in Kent and Northamptonshire towards the end of the nineteenth century and clearly found an ecological niche in the country for it spread rapidly to most of England and Wales. Bucknill could not report any satisfactory records for the county but in June 1900 a pair was seen by Miss C. M. Acland at a probable nest site in Coulsdon. Bentham reported two pairs nesting at Horley in 1907 and in 1911 the keeper at Titsey Park had reported to Bentham that five pairs were breeding there. By this time it seems to have been well established along the North Downs and at Chipstead, Godstone, Kingswood, Oxted and Warlingham. In outer Surrey its spread was comparatively slow and it was still scarce in the Haslemere area in 1920. By 1934 it was described as quite common in the Epsom, Limpsfield and Haslemere districts (*SEBR*) and it was common around Godalming in the 1950s (cNHs).

Nationally, records showed a general decrease following a series of hard winters around 1940 and a further decrease affecting all counties during 1955-61 thought to be due to the effects of pesticide use, with some evidence of recovery by 1965 (Parslow, 1967). The published records from Surrey are insufficient to support or gainsay these trends but the evidence does suggest that it was less common at the end of the review period than in the middle years of the century. It is however widely distributed throughout the county. In the five years 1965-69 breeding was reported from twenty widely scattered areas, seven and eight pairs were present in Richmond Park in 1966 and 1967 and in the 19 Common Birds Census areas studied in the county over the period 1960-69 the species was reported present in five of them. In 1969 it bred in Battersea Cemetery. This appears to be as near to the centre of London as ever breeding has been recorded.

Its optimum habitat requirement seems to be woodland or parkland in close proximity to agricultural land or along river or stream courses. R. K. Chandler found in the Limps-field district that out of seven nests, five were in trees away from woods and two were in woodland about 20 yards from the edge (*The Birds of the London Area*, 1957). J. J. Wheatley in a study of habitat preference around Guildford found nearly all the sites falling into two well-defined categories—scattered trees on the edge of large expanses of arable land with few hedges, and the other—trees near rivers or streams. All the sites he studied were contained in a strip of land embracing the North Downs and open farmland immediately to the south.

Pellets collected in Richmond Park in 1967 contained a preponderance of field voles and at a nest site at Chessington in 1965 there was evidence of predation on juvenile Starlings.

Common resident. **Tawny Owl**

At the end of the review period this species was the *Strix aluco* commonest of the resident owls, widely distributed and abundant in certain areas. It is doubtful however whether this position has always been held. Dixon (1909) considered the species to be rarer than the Barn Owl within the metropolitan limits and gave the inner breeding distribution as restricted to Dulwich, Kew, Richmond Park and Wimbledon. There is little doubt that since then it has improved its position in London's suburbs and breeding has spread nearer to the centre reaching Battersea Park in the 1950s (Cramp and Tomlins, 1966). It is impossible to assess its status in outer Surrey during the first half of the present century on the basis of known records. Bucknill had considered it abundant in well-wooded rural districts and there is nothing to suggest that it has not continued to enjoy the status in these areas up to the end of the period. The species increased generally throughout England from the end of the nineteenth century until at least 1950 after which, in common with other predators it began to decline (Parslow, 1967).

Prestt (1965) considered the species to be 'sparse/common' in Surrey during 1963 and found no evidence of a change in status over the period 1953-63.

An effort was made in 1967 to arrive at an objective assessment of the species' status in the county and evidence of 28 known breeding pairs and 42 suspected breeding pairs widely scattered throughout the whole area was obtained (Parr, 1969). Some interesting concentrations were disclosed during the survey. W. R. Ingram found six definite breeding pairs and 13 suspected pairs in Richmond Park and studies in certain suburban areas containing tree-lined streets and large gardens such as Surbiton, where owls were seen or heard in at least seven localities, indicated that this type of habitat, fairly extensive in suburban Surrey, was important to the species. J. J. Wheatley in an analysis of his records over the period 1959-70 found evidence of the presence of the species in at least 24 areas which were not recorded in the 1967 census and it may well be that numbers were grossly understated. A further indication of the species' comparative abundance in a suitable habitat came in 1968 when at least nine territories were located on Bookham Common.

A detailed and valuable analysis of the food of Tawny Owls in Surrey was made by G. Beven (1967). Pellets of Tawny Owls were examined from a wide range of Surrey habitats: oakwood at Bookham Common, a mixed wood at Earlswood, an alder-oakwood at Holmethorpe, an oak plantation at Richmond Park and a suburb at Morden. The vertebrate prey taken in the oak woodland at Bookham was largely mammalian (90 per cent by weight), that from the alder-oakwood showed some difference due to the presence of a small stream through the area allowing the owls to concentrate on Water Voles (*Aruicola terrestris*) and Brown Rats (*Rattus norvegicus*). The prey in the mixed wood at Earlswood was similar to the oakwood except that more birds were taken. The food taken in Richmond Park showed a high proportion of birds (61 per cent by weight) and might have been due to concentrations of roosting birds in the park. The pellets of the Morden sample indicated a high percentage of earthworms although bird and mammal prey percentages were also high. In short the samples demonstrated the owl's ability to utilize a wide variety of food and so to survive and thrive in a variety of different habitats including the built-up areas around London and the county's larger towns.

Extremely scarce resident.   **Long-eared**
The status of this species in the county had always been **Owl**
rather obscure and to some extent remains so. Bucknill *Asio otus*
thought that a few might have been nesting annually at the
start of the century and he cited nesting at Mickleham in
1898. There is fairly strong evidence that it was not uncommon as a nester in the first decade of this century. N.
Gilroy knew of two or three pairs breeding in the Wisley/
Ockham area in the early 1900s (*per* G. Douglas). It was
often seen at Bagshot in 1901 (*Zool.*, 1904). Dixon (1909)
claimed certain breeding in the Farnham district and
Bentham heard at least seven birds calling in a mile stretch
of road between Waverley and Farnham on 5 August 1911.
Published records after this period become much rarer.
Collenette (1937) drew attention to the inclusion of this
species as a breeding bird in Rudge Harding's list of birds
nesting in the park over the years 1925-27.

In more recent times there have been two reliable records
of breeding. In 1948 F. V. Blackburn found a nest containing three eggs in an old squirrel's drey near Stone hill,
Chobham; unfortunately the nest was robbed. On 29 April
1957 R. Clarke found a family party of this species; all the
birds were of different sizes and on the ground in a mature
conifer plantation near Titsey Wood in the east of the county
under the scarp of the North Downs. Since then there have
been occasional reports of single birds seen at Chobham,
Weybridge, Hackhurst Downs, Petersham and Sanderstead
and the possibility that the bird might still be resident in
the county cannot be entirely ruled out.

Occasional winter visitor. Probable passage migrant.   **Short-eared Owl**
Prior to 1939 this species was recorded in the county only as *Asio flammeus*
a very rare winter visitor. There was a record of a bird present on an unspecified common from 26 March to 15 April
1916 and one from the Haslemere district on 13 March
1920. In 1939 up to five were present on Walton Heath from
12 February to 25 March. In 1946/47 numbers varying from
one to four were observed at Beddington SF from 26 December to 30 March. From the early 1950s the species has been
recorded in the county almost annually although numbers
of over one have been recorded only at Beddington SF where
up to eight were present in January 1959 and up to ten in
the winter of 1970/71, attracted it was thought by a big
increase in vole and mouse numbers. The population of this
species is known to vary considerably yearly in correlation
with vole numbers and it seems likely that these fairly large

influxes follow successful breeding during a good season in the species' European range. The species is not however always dependent on mammal prey and Bentham in 1939 found that 18 pellets cast by the Short-eared Owls present on Walton Heath in that year contained mainly remains of bird species including Starling, Blackbird, Song Thrush and Skylark.

The species has been recorded in every month except June but most records fall in the period October to April with a high incidence in March and from October to December. This suggests that some passage birds may be involved particularly in March. One bird seen at Churt on 1 October 1946 was flying purposefully due south and thought by the observer to be on migration.

Nightjar
Caprimulgus
europaeus

Moderately common but local summer visitor and passage migrant.

There is little doubt that the species has suffered a decrease in the present century due in part to encroachment of urban development on its favoured haunts and to increasing disturbance. Bucknill classed it as a common summer visitor and as a measure of its abundance quoted a record of '47 birds shot' in a very short space of time on High Down Heath. Dixon (1909) stated that it still haunted Dulwich, Streatham, Tooting Bec, Wimbledon and Barnes Commons and Kew and described it as exceptionally common in the Croydon, Banstead, Epsom and Esher areas. Its inner breeding limit has now been pushed to the outer edges of these areas and Oxshott is probably now the breeding locality nearest to London. Some variation in breeding densities appears to take place from year to year with birds suddenly deserting a favourite area and recolonizing it in later years. In the three years 1924-26 G. Douglas found nests on Bookham Common and this site was then deserted till 1957 when two birds were heard churring and a nest found; the bird was again heard in 1958 and 1959 and then again deserted the area. In 1931 the species ceased to breed in Richmond Park (Collenette, 1937) but nested again there in 1950 although the attempt was unsuccessful. By 1934 the species was not often seen in the Epsom and Ewell areas but still considered fairly plentiful on Walton and Headley Heaths (*SEBR*). It has always been considered to be fairly common on the heather commons of that area; other particularly favoured areas are Wisley and Ockham Commons, Limpsfield Chart and Holmbury Hill. In a national enquiry organized by the BTO over the years 1957-58, the species was regarded as common but decreasing in Surrey and chiefly confined to areas of grass, Bracken and birch scrub (Stafford, 1962). This latter statement however, clearly under-estimates the importance of the heather common in the species' habitat preferences. There have been hopeful indications in the second half of the 1960s that the species is improving its position. Localities where the species was recorded in the *SBR* stood at 14 in 1966 and 1967 and rose to 17 in 1968 and 22 in 1969. About 40 different localities have been mentioned since 1957. One particular feature common to certain parts of rural Surrey, which may have operated to its advantage since the end of the Second World War, is the clearance and re-afforestation of certain areas. The species appears to like cleared woodland and the ecological conditions created in areas replanted. Thus in the later 1940s when thick woodland at Prince's Coverts, Oxshott was cleared and replanted, largely with conifers, the area had been colonized by Nightjars by the early 1950s and nesting was still recorded in the area at the end of the review period despite the growth of the new trees. Similarly beech woodland on the North Downs at Netley Heath which was cleared in the mid-1960s had been colonized by the species by 1969. Such areas are little disturbed whereas those subject to greater use by the public as in the Box Hill-Headley district are known to have lost or suffered an appreciable decline in their Nightjar populations.

The species is not usually recorded till mid-May although there are odd records from early May. *The Handbook* mentions two early Surrey records on 15 April 1908 and 16 April 1909 and there was a very early record from Hydon Heath on 12 April 1949. It departs in August and September. The latest recorded date is 18 September 1966 at West Humble.

Swift
Apus apus

Locally abundant summer visitor and passage migrant. The Swift has been common and widespread in the county as long as records have been kept. It still appears to be very numerous although with the modernization of some old buildings and the demolition of others (especially the types of buildings where entry under the eaves gives direct access to the roofspace), long-used nest sites are disappearing.

The dates of spring arrival fall within a narrow compass. Nearly always the first birds are reported on dates between 16 April and 29 April and the main influx is usually in early May.

During the summer very large concentrations of Swifts build up at times over the sewage farms and reservoirs, as for instance in the first week of July 1956 when 1,000 birds were seen over the R. Hogsmill and there were as many over the Walton Reservoir in June and July 1965. No less than 3,000 were estimated at Barn Elms Reservoir on 25 June 1966. In one or two cases swarms of flying ants (*Formicidae spp.*) were present at the same time. No doubt the large sheets of water attract many birds from a distance when insects are abundant but these gatherings of Swifts are believed to consist mainly of non-breeding birds and yearlings (Lack, 1956) and they do not necessarily reflect the number of locally nesting birds.

Visible migration of small groups of birds is often observed in early August. Examples are the movement east of c. 100 Swifts in parties of five or six at Thorpe in the space of an hour on 13 August 1966, the movement sw of c. 400 in two hours at Burgh Heath on 1 August 1967 and parties of 20-30 birds passing at the rate of 50-60 a minute at Farnham in the late afternoon on 11 August 1968. While the majority of Swifts depart in August, every year there are lingerers present in September or even October and November; the latest date recorded in Surrey in the review period is 7 November 1970 at Povey Cross near Gatwick.

A considerable amount of ringing has been carried out; at West Ewell alone over 2,000 Swifts were caught and ringed in the course of four seasons. The majority of recoveries have been in the same locality, some up to six years later. Overseas recoveries of Surrey-ringed Swifts reflect in the main their migration to and from Africa. Recoveries have been as follows: one from the North Frisian Islands in May, one from north France in May, five from Spain (one in May and four in August), two from the Pyrenees (May and August) and the first two recoveries of British-ringed birds in Morocco, ringed at Mitcham and Barn Elms in 1962 and 1964 respectively, recovered in May and September 1969. Finally there have been three recoveries from the species' winter quarters: one from Malawi in January and two from the Congo in early April, one of these birds having had the dubious distinction of being shot with a bow and arrow.

Alpine Swift Extremely scarce vagrant.
Apus melba There are only six recorded occurrences of this species in Surrey, two being within the period under review. The *SBR* for 1954 mentioned one record in 1951 but gives no supporting details. In 1967 a bird was observed by P. R. Colston on three occasions with c. 1,500 Swifts at Beddington sf on the afternoon of 18 June.

Moderately common resident. **Kingfisher**
The Kingfisher of the nineteenth century lived a hazardous *Alcedo atthis*
life, much prized by 'sportsmen' as a trophy to embellish a
glass case or even to decorate, complete, a lady's hat. It is
not surprising therefore that in 1900 it was said to be decreasing. Since then it appears largely to have held its own
in the county although suffering severe drops in numbers
after periods of prolonged hard weather as for instance the
winter of 1962/63. At the end of the review period however
it was widespread as a breeding species throughout the
county along the main river courses, the smaller tributaries
and occasionally at gravel or sand pits. The Rivers Wey and
Mole have always been favoured but on the latter there has
been considerable loss of habitat in the Hersham/Molesey
area owing to the dredging and concreting of the river after
the severe floods of 1968.

Young birds may disperse widely from their nesting areas.
One of a brood reared at Godstone was recovered a month
later in the Isle of Wight, while at virtually the same time
another of the same brood was found dead at Tunbridge
Wells.

In the winter months birds often move away from breeding areas, visiting quite small ponds as in gardens, parks
and village greens.

There is one record of the Bee-eater in the county in the **Bee-eater**
review period. An adult was recorded at Beddington SF on *Merops*
5 August 1958 (*BB*, 53:167). *apiaster*

Extremely scarce vagrant. **Roller**
There are two records of this species for the county both *Coracias*
after the mid-point of the present century. One was recorded *garrulus*
on forestry land at Oxshott from 23-29 May 1959 (*BB*,
52:421) and one was on Chobham Common from 17-20
June 1970 (*BB*, 64:357).

Irregular summer visitor and vagrant. **Hoopoe**
Until the 1950s this species was regarded as a scarce visitor *Upupa epops*
to the county but in the last 20 years of the review period
the Hoopoe has been recorded almost annually. Numbers
vary from year to year; a particularly good year was 1956
when birds were reported at Albury Heath, Blackheath,
Epsom SF, Harnley Common, Kenley, Kingswood and
Windsor Great Park.

Most records are of birds that have apparently overshot
their normal breeding range in spring, the majority having
occurred in May, a good number in April and a few even in

March. There are also a few records in every month up to
October. Nearly all the birds arrive singly, though there
were two at Hankley for several days in 1956 and in April
1949 four were seen at Oxted, two of which stayed for
several weeks, while one, the remains of which were found
later, had apparently been killed by a Sparrow Hawk.

There is no evidence in Surrey of attempts at nesting in
the review period. In 1841 a pair nested near Dorking—the
eggs being taken—and before the turn of the century a pair
nested at Leatherhead and successfully reared young. A male
bird remained at Frensham for the whole of the summer of
1963 and was frequently seen at the entrance to a large
hole in an old oak.

**Green
Woodpecker
*Picus viridis***
Moderately common resident.
The Green Woodpecker is well established as a breed-
ing species in very many parts of the county. The older
records speak of it as common and there is little or no docu-
mentary evidence to suggest any great change of status.

It has a wide range of habitat, frequenting not only woods
and parkland but also conifers on the edge of open heathland, where it is often seen feeding on the ground on ants
(*Formicidae spp.*) and on pine cones which it wedges into
a crack in a tree trunk in order to extract the seeds.

The species suffered very severely in the hard winter of
1962/63 and greatly reduced numbers were reported everywhere during the next few years. However, in many parts
it had recovered by 1965 though in some parts of the county
recovery was slow. At the end of the review period its local
status was variously reported.

**Great Spotted
Woodpecker
*Dendrocopos
major***
Common resident.
The Great Spotted Woodpecker is one of the few species
that has increased considerably during the present century.
In 1900 it was said to be rather rare in Surrey and though
moderately plentiful in undisturbed localities its nest was
always considered a good find. Since that time it has appeared
in increasing numbers all over the county and spread to
the suburbs and central London parklands while it became
as common or commoner than the Green Woodpecker in
the large open spaces a little out of inner London (*The Birds
of the London Area*, 1957). A general increase throughout
southern England has been noted particularly since 1920
(Parslow, 1967).

The species has become exceedingly bold, bringing its
young to feed at bird tables close to houses, even attacking
milk bottles on the doorstep and frequently enlarging the

28 *Wryneck.* Once common, now on the verge of extinction in Surrey (*M. D. England*)

entrance holes of nest boxes in order to extract nestlings. Its catholic taste in food has no doubt enabled it to exploit any source of supply and it was probably due to the bird table habit that it survived the hard winter of 1962/63 so well.

Ringing has not brought to light any long-distance movement but birds ringed at Ewhurst have been recovered at Eton (Berkshire) and Datchet (Buckinghamshire); one at Addington was recovered at Erith (Kent) and one at Weybridge was recovered there five years later. A local population may not be as static as it appears. One observer believed that a mere pair of Great Spotted Woodpeckers was frequenting his bird table but ringing revealed that there were in fact at least 11 different birds.

Lesser Spotted Woodpecker *Dendrocopos minor*

Moderately common resident.
Observations show that the Lesser Spotted Woodpecker is widely though thinly distributed all over the county apart from the heavily built-up areas close to London. The relative abundance of this species and the Great Spotted Woodpecker has undergone a change. In 1900 Bucknill asserted that the Lesser Spotted Woodpecker was far more numerous and more generally distributed than the Great Spotted Woodpecker and usually commoner than the Green Woodpecker while in 1909 the Lesser Spotted Woodpecker was still said to be far the most plentiful woodpecker in the metropolitan area. This is certainly not the case today and the Lesser Spotted must be reckoned the least abundant of the three woodpeckers resident in the county. The change in relative numbers of course reflects the remarkable increase in numbers of the Great Spotted Woodpecker as much as any decrease in those of the Lesser Spotted. The latter in any case is less conspicuous and less noisy than the Great Spotted Woodpecker. Again, visits to the bird tables are infrequent, though one bird was observed roosting in a nest box close to a house throughout the winter.

An indication of the comparative abundance of the three woodpeckers in Surrey at the end of the review period was to be found in the figures of the Common Birds Census studies in the county during the 1960s made in 19 areas of varied habitats. Out of a total of 11,078 territories in over 9,992 acres in 84 census plot years, the Great Spotted Woodpecker was the most numerous, with 54 territories spread over nine areas, next was the Green Woodpecker with 28 territories in six areas while the Lesser Spotted Woodpecker had 15 territories in four areas. The largest concentrations

29 *Woodlark*. Now far less common than in mid-century and confined to a few favoured heathlands (*F. V. Blackburn*)

178

of all three species occurred in oak woodland at Bookham (*per* D. Griffin).

One observer has detected in the Lesser Spotted Woodpecker a marked preference for sites along the rivers Wey and Mole—this may be associated with the bird's liking for Alder trees.

Wryneck
Jynx
torquilla
Formerly a summer resident, now a scarce passage migrant. Probably no bird has suffered a more drastic change of status in recent years than the Wryneck. At the beginning of the century it was described as a common summer visitor to the rural districts and in 1909 it was said to visit more of the central London areas than the other members of the woodpecker family. Its popular names, Snake-bird, Cuckoo's Mate and Emmett show it was familiar to country folk. During the first three decades of the century it was reported from a number of places in Surrey. Many of the nests were in nest boxes, and at Limpsfield a nest box was occupied for seventeen consecutive years. During this period the bird was usually first noted in the second or third week of April; early arrivals were one on 12 March 1911 (*The Handbook*, II:294) and at Shalford Common on 31 March 1923. In the autumn it has been recorded as late as 3 October in 1931 (*The Handbook*, II:294).

Monk 1963 traced the steady decline of this species in Britain. Surrey was one of the latest areas to be affected but an undoubted decrease had set in by 1948 and by 1953 it could only be found regularly in the north-east of the county and on the Hampshire border. Over the period of his survey (1954-58) Monk discovered eight proved breeding records and 54 possible breeding records in Surrey. Some of the last records were from garden nest boxes as for instance in 1951 at Purley and in 1952-54 at Bookham. Breeding was recorded at Chipstead until 1960 and two pairs nested in the north-east of the county in 1966. The last known breeding record for the county was in 1968 at Warlingham. The only four occurrences in 1969 were in the autumn while in 1970 one was recorded in a garden at Dulwich on 13 June but could not be traced subsequently and there were three other records in the autumn.

It must be concluded that at the end of the review period it seemed unlikely that the Wryneck was a breeding bird in Surrey.

Short-toed Lark
Calandrella
cinerea
Extremely scarce vagrant. There is one record only of this species for the county—a single bird at Beddington SF on 24 April 1966 (*BB*, 60:323).

The only record of this species that might be claimed for **Crested Lark**
the county is of two birds on an unspecified foreshore of the *Galerida*
Thames between Chiswick Eyot and Hammersmith Bridge *cristata*
on 8 March 1947 at the end of a long spell of very cold
weather (*BB*, 41:345).

Scarce and very local resident. **Woodlark**
The population of this species in Surrey has been subject *Lullula arborea*
to considerable fluctuations. Whatever its status throughout
the nineteenth century (and this is an open question) the
indications are that the Woodlark was at a low ebb in 1900
and that in the first twenty years of the review period it
remained extremely local and uncommon.

About 1920 numbers began to increase and a considerable
expansion took place in the next three decades or so, apart
from something of a setback in the late 1930s. A peak
appears to have been reached in the late 1950s the years in
which it was recorded in the breeding season in about 40
localities. Although the species' decline in the early 1960s
is usually related to the hard winter of 1962/63 a general
decrease throughout Surrey was noted in the *Surrey
Bird Report* for 1961. The number of areas with breeding
season records continued to decline as the 1960s progressed
and in 1969 breeding was confirmed in only three areas and
breeding season records were for west Surrey only where the
preferred habitat is found (see below). Changes in status
of the Woodlark in Surrey approximate to the 'national
changes' given by Parslow (1967).

These considerable status changes have not been fully
accounted for. It has been shown that the effects of a hard
winter are not solely responsible for decreases in numbers.
Harrison (1961) established a broad correlation between
Woodlark numbers and mean annual temperature. Certainly
there would appear to be factors involved other than habitat,
which probably causes only very local changes such as were
shown by Venables (1937) (see below). Given open ground
and scattered trees (light cover is not essential) the Woodlark still adapts to a variety of habitats and when numbers
in Surrey have been high the species has bred in habitats
ranging from dry fields in the Haslemere area to urban
heathland pockets. It bred on Putney Heath six and a half
miles from St Paul's Cathedral, within the period 1945-50.

The preferred habitat is heathland with light well-drained
soil, heather as nesting cover and with scattered trees, such
as is widely found in west and north-west Surrey in areas
such as Chobham, Frensham and Thursley where the species

has been consistently recorded. Venables (1937) showed that its distribution on the Surrey greensand heaths was linked with the occurrences of open spaces made by heath fires. Such fires not only prevent afforestation but also keep down the ground cover. L. J. Raynsford recorded at least 11 pairs on Witley Common in 1958.

Chalk downland is rather far behind in second place as a Woodlark breeding habitat in Surrey. However, when the Surrey population has been comparatively high, breeding has occurred in many localities on the North Downs including Banstead Heath, the areas of Box Hill and Ranmore Common and White Downs. The incidence of breeding in the Box Hill area has been variously reported but it seems unlikely that breeding densities have ever been high there.

Other heathlands, notably Esher Common, Oxshott Heath, Reigate Heath, Wimbledon Common and Walton Heath, have also held breeding populations at times. Most of these heaths are found on a mixture of sand-gravel soils, some including clay-with-flints, but nevertheless providing the good drainage which as Harrison (1961) points out is probably an important factor for a bird that spends most of its time on the ground in areas with sparse vegetation.

Breeding on clay is uncommon. In Surrey the species has been recorded nesting and breeding sporadically on London Clay in Richmond Park and elsewhere but appears to have been virtually absent from the areas of Wealden clay although Bentham had one breeding season record near Vachery Pond in 1924.

The species has been recorded in all months of the year and has frequently been recorded singing at both ends of the song period given in *The Handbook*, as for instance in January and February when few other birds can be heard. In the autumn and winter small flocks are sometimes recorded, occasionally of over 20 birds. There is no evidence to suggest that these flocks are of other than local origin.

Skylark
Alauda
arvensis
Abundant resident. Passage migrant and winter immigrant. There has been no apparent change of status for the Skylark in Surrey during the review period except in so far as it has retreated from the inner London areas as the Metropolis has advanced. Common and widespread in the county, it breeds in the open spaces of outer suburbia and rural Surrey particularly favouring agricultural land and rough grass or common land.

In the Common Birds Census studies made in the county

during the 1960s average densities on farmland varied between one pair per 28 acres (Wey Manor Farm, near Weybridge) and one pair per six acres (Chessington). On farmland at Norbury Park where the Skylark was found to be about the most abundant species, the average density was one pair per 15 acres. On downland at Banstead the average density was one pair per eight acres, almost as high as for the optimum farmland habitat (Griffin, 1970).

There was a reduction in the breeding population in most areas of the county after the hard winter of 1962/63 but there were no indications of a serious set-back.

Autumn passage, which begins towards the end of September generally reaches a peak in the middle of October and continues to the end of the month. Most of the movements are in a south or westerly direction and generally involve the passage of a succession of small flocks but parties of up to about 100 birds are sometimes seen. It would seem that some of the flocks are of immigrants from the Continent. The extent to which they remain in the county during the winter is not known.

Winter flocks are commonly seen up to the end of February, often feeding on stubble fields and at sewage farms; up to 500 are sometimes recorded, hard weather movements apart. Spectacular flocking and movements have been recorded in hard weather. At the end of 1938 Skylarks at Beddington SF were estimated in thousands while hundreds died of cold and starvation. Again in 1963 very large numbers were found there with a maximum number of c. 3,000 at the end of January. On 31 December 1961 a day of heavy snow showers, many movements of Skylarks were recorded including c. 1,000 south at Addington and c. 1,000 ssw at Leatherhead, while c. 2,000 flew south at Shirley the following day. On 6 and 7 January 1962 c. 650 were recorded flying in the opposite direction, north. Very many lesser hard weather movements have been recorded during the review period. Extreme cold also forces Skylarks into gardens in search of food. Spring passage has not been recorded in the county.

Shore Lark
Eremophila alpestris

Extremely scarce vagrant.
There has been only one record of this species in this century. On 28 October 1961 three were observed at Queen Elizabeth II Reservoir whilst it was under construction. Bucknill referred to two undated specimens—one shot at Merrow Downs and the other labelled 'shot in Surrey'.

Swallow Common summer visitor and passage migrant.
Hirundo The Swallow breeds widely in the county in open country
rustica particularly near water but will only rarely tolerate really
built-up conditions and so has retreated from former breeding areas in London as the Metropolis has advanced. It
ceased to be a breeding bird in Richmond Park three decades
or so before the end of the review period.

There is insufficient evidence available to show whether
its status has declined overall during the review period
although numbers would seem to have fluctuated and some
observers think that numbers are decreasing. The *Haslemere
Review* (1968) gave it as not so numerous as the House
Martin in the area and this probably holds good for the
county as a whole, although the difference is most marked
in suburban areas.

The species usually nests in out-buildings which give
ready access and sometimes under bridges and similar struc-
tures and there is a record of a pair nesting on a fluorescent
lamp at Thorpe in 1967. Stables and farm buildings in rural
areas are particularly favoured.

In most years the first birds are recorded in early April
although there are several March records, the earliest being
19 March 1961 at Frensham. Numbers up to 500 are sometimes recorded on spring passage in April. Passage has not
been much reported in May.

Return passage covers a very wide period. There was a
gathering of c. 500 at Guildford SF on 5 July 1966 but autumn
movement is at its strongest in August and September.
Heavy movement may involve hundreds of birds as in 1957
when 1,000-1,200 per hour were recorded passing SW over
Richmond Park on 26 August and 9 September and in 1969
when 1,400 were counted between 0730 and 0930 hours on
19 September at Worcester Park. Roosts in late summer and
autumn have been recorded in a variety of situations including the sewage farm at Epsom (5,000 birds on 7 September 1955), a young conifer plantation at Oxshott (200 birds
on 22 July 1959), Bracken at Walton Heath (20 juveniles on
31 July 1964) and at a small pond at Elstead (c. 1,000 birds
on 18 September 1967). Numbers in October are much reduced and probably include late breeding birds (the species
is occasionally triple-brooded, and one pair was found feeding young as late as 11 October at Haslemere in 1950. There
have been a number of isolated records in November and
December, the latest record since 1900 being of birds present
up to 9 December 1970 at Thorpe.

Ringing has thrown some light on migration. Surrey-ringed juveniles have been shown to be wintering in South Africa viz: one ringed at Ewhurst on 11 September 1962 was recovered 30 miles from Kimberley on 17 November 1962 and another ringed at Ewhurst on 22 August 1968 was recovered in the Transvaal on 13 November 1968. Conversely an adult ringed near Cape Town on 30 December 1965 was retrapped at Farnham on 12 June 1966. Autumn movement of Surrey-ringed birds via Sandwich Bay, Kent has been demonstrated and one bird has been recovered in October at Perpignan, France. A Swallow ringed in Belgium on 11 May 1963 was recovered at Albury on 2 August 1965 and one ringed at Hersham on 5 May 1963 was recovered in County Clare, Eire on 15 April 1966.

House Martin
Delichon urbica

Very common summer visitor. Passage migrant. There are no definite indications of a significant change of status for this species in Surrey during the review period. It breeds widely in the county generally nesting under the eaves of houses and readily colonizes new housing estates. Bucknill gave it as breeding on ledges of chalk quarries, its nest being composed largely of chalk, but this phenomenon is unknown in the present century.

The Birds of the London Area (1957) referred to a slow retreat from the inner districts of London up to about 1950 but Cramp and Gooders (1967) described how by the late 1960s an increase was taking place in inner London, nesting being recorded, for example at Hammersmith and Putney and small colonies being present in 1965 at Streatham and Tooting. The increase was attributed to cleaner air following the introduction of smoke control legislation and the consequent increase in flying insects.

Colonies generally contain up to 20 nests but some are much larger. Early in the century there was a colony of c. 70 pairs at Oxted Mill and in 1969 and 1970 between 50 and 70 nests were in use on the Memorial Gates at Polesden Lacey. In a special survey of nests at Alfold, Bramley, Chilworth, Cranleigh, Dunsfold and Ewhurst in 1968, 405 nests were counted of which 198 were successful with one brood and 33 with a second. The species is not uncommonly triple-brooded and this no doubt the reason for the several records of young still in the nest in October.

The main arrival of House Martins occurs about the third week of April. Occasionally earlier arrivals are reported, the earliest for the county in the review period being 19 March 1938 (*The Handbook*, 11:237). When they first arrive House Martins are often seen hawking for insects over open water with other hirundines. Spring passage is recorded up to the end of May.

Pre-departure concentrations are recorded from mid-July onwards and passage is spread over several months. Flocks of several hundred are frequently reported. A thousand were seen flying NE preceding rain clouds at Worcester Park on 25 September 1968. Good numbers are often maintained in October as at Beddington SF in 1938 when 500 were seen on 18 October. From time to time odd birds are recorded in November and a bird in a weakened condition was seen flying at Milford on 4 December 1962.

Birds ringed in Surrey in May and June (before the possibility of post-breeding dispersal) have been shown to return to the same locality in later years but there is insufficient data to determine the extent of faithfulness to breeding sites. A juvenile bird ringed at Epsom on 18 August 1957 and recovered at Cartama, near Malaga in Spain on 18 October of the same year is the only foreign recovery of a 'Surrey' bird.

Sand Martin
Riparia
riparia

Summer visitor, locally common. Passage migrant.

Breeding colonies of the Sand Martin have occurred in widely scattered areas of the county where local conditions offer suitable breeding sites but the major colonies in the later years of the review period have been in sand pits in the greensand belt running across the county from Frensham in the west to Godstone in the east. Colonies at Farnham and Holmethorpe SPS have held up to 500 pairs. There are many records of colonies of 50 to 400 pairs. A number of these colonies are long established but Sand Martins frequently form new colonies when excavation of new pits create new possible sites. In 1963 Sand Martins at a working pit dug new holes every evening for several weeks after the workmen had left only to have their efforts brought to nought the following day by further excavating.

Although sand pits are most used as nesting sites in the county there are several colonies in gravel and chalk pits and breeding has been suspected at a clay pit in the former Oxshott brick works. Other sites recorded are drain pipes on the sides of reservoirs and railway embankments. River banks are used locally by small colonies.

Sand Martins arrive in late March or early April and passage continues into May. When first recorded they are usually seen over open water. The earliest record for the review period was of one at Fetcham Mill Pond on 12 March 1961.

From about the middle of July and through August and September birds begin to congregate in preparation for the autumn migration and gatherings of 500 or more are regularly reported over reservoirs and other stretches of open water. Most birds have left by the end of September although there are scattered records of odd birds during October; the latest Surrey record is of one at Beddington SF on 30 October 1932. A roost of 300 birds at Frensham Little Pond on the late date of 20 October 1962 was exceptional.

There has been extensive ringing of this species in the county, stimulated by a grant-aided scheme operated by the BTO in the 1960s. In each of several years more than 1,000 birds were ringed at various sites in Surrey. Juveniles showed a distinct tendency to disperse widely after fledging and before migrating but also displayed a predisposition to return for breeding to a colony near to where they were hatched. There was some interchange from year to year between colonies in south-east England but the majority of adult birds returned annually to the same colony. In autumn a number of Surrey birds were retrapped at a very large roost at the Chichester GPS (Sussex) (L. J. and J. J. Weller, 1964). Foreign recoveries of Surrey-ringed birds include many from France, one from Spain, two from Morocco and one from Tunisia, some being on the outward journey and others on the return spring movement.

Golden Oriole
Oriolus oriolus

Very scarce visitor. Occasionally breeding. Bucknill could give no authentic breeding records although he considered that the Golden Oriole had probably bred in the county during the last three decades of the nineteenth century. He accorded it the status of rare summer visitor.

In the present century there have been a dozen or so records. On 19 April 1911 one was reported from Farnham. The next record, the only acceptable one of successful breeding during the review period, was in 1930 when a pair raised a brood of four (*BB*, 24:226). The locality may well have been Godstone where the species was said to have nested unsuccessfully before 1939. In any event *The Birds of the London Area* (1957) gave the successful breeding record as within the London Natural History Society's area and added that pairs were seen in the breeding area in at least two subsequent years.

There were records at Kew Gardens and Mitcham in 1934 and a pair was at Chiddingfold in May 1936. In 1940 when a pair attempted to nest across the Thames at Chiswick House but abandoned the site about 6 May, a female was seen on Wimbledon Common on 11 May and may have been one of the Chiswick birds. Eric Parker (*World of Birds*) referred to one in a garden at Guildford in the same year. In 1955 there were records of a male at Runfold on 12 April and of a seemingly immature male on Wimbledon Common on 20 May and 18 June. The next year there was a record of one given as a 'young male or brightly coloured female' at Watermeads, Morden, on 21 June 1956. In 1963 a pair nested near Farleigh Common; eggs were laid but the nest was robbed (A. S. Turner). The last record in the review period was of a male seen on Banstead Downs on 13 May 1969.

Raven Extremely scarce visitor.
Corvus Although it is probable that the Raven bred in small
corax numbers in Surrey up to at least the middle of the nineteenth century, documentation is lacking. A note by W. A. Shaw (*Haslemere List*, 1921) that the species was recorded from Hindhead is rather indefinite. The only positive records to hand for this century are of one bird at Esher on 12 September 1909 (*Zool.*, 1909) and one at Frensham on 16 November 1956.

Carrion Very common resident.
Crow At the turn of the century the species was probably not
Corvus particularly common in most of Surrey, though in 1910
corone Bentham regarded it as abundant in the south-west. P. F.
corone Bunyard (*BB*, 17:198) noted a considerable increase during the First World War but a marked decrease afterwards due to shooting and poisoning. By 1930 the species was probably generally fairly common. After the Second World War it increased enormously and by the mid-1950s had established itself as a common resident. A slight increase in the county was noted for the next decade (Prestt, 1965) and a small increase in 1967 over 1966 was indicated by a Common Birds Questionnaire in the *Surrey Bird Report* (Summers, 1969). By the end of the review period the species appeared to be very common and widespread.

The species' success has been due to a general reduction in persecution and its ability to exploit various situations as for example a spread into urban areas, parks and gardens following its expansion in rural areas. However, its chief natural advantage lies in the fact that it is an adaptable scavenger and it is commonly seen feeding at sewage farms and rubbish dumps. G. H. Gush observed 14 feeding on a deer carcass at Thursley Common on 18 February 1962. Flocks are generally recorded in the winter months. Among the records available the largest flock before the 1940s was of 50 at Kew on 19 January 1918 seen by Bentham, who recorded several flocks of 50-100 plus in the 1940s at Beddington and Epsom SFS. Flocks of this size were recorded several times in the last two decades of the review period in various localities. The only record to hand of a flock well over this size is that of c. 400 on Wimbledon Common on 19 December 1964.

At Beddington SF between 1946-49 the average size of the flocks varied little at different seasons, being within the range 50-60. Several years later K. C. Osborne, referring to 60 birds on 29 May 1967 at this same sewage farm, postulated that 'this summer flock of non-breeders may account for lack of breeding success of Snipe, Redshanks and Lapwing in recent years'.

There are a few records of roosts of up to 100 and two records of roosts over 200, the largest being 230 plus in an oakwood at Motspur Park on 27 January 1969. However it is probable that some roosts are larger still in view of counts made in recent years of birds flighting to roost. At Carshalton Beeches during January 1963 up to c. 700 were counted on a flight line to a roost in the area.

Hooded Crow
Corvus corone cornix

Scarce winter visitor.
The Hooded Crow had become rather scarce in Surrey before 1900. In the early years of the present century the species was only regularly recorded in the extreme eastern areas of the county mainly on the North Downs in the Warlingham district, in Titsey Park, at Limpsfield and south to the Surrey-Sussex border, but not west of a line Caterham/Godstone/Felbridge. The species was unusually numerous in the winter of 1906/07 but by 1912 it appeared to be again getting scarce, though it was regularly recorded in the east up to the very early 1920s and A. Beadell recorded 60 in the Beddlestead Valley on 22 February 1920 and 20 at Warlingham on 20 February 1921. (These numbers are larger than any given by Bentham for the period before 1912, his maximum being 12.) Since 1921 there have been hardly any records for this general area. Elsewhere in the county, the species was seen with some regularity in numbers up to three along the Thames at Chelsea Reach from 1919 up to about 1928.

From 1930 to the end of the review period the species was recorded in about six of the years in each decade in various localities in the county, most frequently at a sewage farm. In some years there was only a single sighting of one bird but more often two or three birds were seen in the county. In the winter of 1953/54 there were records from six separate localities and in the 1957/58 winter there were six at Milford.

Birds were almost all recorded from the end of October to March. There were two records for April and one bird was seen near Frensham Ponds in June 1949.

Rook
Corvus
frugilegus
Common resident. Probable winter immigrant. The Rook was described as an abundant resident throughout Surrey in 1900 and it apparently remained so in most of the county in the first few decades of the nineteenth century though disappearing from its breeding areas in London as the city expanded. It held on at Herne Hill until 1919, Wandsworth until about 1924 and Dulwich until about 1930. It seems probable that it was generally plentiful in rural Surrey between 1911-30.

In 1931 P. A. D. Hollom conducted a census of rookeries in an area of 32 square miles centred on Addlestone. Nine rookeries, containing in total 421 nests, were counted. In the same area in 1970 no more than two rookeries with a total of 40-50 nests were known, this pointing to a severe reduction in numbers in that area during the past 40 years.

It is open to doubt whether the fairly general increase in England between 1930 and 1960 (Parslow, 1967) was in fact reflected in Surrey and unlikely that any possible increase continued beyond the late 1940s.

No very large regular numbers have been recorded since 1949 although *The Birds of the London Area* (1957) cited a Rook/Jackdaw roost at Titsey, the indication being that it was rather large. Very large roosts previously recorded include 3,500 corvids (90 per cent Rooks) near Marden Park on 16 December 1911, c. 7,500 Rooks and Jackdaws at Birtley in December 1936 and at least 3,000 Rooks and Jackdaws in pines overlooking Frensham Little Pond in the years before 1939. A very large Rook/Jackdaw roost over 60 years old at Gatton Park was abandoned towards the end of 1949. (See under Jackdaw for further details.)

There are indications that the species was at a low ebb in Surrey in the very early 1960s, possibly due to the use of toxic chemicals in agriculture. However there was a sharp increase in the number of rookeries recorded at the end of c. 700 nests were reported from widespread areas as follows: the 1960s and in 1969, 40 occupied rookeries totalling one to ten nests: 12, 11-20 nests: 14, 21-50 nests: eight, 51-100 nests: three, others in which the number of nests was not determined: three. At this time the largest rookery recorded was at Addington, the number of nests varying between 76 and 108. There are no rookeries for which a history for the whole of the review period can be given, but in the Clandon/Effingham area several small rookeries first recorded in the early 1930s could still be seen in 1970, the open agricultural downland with woods and roadside trees of that area being typically 'Rook country'. The largest Rook roost recorded from 1950 to 1970 was of at least 600 birds at Oxted in 1967 although other roosts were recorded as large.

Ringing in the county has proved longevity—a fully grown bird ringed at Ewhurst on 13 July 1949 was found dead at Ockley on 21 September 1963. It has not thrown much light upon post-breeding dispersal and no foreign-ringed birds have been recovered in Surrey, although it is probable that some winter visitors from northern and central Europe and Scandinavia which arrive on the east coast in the autumn spread into the county. A hard weather movement was noted on 30 November 1969 when several hundreds flew north-east during a snowstorm at Brockham Green.

Jackdaw *Corvus monedula*

Common resident. Winter immigrant.
Although it was described as common at the turn of the century there is evidence that the species increased in numbers up to the mid-1950s. Localities where it was described as very numerous at different times during this period include Abinger Hammer, the Clandon/Merrow area, Gatton Park, Limpsfield and Richmond Park.

There is little information available for the period from the mid-1950s to the mid-1960s. No local increases were reported and it is just possible that the species became a little less common. However by the end of the review period the species appeared to be decidedly common and by 1970 was breeding in all the ten kilometre squares in the county.

Although perhaps more plentiful in the rural areas, the species is very adaptable and is able to thrive in built-up areas too. It nests readily in old trees and buildings but will use other sites such as chalk quarries along the North Downs or sand pits as recorded at Limpsfield. The increasing use of chimney pots for nesting at Sanderstead at the end of the review period has been associated with the increase in certain types of central heating, the chimney pots having fallen into disuse.

Some very large Jackdaw/Rook roosts have been described under the Rook but some details of the one that used to be in Gatton Park and of special significance for the Jackdaw is given below. A count in February 1947 gave a roughly estimated figure of 5,000 with Jackdaws outnumbering Rooks by about five to three. There were flight lines to this roost over Kingswood, Redhill, Reigate and Walton Heath and Jackdaws from Richmond Park almost certainly joined this roost. Shortly after it was abandoned (this was towards the end of 1949) 1,000 Jackdaws were seen on the same Motspur Park-Banstead flight line presumably going to roost somewhere else. On dates in September and October 1956, c. 5,000 birds (presumably all Jackdaws) were estimated roosting at Oak Park near Sanderstead but on 12 December none remained. No concentration of this nature appears to have been recorded since. In 1969, over 600 were roosting in an oakwood at Motspur Park on 27 January. The combined Rook and Jackdaw population of the county is a large one and there are no doubt other undocumented roosts of similar magnitude.

Hard weather movements are sometimes observed—there was rather a large movement of c. 1,000 birds flying east to west over Windlesham on 1 December 1954. The species is known to be a winter immigrant but with no recoveries in the county of foreign-ringed birds, the lack of records of winter flocks and the complication of hard weather movements, it is impossible to present a picture of present immigration. However, Bentham regarded the large flocks seen around Tadworth in the winter in the 1920s as probably of Continental origin.

Magpie
Pica
pica

Very common resident.
During the first decade of the present century the Magpie was described as one of the rarest breeding birds in the county. It was chiefly confined to the extreme western and south-western areas and only locally at all common, as at Frimley in 1911. When on 6 March 1910 Bentham saw 11 on a morning's walk from Hankley Common to Waverley he regarded it as 'most unusual for Surrey'.

During the First World War and the years that followed there was a relaxation of persecution by gamekeepers and the species increased rapidly in some areas and its range expanded steadily up to about 1930. It spread for example, into north-east Surrey where towards 1930 the species had become 'numerous' at Chelsham. Numbers over 40 recorded before 1930 are 43 at Vachery Pond on 13 March 1919, 50 at Cranleigh in March 1919 and at least 60 within a mile of Ongar Hill in the Addlestone district in September 1929.

Expansion continued in the 1930s but up to 1939 there were still rural areas where the species was very rare, notably in central Surrey and G. Douglas stated that it was probably absent from Bookham, Effingham and Fetcham as late as 1939. By 1951 however it was a familiar sight in these areas and was probably common over most of the county. The species was gradually spreading into London and breeding was suspected for the first time in Kew Gardens in 1969. Prestt (1965) gave a moderate increase in the county during 1953-63 and showed that the species' general increase in the county was largely attributed to a decrease in game preservation. Game preservation was still a locally important factor and as recently as 1946 one keeper accounted for 57 in three months at Addington (Pounds, 1952). There were indications of a substantial increase in the species in 1967 over 1966 in the county (Summers, 1969) and by the end of the review period there was no doubt that the species was very common and widespread except in the inner London area.

The largest roost recorded in the county is of 50-60 in Alders at Eashing up to 1939. Despite the apparent increase up to the end of the review period no large flock or roost (over 40) was recorded in the last two decades.

Extremely scarce vagrant.   **Nutcracker**
Authentic records of vagrant Nutcrackers in Surrey in the *Nucifraga*
review period are as follows: one was shot at Addington *caryocatactes*
Park, Croydon on 13 October 1913 and was found to be of the slender-billed race (*N. c. macrorhynchos*) to which most Nutcrackers recorded in Britain belong; one was recorded at Frensham on 12 November 1957 and during 1968, the exceptional invasion year when over 300 birds arrived in Britain from, it was thought, Russia and Siberia, one was seen at South Croydon on at least five occasions between 8 August and 7 September and one was recorded at Headley on 10, 22 and 26 September.

There are unsubstantiated records of a sighting at Dulwich on 14 April 1905, one at Frensham Vale in June 1948 as reported in *Country Life* (*October* 1948:887) and one at Banstead on 16 December 1968. The indications are that this last record would have proved acceptable had details been submitted. A Nutcracker seen at Kew Green on 6 July 1936 was probably an escaped bird. There were four records for the county prior to 1900.

Jay Very common resident. Winter immigrant.

Garrulus The Jay was not scarce as was the Magpie early in the
glandarius present century but nevertheless it experienced a similar
considerable increase. The Jay was a common resident in
Kew Gardens in 1906 (the Magpie not being suspected of
breeding there until 1969) and it colonized inner London
in the 1930s and 1940s. The species was increasing in the
county around 1910 and increased greatly during the First
World War and in the years that followed when persecution
(never so strong as with the Magpie) was relaxed. By 1935
it was probably generally common.

There appears to have been a further increases during
the Second World War and Prestt (1965) gave a slight to
moderate increase in the county in the period 1953-63. A
moderate increase in 1967 over 1966 was indicated too by
the Common Birds Questionnaire in the *Surrey Bird Report*
(Summers, 1969) and at the end of the review period the
species was very common and widespread.

The species' success may be due to a relaxation in persecution but in Surrey the species has benefited too from
the new habitat provided by maturing forestry plantations;
it has also adapted itself to scrubland so long as the trees
are present in small numbers and is common in the suburbs
where predation on garden birds such as the Blackbird and
Song Thrush has become increasingly common.

Flocks and passage recorded may be local movement or
immigration. Parties of 20-30 are not infrequently recorded
in the winter months and small movements south, east or
west are often recorded in September and October. The
years in which considerable passage or special indications
of immigration were observed in Surrey during the review
period were 1913, 1947, 1957, 1963, and 1965. In 1957 there
was an exceptional immigration of Continental Jays into
Britain and a considerable passage of the species was noted
in Surrey in late September and in October. At Dulwich
numbers up to 32 were seen on four dates passing over in
a predominantly WNW direction. Large numbers were also
noted in the local woods, there being a flock of 64 present
on 24 November.

There is one longevity record of a bird ringed as an adult
at Tadworth on 13 June 1954 and retrapped in the same
place on 17 April 1966.

Chough There is no evidence that the Chough has occurred natur-
Coracia ally in Surrey. On the other hand not all records for the
pyrrhocorax county have been of birds that had obviously escaped.

Bucknill gave five records and was of the opinion 'it is by no means unlikely that none … are really wild birds. On the other hand, there is no evidence to show that this is the case….' His opinion holds good for the twentieth century. Eric Parker (*English Wild Life*) described a rather strange incident when a seemingly wild Chough visited a tame Chough in a Surrey garden early in the century. The likelihood that one seen in Marden Park, near Woldingham in the early 1950s was an escaped bird is far greater.

Abundant resident. Probable autumn passage migrant and winter immigrant. **Great Tit** *Parus major*

The species is numerous and widespread in the county in all but the most heavily built-up areas of London, although less abundant than the Blue Tit. There is no evidence of any change of status during the period under review. Catholic in its choice of food and nesting site, the species breeds successfully in any habitat providing a fair number of trees or bushes with holes or boxes for nest sites. In 19 Common Birds Census study areas in the county during the 1960s the Great Tit was the seventh most common breeding species with 571 territories out of a grand total of 11,078 in 84 census plot years; the areas were in various habitats and the species was present in all of them. The highest densities were in woodland and in 40 acres of woodland on Bookham Common where the highest average density was recorded, between 11 and 19 pairs were in territory each year. This gives a 'breeding density' of up to one pair per two acres (Griffin, 1970).

Outside the breeding season Great Tits are sometimes seen in small flocks often with other species of tits. The highest number in the available records is c. 50 which were feeding at a rubbish dump at Cranleigh on 19 January 1964 in company with Blue Tits and other birds.

A melanistic form of this species, having a completely black head, was recorded during the 1950s and 1960s from Hersham/Weybridge and the Oxshott/Leatherhead/Fetcham areas.

There is a small amount of evidence suggesting probable passage migrant/winter immigrant status, notably by recovery of an adult ringed at Esher on 22 October 1959, at Mellun, East Frisian Islands, Germany on 9 April 1960 when it was controlled. Other recoveries of Surrey-ringed birds have been few and mostly near the place of ringing but one noteworthy record was of an adult female ringed at Weybridge on 3 March 1967 found dead at Solihull,

Warwickshire 90 miles NW on 21 May 1967. At Selsdon a ringed female returned to the same nest box in six successive years between 1958 and 1963, with a different male each time.

Blue Tit
Parus
caeruleus
Abundant resident. Autumn passage migrant and winter immigrant.

This species is very numerous and widespread throughout the county including the built-up areas of London for it is very tolerant of man and adapts to any habitat that provides some vegetation and holes for nesting. It is most abundant in the deciduous woodland and gardens of Surrey. It was found to be the third commonest species in the 19 Common Birds Census areas studied in the county in the 1960s. In five of the areas there was more than one territory per ten acres and in 40 acres of deciduous woodland at Bookham the number of territories varied between 16 and 22, thus giving a maximum territorial density of over one pair per two acres (Griffin, 1970). This territorial density is by no means unusual in woodland. Eleven acres of woodland in Stoke Park, Guildford has held up to eight pairs.

Outside the breeding season the species is often recorded in flocks sometimes in association with other species. Numbers up to 100 are not uncommon. The largest number in the available records for the review period is 200 at Oxshott on 30 November 1963.

Evidence of Continental immigration includes the trapping (for ringing) in autumn and winter of birds showing the characteristics of the race *P. c. caeruleus*. Autumn passage is sometimes seen and it was well recorded in 1957 the year of large scale immigration of Continental birds into Britain.

Of the many Blue Tits ringed in the county most recoveries have been local and there was no foreign recovery in the review period.

Orange-tinted birds were observed near Dorking during the 1960s and the tint was thought to be due to some carotenoid substance in the diet (*SBCQB*, 45 *March* 1968)

Coal Tit
Parus
ater
Common resident.

The Coal Tit is generally less common than the Blue Tit and Great Tit but it is well distributed in the county and is locally very numerous exceeding both Blue and Great Tit in pine forest. There is no evidence to suggest a marked change of status during the review period except in so far as the species has decreased close to London. Parslow (1967) referred to a general increase in the country and gave conifer afforestation as a contributory factor. However the dense, half-grown conifer plantations now common in Surrey do not appear particularly attractive to the species. The preferred habitat is a less dense and well-grown coniferous woodland such as is found widely with the heaths of west Surrey. In 1907 Bentham considered it to be the most abundant species in the Thursley area and certainly, it was at the end of the review period, very common there. It is well but more thinly distributed as a breeding bird in many of the deciduous and mixed woodlands in the county as for example those along the North Downs. It is also common in suburban gardens and urban areas with a scatter of conifers among the deciduous trees as at Ashtead, Esher and Guildford.

It commonly nests in banks rather than tree holes. An unusual nest site recorded in the county was in the roof of a house at Sanderstead in 1968.

At the end of the breeding season small flocks are sometimes recorded. There is some evidence to support passage migrant status for the species in the county—most recently a large south to south west movement all morning on 15 November 1959 at Wisley. In winter larger numbers are recorded than in late summer/autumn and Continental immigration has been postulated, notably by Bunyard (1919) who was able to discount hard weather movement on one occasion. However, proof is lacking and it would be wise to be cautious on this issue. The larger flocks recorded in winter include 140 on Pirbright Common on 31 December 1965 and c. 150 at Cleygate Common on 23 January 1966.

Crested Tit
Parus cristatus

Bucknill cited one unsatisfactory sight record of this species for the county and indicated that one of a pair in the Charterhouse Collection was supposedly shot in Surrey but that this was open to doubt. In the present century C. W. Colthrup saw and heard the call of a tit which he considered to be of this species on 24 April 1904 near Croydon. The record was published as a 'probable' (*BB*, 16:161). Again on 10 April 1945 Miss D. Burridge took a satisfactory description of one she had seen at close quarters near Godstone. (*The Birds of the London Area*, 1957). It is likely that birds seen in southern England are of the northern or central European races (*P. c. cristatus/mitratus*) rather than the Scottish race (*P. c. scoticus*).

Marsh Tit
Parus palustris

Moderately common resident.

In 1900 Bucknill considered this species to be a moderately common resident, locally distributed. At that time however the Willow Tit had not been recognized in Britain, so all black-capped tits were thought to be Marsh Tits. However, the status given by Bucknill to the species was certainly appropriate at the end of the review period.

The habitat preference is for dry, birch-dominated commons and mixed deciduous woods with a fair amount of secondary cover. It likes too the wooded edges of small ponds and lakes such as those at Cutt Mill. It is locally common in the mixed woodland of the North Downs and in one such wood at Headley containing thick ground cover of bramble and Bracken and a number of small ponds, at least four pairs were found breeding in 1969 within 100 yards of each other; the nest sites were—in existing holes at ground level in a hollow birch stump, five feet high in a hole of dead birch on a pond edge and 50 feet high in a hole in a dead chestnut. A pair that raised five young was reported using a nest box at Hydon Heath in 1966.

The species has been reported breeding from many parts of the county with the exception of the inner metropolitan areas and occasionally breeding has been reported from suitable habitats as far in as Dulwich and Kew.

For a comparison in status between the Marsh Tit and the Willow Tit see under Willow Tit.

Willow Tit Moderately common resident.

Parus montanus This species was not recognized in Britain until the end of the nineteenth century when the first British specimen was described (*BB*, 1:23-24, 44-47). The first reference to the species in Surrey was of one seen in Reigate in 1910 (*The Birds of the London Area*, 1957) and the first breeding record traced has been of a nest convincingly described by Bentham in an entry in his diary for 27 May 1914, the nest being situated in a rotten tree stump in the garden of a cottage in Brockham. He also recorded a second nest found on 15 May 1919 at Leigh Mill Wood, Godstone. By 1935 the species was described as quite common in the Haslemere area and as having an apparent liking for the edges of the greensand commons though it was very scarce on the Wealden clay where it was being outnumbered by Marsh Tits in a proportion of five to one. The species was also found to have a liking for marshy places such as the environs of wooded streams and to be nesting in the rotten tree stumps usually found in such places (*SEBR*). In a report of a countrywide survey by Witherby and Nicholson (1937) the Willow Tit was adjudged to be equal in number to the Marsh Tit in the Farnham/Haslemere area and it was found to be fairly numerous in the areas south of Croydon and Epsom/Dorking. It was recorded only at one or two points in the area between the North Downs and the Thames. An analysis of the records submitted to the Surrey Bird Club in the decade 1960-69 suggests that during this period the Willow Tit was more widely distributed and numerous than the Marsh Tit. The number of localities where breeding was proved varied between four and ten compared with between two and six for the Marsh Tit. In 1969 breeding was reported from ten areas ranging from the alluvial gravels at Thorpe, Bagshot Sands at Oxshott, clay commonland at Ashtead, the North Downs and the Wey Valley at Eashing and Godalming. In addition birds were also seen in nine other areas during the breeding season.

In autumn and winter the species is seen in a wide variety of habitats away from its usual breeding areas and it regularly visits bird tables in outlying suburban gardens.

It is possible that even in 1970 there was some confusion between Willow and Marsh Tits. The two species are not easy to differentiate in the field especially if the observer is not familiar with calls and songs. The somewhat conflicting picture presented by past records has no doubt been caused by this confusion. Again to some extent too the habitat preferences of the two species overlap as in certain woodlands of the North Downs and this has no doubt added to the confusion. In view of these factors, it would probably be prudent to entertain some reservations concerning the status of the two species as described above, in the 1960s. There is scope for some fruitful study in the future on the status of this and the preceding species in the county.

Common resident.
This species is subject to considerable fluctuations in numbers because it is particularly vulnerable in hard winters. After the winters of 1916/17, 1946/47 and 1962/63 populations in the county were greatly reduced and each time took several years to recover. In 1963 there was none on Bookham Common, whereas there had been ten pairs in 1962.

It is not possible to say to what extent numbers build up between one 'crash' and the next or whether there has been any long-term change of status. However numbers of the species were at a high level in the county in 1960 and 1961 when 'exceptional numbers were present in the breeding season' (*SBR*, 9:17).

Long-tailed Tit
Aegithalos caudatus

Following the 1962/63 hard winter crash in the population, increasing numbers were reported from the mid-1960s to the end of the review period and in 1969 a total of c. 60 breeding pairs was reported and whilst this cannot be taken as anything like the actual total of breeding pairs it indicated that the species was again at or near a peak level. During the review period the species retreated from many breeding areas in London as development expanded.

It requires something of a rural setting for breeding and is found mainly in hedgerows, thickets, bushes and open woodland but in recent years it has been increasingly reported breeding in suburban gardens as in the areas of Ashtead, Banstead and Oxshott. At the end of the review period it was widespread in suitable habitats in the county.

Exceptionally early nest building was recorded at Haslemere on 19 February 1943. One bird of a pair nesting near Chelsham on the North Downs in April 1954 had the characteristics of the white-headed race (*A. c. caudatus*) (*BB*, 48:92).

One bird ringed at Cranborne, Dorset on 14 October 1959 was recovered at Ewhurst on 19 January 1961.

Bearded Tit *Panurus biarmicus* Extremely scarce visitor.

Three records of this species have been accepted during the review period; two were in 1964 and 1965 in a period when populations in East Anglia and on the Continent showed a tendency to irrupt in the autumn involving dispersal to many areas of southern England; two birds were seen in the reed bed at Frensham Little Pond on 25 October 1964 and a male was seen briefly at Lower Pen Pond, Richmond Park on 6 November 1965. The third record was of a single bird at Frensham Great Pond on 18 October 1970.

There is also an unsubstantiated report of Bearded Tits on the R. Wey between Guildford and Pyrford between 1936 and 1946 (*SEBR*). Bucknill gave a number of occurrences in the nineteenth century and regarded it as probable that the species had bred in the county but not later than the first decade of that century.

Nuthatch *Sitta europaea* Common resident.

The Nuthatch is generally distributed in the county mainly in deciduous woodland and other wooded areas including parks and the large gardens of outer suburbia where it is regularly seen as a visitor to the garden bird table. In the built-up areas of London it is generally found only where there are substantial pockets of woodland such as Dulwich

Woods. The Common Birds Census study in Surrey in the 1960s showed that in 40 acres of deciduous woodland at Bookham Common the average number of pairs in territory was five, this giving a density of one pair per eight acres, slightly higher than that found in a similar habitat at Ashtead Woods (Griffin, 1970). Other woodland areas have shown similar densities.

The species sometimes nests in nest boxes, enlarging the entrance hole of tit boxes, or where the hole has been enlarged by Starlings or squirrels, reducing it by mud plaster. On one occasion a bird was seen carrying nesting material into a letter box and plastering the entrance.

There is no evidence to suggest a change of status during the review period.

Common resident. **Treecreeper**
The Treecreeper is generally distributed in the county in *Certhia* mature woodland and in other areas including gardens, *familiaris* provided that trees are present. It lives almost entirely on insects extracted from cracks in the bark of trees and it nests in crevices. It is less exacting in its requirements than the Nuthatch and probably more widespread. Because of its secretive behaviour and quiet call it is probably very much overlooked.

After the hard winter of 1962/63 when observers made a special effort to record the birds in Surrey to see how numbers had been affected, there were 60-70 records of Treecreepers and the species appeared to be fairly widespread though possibly reduced in numbers. The *Haslemere Review* (1968) however gave it as 'nearly wiped out in the freeze-up of 1963' in the Haslemere area. Nevertheless by the end of the review period the species was common and there is no evidence to suggest any marked change of status. It was present in the breeding season in 12 out of the 19 Common Birds Census areas studied in the county in the 1960s, being unrecorded only in certain of the farmland, downland and mixed scrub areas, a hawthorn/oak copse of 29 acres, and at Clapham Common in London (Griffin, 1970). Breeding densities can occasionally be quite high. In 1970 there were at least five nests in about 25 acres of damp woodland at Stoke, Guildford. Two of the nests were in willow. At least seven pairs were located in Richmond Park in 1969.

Family parties are frequently seen in the late summer and in the winter it often joins roving parties of tits. In 1967 there were seven together in one oak tree at Weybridge

Heath on 1 November. Records in the London area show that outside the breeding season there is some local movement as the Treecreeper is then recorded in some of the open spaces of the inner suburbs such as Clapham Common.

Wren
Troglodytes troglodytes

Abundant resident.
The Wren is generally common throughout the county wherever there is adequate low cover. It is found in heathland and in woodland, in parks and gardens, at gravel pits, sewage farms and in waste places but is absent from the very heavily built-up areas of London. In the Common Birds Census studies in Surrey in the 1960s, the Wren was the sixth most abundant of the recorded species, with a total of 636 territories out of a grand total of 11,078 in 84 census plot years in the 19 study areas. It was absent only from Clapham Common. It was recorded in territory in only one year (1967) on Banstead Downs which is noteworthy as the study area included tangled undergrowth and hawthorn copses. The highest breeding density was found in 40 acres of oakwood at Bookham where in 1968 there were 26 territories, this giving a breeding density of 6.5 pairs per ten acres (Griffin, 1970). However, the species suffers great loss in very severe winters and, by way of illustration, only one singing male was recorded during the 1963 breeding season in the 40 acres of oakwood at Bookham (referred to above) where 12 had been recorded in 1962.

A noteworthy ringing recovery was of a bird ringed at Shoreham by Sea, Sussex, on 23 October 1959 and recovered at Great Bookham on 31 January 1960. Otherwise very little is known of movements or dispersal of the Wren in Surrey.

Dipper
Cinclus cinclus

Extremely scarce vagrant.
There have been only three authenticated records of the species in the review period. One Dipper was seen on 28 March 1915 on the R. Mole between Leatherhead and Cobham (*BB*, 8:292) and a bird was reported at Leatherhead Railway Bridge on 3 May 1926 (*BB*, 20:107). On 13 April 1965 one was trapped and ringed at Leigh Mill Pond by R. F. Durman.

Bucknill referred to two probable occurrences of the species on the R. Mole.

Mistle Thrush
Turdus viscivorus

Very common resident. Winter immigrant and passage migrant.
The Mistle Thrush is well distributed throughout the county including the built-up areas of London, wherever

there is open ground for feeding and some high trees. The indications are that there has been a gradual increase in the county during the review period in keeping with the national trend given by Parslow (1967). In the last century it was more of a bird of the rural areas but in the present century it has become increasingly common within the area of the outer London suburbs, as at Ashtead where it is high on the 'bird table' list. Bentham, at his home in Tadworth where he had been in residence since 1934, noted the species on the bird table for the first time on 12 February 1958.

An increasing trend was shown by Common Birds Census studies in the county in the 1960s. The species was present in all but two of the 19 areas studied, being absent only from downland at Banstead (rough grassland with scrub) and scrubland at Holmbury Hill; it was also virtually absent from Frensham Great Pond (with heathland). Almost the highest breeding density was on Clapham Common which had one pair per 16 acres in 1965. A similar density was found in Ashtead Woods in 1966 and the highest density of the study was on the 40 acres of oak woodland at Bookham in 1965 (one pair per 13 acres) (Griffin, 1970).

The effects of hard winters on the species would appear to be variable. Bunyard (1919) considered the species very scarce after the hard winter of 1916/17. There was no evidence in Surrey however that the breeding strength was seriously affected by the severe weather of the 1962/63 winter.

The Mistle Thrush nests early and post-breeding flocks are observed from June onwards. There were 89 at Beddington SF on 26 June 1932 and 50 or so birds have often been recorded in June and July (and indeed from then onwards to the end of the year). There were upwards of 50 juveniles in Banstead Woods on 11 June 1955.

Reports of influxes and movements are sometimes made in autumn and winter and it is probable that birds from the Continent and/or northern Britain are involved; however, it is not always possible to be certain what the records signify. For example, a large movement, possibly of several hundred, apparently heading northwards, was observed around Albury on 19 September 1954. Other records indicating influx and movement include 'numbers' going south at Ewell on 14 August 1923, 280 birds counted in one hour on Limpsfield Common on 12 September 1954, a large influx at Banstead and Walton Heaths from 22 to 27

October 1968 (followed by a marked decrease) and 'fully 1,000 birds' at Selsdon on 6 December 1942.

Ringing has demonstrated emigration or dispersal to France; a nestling ringed at Ewhurst on 5 May 1952 was recovered in December 1952 at Caen, 145 miles south and a juvenile ringed at Haslemere on 3 August 1962 was recovered on 2 February 1963 at Olonne-sur-mer (Vendée) over 300 miles sw.

Fieldfare Common winter visitor. Passage migrant.
Turdus The Fieldfare is a common winter visitor in Surrey al-
pilaris though numbers fluctuate considerably from year to year. In most years the main period of arrival and passage commences in the latter part of October although a few birds have been recorded in September and there is one exceptional record of a bird at Beddington Park on 2 July 1969. Birds seen in October and November are usually in small parties of up to 50 moving generally in a westerly direction. In 1961 immigration was late but on a vast scale reaching a 'high' on 6 November when c. 1,500 were recorded sw over Sutton and passage at the rate of 300-400 per hour was reported from a number of other localities.

During the winter months the species is generally well distributed in the more rural parts of the county and is commonly seen feeding in fields in association with Redwings and other thrushes. Not infrequently it visits gardens and orchards and will readily feed on fallen apples especially in hard weather. Very large concentrations are recorded in some years. Bentham recorded 2,000-3,000 in Yew trees in Norbury Park on 15 December 1946 and a flock of 1,500-2,000 was noted in the Mitcham Common area on 12 December 1955. The largest concentration recorded in the review period was of 5,000 plus on ploughed fields at Shere on 21 February 1969.

The species is subject to hard weather movements during the winter when further immigration might occur from the Continent. In one such movement c. 1,000 were counted flying south over Addington on 31 December 1961.

The spring passage is not as conspicuous as that in the autumn but sometimes large numbers of presumed migrants are recorded, as for instance 1,000 at Stoke D'Abernon on 2 April 1969. Single birds are often recorded up to 15 May and Bentham recorded an unusually late party of c. 50 birds remaining on Walton Heath until 7 May.

The few ringing recoveries both indicate the countries of origin of our visitors and demonstrate the wide-ranging nature of the species' winter movements; a bird ringed at Ewhurst on 24 February 1956 was recovered at Reinsvoll, Norway on 23 July of the same year; one ringed at a roost on Wisley Common on 24 December 1966 was shot at Ravina, Italy, on 13 December 1968 and one ringed at Godalming on 6 February 1954 was recovered at Ribatschi, USSR on 9 April 1960.

Song Thrush *Turdus ericetorum*

Abundant resident. Winter immigrant and passage migrant. This species is widely distributed and common throughout the county. The relative abundance of the Song Thrush and Blackbird is discussed under the latter species. There is some evidence that in the early years of the century the Song Thrush was more abundant than the Blackbird at least in metropolitan Surrey and that since then it has lost ground to the Blackbird and suffered a marked decrease in areas close to London, this becoming evident by the 1930s (*The Birds of the London Area*, 1957).

For outer and rural Surrey there are few data from which to evaluate status changes since 1900 when Bucknill considered the species abundant throughout the county. The *Haslemere Review* (1968) reported the species as common at Beacon Hill, Hindhead, where even as recently as 1940 it had been rarely seen and suggested this might be due to housing development and the consequent increase in gardens. It was not, however, until the 1960s when material from the Common Birds Census became available that it was possible to assess the species' county status realistically. Over the period 1960-69 the species had been recorded in all 19 areas studied (Griffin, 1970). The two areas with the heaviest breeding densities were at Bookham in oak woodland with an average density of 1.6 pairs per ten acres and Walton in a hawthorn/oak copse with a density of 2.1 pairs per ten acres. Breeding numbers in 1963 showed an appreciable drop in many areas following the hard winter of 1962/63 but by 1964 numbers had apparently recovered to the previous level.

During the winter there is a considerable shift of populations. Many of the resident birds fly south and the numbers of birds that do over-winter are augmented by immigrants from the Continent. As with the Blackbird diurnal passage is not often recorded and movement is usually noticed by significant local 'falls' following nocturnal influxes, such increases being regularly noted from September to November. Hard weather movements are also frequently reported and numbers recorded at sewage farms, particularly during the winter, vary greatly in response to weather changes.

A number of ringing recoveries reflect the movement of resident birds southwards in the winter. There are recoveries of birds ringed as juveniles and nestlings from France, Spain and Portugal though in fact most recoveries of birds ringed when fully grown are from north or west France. Occasionally westerly movements are reflected in a recovery, as for instance by a bird ringed at Ewhurst on 15 November 1962 which was recovered at South Milton, Devon on 4 January 1963.

Redwing Common winter visitor. Passage migrant.
Turdus As with the Fieldfare, numbers and winter movements of
musicus the Redwing vary considerably. It is commonly seen in winter feeding in fields and on berry-bearing trees, particularly Yew and hawthorn, in the more rural parts of the county and the two species are often seen together. It sometimes visits gardens and orchards in cold spells seeking berries and fruit. Overall the Redwing has been somewhat more numerous than the Fieldfare in Surrey during the review period and has been regarded as occurring much more frequently in the metropolitan area than the Fieldfare.

Although occasionally the Redwing is first recorded in late September, first sightings in autumn are usually in October. Influx and passage are generally at a height towards the end of the month and sometimes involve large numbers; for example, 4,000 flew westwards between 0900 hours and 1300 hours at Headley Heath on 15 October 1963 and 3,500-4,500 were recorded moving south between dawn and midday at Thorpe on 12 October 1969. Nocturnal passage is regularly heard in the autumn, often starting in the early evening and continuing to midnight or later.

Flocks of 300 or so birds are commonly reported in November, December and the early months of the New Year and in some years very large flocks involving several hundred birds, are recorded. These generally occur at times of hard weather when there are also very many records of movements and local increases. For example in 1962/63, c. 4,000 were present in hawthorns at Caterham on 19 December 1962 and in early January 1963 movements involving up to 600 birds were widely reported in the county. At Beddington SF numbers reached a peak on 8 January when c. 5,000 were recorded.

In spring, numbers of up to 500 have been recorded as

late as the end of March and in many years last records for the spring are in the first week of April. There are very few later records and the latest birds recorded during the review period were c. 20 at Haslemere on 8 May 1969. Generally, passage is almost complete by the end of March and in some years by the middle of that month.

The Handbook gives 'no clear evidence that (full) song is ever heard in its entirety in this country'. However, there is a record of 'as complete a song as any ... heard in the Icelandic breeding grounds' by Mr and Mrs D. A. White at Haslemere on 26 March 1963; again Bentham and P. A. D. Hollom have recorded good song in Surrey during the review period, Bentham equating the song almost, with that heard in Norway. A bird showing the characteristics of the Icelandic race (*T. m. coburni*) was trapped and ringed on Wisley Common on 15 January 1967.

Birds ringed in Surrey have been recovered in France, Italy and Spain in subsequent winters, the recoveries suggesting that Redwings wintering in Britain in one year may well winter elsewhere in other years. One ringed at Worcester Park on 18 February 1956 was recovered near Preetzen, Mechlenburg, Germany on 27 April 1956 and one ringed at Epsom on 25 January 1958 was recovered on 19 March 1959 at Makharadze, Georgia, USSR; these birds were presumably returning to breeding grounds in eastern Europe.

Ring Ouzel
Turdus torquatus

Scarce passage migrant.
There is little evidence of any marked change of status in the present century for this species. It is a scarce double passage migrant occurring in most years usually on the higher ground of the North Downs or the greensand hills.

In the first half century there was 29 records in the London area of Surrey mostly from the North Downs around Headley, Caterham and Oxted. In 1934 the *South Eastern Bird Report* described the species as a fairly regular autumn visitor in the Haslemere district particularly at Hindhead where small flocks were sometimes seen feeding on rowan berries. In 1951 birds were present on Walton Heath for over three weeks with a maximum of ten on 8 October and this is the highest number ever recorded as seen at one time in the county. Records in the later years of the 1950s and in the 1960s have been of ones, twos or threes and in the ten years from 1960 to 1969 there was a total of 18 spring and an equal number of autumn records, mainly from the downs and higher western hills but also from Beddington SF, Chessington, Frensham and Richmond Park. Spring passage is observed from the end of March to early May, most birds being recorded in April. Autumn passage records cover September and October (but there is one earlier record of one bird at Frensham on 18 August 1968), birds sometimes lingering for a week or more when berries are available.

American Robin *Turdus migratorius* Extremely scarce vagrant. This New World species has been recorded once in the county at Wick Pond, Windsor Great Park from 12 February to 5 March 1966 (*BB*, 61 : 363).

Blackbird *Turdus merula* Abundant resident. Winter immigrant and passage migrant. The familiar Blackbird is one of the commonest resident birds in the county, as common in parks, gardens and built-up areas of the suburbs as in the rural areas. Bucknill considered it to be the commonest thrush species and noted that it had penetrated the thickly populated districts in greater numbers than the Song Thrush—a fact that has been confirmed by more systematic studies in the London area in the present century. In the outer rural areas some observers have considered that in the earlier years of the century the Song Thrush did in fact outnumber the Blackbird. G. Douglas considered that before 1940 the Song Thrush outnumbered the Blackbird in the Bookham area by two to one whereas by 1970 the reverse was true. However with no reliable statistical evidence available such opinions can only be regarded as conjectural. What is certain is that in the 1960s the Blackbird was one of our commonest and most widely distributed breeding birds. The species was present in each of the 19 Common Birds Census areas over the years 1960-69, accounting for almost 12 per cent of the total number of territories recorded and outnumbering the Song Thrush by almost three to one. On Clapham Common, Blackbird territories formed 43 per cent of the total and in a hawthorn/oak copse at Walton the density was 4·1 pairs per ten acres (Griffin, 1970).

The resident population is considerably augmented in the autumn by immigrants from the Continent. Diurnal migration is not often reported for this species but significant increases are frequently recorded from certain areas particularly in September and October, the birds having arrived in overnight falls. For example an influx of 250-300 was noted in Dulwich Woods in October 1957. Similar instances are regularly reported from a hawthorn/oak copse at the Walton Reservoirs where the birds congregate from late August onwards to feed on the berry crop, numbers usually reaching a peak of 300-500 in November and early December. Hard weather influxes are also occasionally reported and a number of such occurred in November and December 1961 at Beddington SF and in December at Holmethorpe SPS.

Ringing recoveries have also provided ample evidence of the influx of winter visitors and seven birds ringed during the winter months in Surrey have been recovered as follows: Spain: one, Sweden: two, Finland: one, France: one and the Netherlands: two. A bird ringed as a nestling at Antwerp, Belgium was trapped on three occasions at Woldingham in the winter of 1959/60. At least one locally bred bird has subsequently been recovered on the Continent—a juvenile ringed at Wimbledon on 13 May 1945 found at Brest, France on 25 January 1949. That birds also pass through the county to wintering areas further westwards has also been demonstrated by ringing; a bird trapped at Ewhurst on 9 January 1963 was recovered six weeks later at Launceston, Cornwall, 180 miles wsw.

Wheatear
Oenanthe
oenanthe

Extremely scarce summer visitor. Passage migrant.
As a summer visitor this species has suffered a sad decline in the present century. In Bucknill's time it was still quite common, breeding regularly in localities such as Epsom Downs and Common, Reigate, Walton, Banstead and Headley Heath, Box Hill, Leith Hill and most of the hills of west Surrey. Annual nesting was recorded in Richmond Park until 1908. The species had regularly nested in rabbit burrows in the Park but in 1904 the rabbits were killed off and their burrows outside the plantations filled in, depriving the Wheatears of their nesting sites (Collenette, 1937). Bentham found eight pairs nesting in the vicinity of the Frensham Ponds in 1909. One or two pairs continued to breed on Park Downs, Banstead, up to 1930 and in the following years a few pairs were present in May and June and probably nesting in north-west Surrey (*SEBR*). In 1934 eight nesting pairs could still be located in the Haslemere district. The Second World War seems to have marked the demise of the species as a regular breeding bird in the county and since 1950 breeding has only been recorded in three years: in 1955 in Richmond Park, in 1961 at Frensham and in 1969 on Hankley Common.

Parslow (1967) described a marked decrease in southern England in the present century; the species had disappeared or become very scarce as a breeding bird in several counties besides Surrey, where previously it had been locally common. The decline accelerated after the Second World War due to the loss of marginal land to agriculture and forestry and, in the mid-1950s the reduction of the rabbit population.

It is now most likely to be seen as a double passage migrant and such records appear to have increased in the 1950s and 1960s. In spring the species is one of the earliest arrivals and is regularly seen in March, early records being one at Milford on 16 March 1969 and two at Frensham on 19 March 1961. Main passage usually begins in April and lasts till the end of May. There is one record of a migrant on 10 June 1961 at Beddington SF. The largest number recorded in the spring has been 58 near Horley just north of Gatwick Airport on 14 March 1967 (N. V. McCanch). Autumn passage usually starts in the third week of July with peak numbers recorded in August and early September when parties of up to 20 birds are not uncommon in suitable localities on the North Downs and other open spaces. Passage lasts throughout October and occasionally into November, the latest record being one at Mitcham on 21 and 22 November 1959.

Reports are occasionally received, usually in the spring, of large birds thought to be of the Greenland race (*O.o. leucorrhoa*). There is little doubt that a few birds of this race do pass through Surrey in both migration seasons.

Stonechat
Saxicola torquata
Moderately common resident, locally distributed and partially migratory.

As with other chats this species has suffered a marked decline in numbers in the present century but its decline has been less marked than that of the Wheatear and Whinchat. At the end of the review period it appeared to be holding its own in the county. The breeding population has always been subject to considerable fluctuation in numbers and the species is particularly vulnerable in a hard winter when many overwintering birds are lost. It is interesting to note that work on the BTO Atlas Survey (1968-1972) has shown that Surrey is the only inland county supporting a good-sized breeding population.

Information from the first quarter of the present century is thin. Bucknill had described it, surprisingly, as much less common than the Whinchat but stated that it frequented most of the large furze-clad commons and bred regularly at Banstead, Epsom, Headley, Mitcham and Reigate. Dixon (1909) regarded it as locally distributed at Croydon, Tooting Bec and Richmond. Bentham referred to four or more pairs at Limpsfield in 1906 and thought it abundant at Thursley in 1907 and numerous around the Frensham Ponds in 1911. By 1913 Bentham claimed that in the Elstead area it outnumbered the Whinchat by 20 to one.

30 *Willow Tit*. This species has a widespread distribution in Surrey with a liking for damp, marshy areas where rotting tree stumps abound (*S. N. Dalton*)

There was a severe winter in 1916/17 which apparently
drastically reduced the breeding population but Bunyard in
1919 noted a slight recovery which was continuing in 1923
(*BB*, 13:229, 17:201). G. Douglas found that the species
was not uncommon in central Surrey prior to the Second
World War and up to ten pairs could usually be found on
Epsom Common. In 1933 the London Natural History
Society carried out a special investigation into its status;
within the Society's area in Surrey it was found to be present
only in seven localities of the North Downs, in Richmond
Park and on Mitcham and Wimbledon Commons. In the
mid-1930s the Stonechat appeared to be still holding its own
in west Surrey; in 1934 ten pairs were located on one heath,
it was still abundant in north-west Surrey in 1935 and well
distributed in the Thursley/Ockley area in 1936 (*SEBR*).
A series of hard winters in the following decade had a very
severe effect on breeding populations and in Surrey in the
LNHS Recording Area only one pair at Walton Heath was
known to have nested in 1947. This was the only record of
nesting in the whole of the London area. Some recovery
clearly took place in the 1950s and in 1961 as a result of a
special enquiry by L. J. Raynsford into the status of the
species in Surrey, 41 pairs were found distributed as follows:

Esher Common	1
Headley Heath	1
Worms Heath	1
Ash-Pirbright	8
Bagshot area	3
Blackheath	2
Chobham Common	4
Hindhead and Frensham	4
Milford-Tilford	16
Redlands (Dorking)	1
	41

The first three pairs cited above were in the LNHS Recording Area. Breeding was proved in the first two localities
and these were the first breeding records for the area since
1952. Clearly the species' strongholds in the county were the
heaths of west and north-west Surrey.

In the second half of the 1960s the species was shown to
be holding its own reasonably well despite the severe winter
of 1962/63. In 1965 P. G. Davies ringed 60 nestlings in the
Haslemere area, indicating a good-sized population there

31 *Cock Stonechat*. Still common on the western heaths of Surrey but sensitive to hard
weather (*R. K. Murton*)

and in 1969 at least 30 breeding pairs were reported to the Surrey Bird Club in the West Surrey Recording Area although there was evidence of only one other breeding pair in the county.

Magee (1965) in a report to the BTO discussed the national status of the species as shown in a census in 1961 and the causes of its general decline in Britain in the present century. He attributed some blame to the series of hard winters in mid-century, particularly the three winters from 1939 to 1942 when the species was given no time to recover its winter losses and also blamed loss of habitat although, as for instance in Surrey, the species had taken to a newly created habitat of a temporary nature—young conifer plantations in early stages of growth. Venables (1937) described its habitat requirement as mature, thick, tall heather with a bush or small tree for a song post, an association which has suffered severely in the county since 1950 due to fires and disturbance. Raynsford (1961) also drew attention to the limiting effect of scrub encroachment on the species' main heathland habitats.

Winter records of Stonechats are fairly commonplace but it is clear that many birds move away from their breeding areas during the winter months and winter sightings are often from areas that do not hold breeding pairs, as for instance Beddington SF, Thorpe GPS and Hersham SF, where two to four birds were recorded in the winter of 1969/70. That a proportion of the Surrey breeding population does migrate is suggested by a ringing recovery; a bird ringed at Frensham on 25 April 1965 was recovered in Spain on 15 December 1965.

Whinchat Very scarce summer visitor. Passage migrant.

Saxicola Like that of the Wheatear, the Whinchat's status has de-
rubetra clined drastically during the course of the review period. In 1900 it was a common nesting species but in 1970 one of the rarest breeding birds of the county. Bucknill described it as being less restricted in its haunts than the Wheatear and in his day it frequented almost any fairly large patch of furze or rough ground and undisturbed meadowland. It continued to nest in reasonable numbers in the first two or three decades of the present century. Bentham recorded five or six pairs breeding regularly on Walton Heath, breeding occurred on Bookham Common in 1933 and 1934 (G. Douglas), up to four pairs nested regularly in Richmond Park until 1940, but there were no further breeding records in the Surrey part of the LNHS Recording Area until one or

two pairs were reported breeding in a gravel pit area at
Walton for a number of years beginning in 1951. In outer
Surrey, as for the other chats, the western heaths have been
the strongholds of the species. In the early years of the
century it was abundant in the Farnham and Thursley/
Ockley Common areas and Bentham recorded numerous
nests found sometimes at a high density, as for instance
four nests in three acres (at Ockley in 1913). The published
records suggest a severe decline in numbers nesting in the
county from the mid-1930s to the early 1950s. Four pairs
were recorded at Bisley in 1952 and in the late 1950s breeding was occurring in three to five different localities. The
species was at its lowest ebb as a breeding bird in the early
1960s. No nesting pairs were recorded from 1961 to 1963,
one pair was proved to breed in 1964 but no breeding was
reported in 1965. Since then there has been a slight improvement with three to five pairs in territory in the period 1967-69
and two pairs proved to be breeding in 1967 and 1970.
Parslow (1967) reported a general decline in the Midlands
and south-east England in the present century, attributed
in part to the loss of suitable habitat. Loss of habitat has
been very evident in Surrey but this cannot account fully
for the severe drop in numbers that has occurred in the
county.

As a passage migrant the species is considerably later than
the Wheatear, with first arrivals not usually recorded till
the last week of April although in two of the ten years from
1959-68 birds were recorded in the second week—one at
Beddington on 13 April 1959 and one at Weybridge on 14
April 1968. There is one March record for the county;
H. E. Pounds recorded one at Addington on 9 March 1930.
Numbers of up to 20 birds occur in the first or second week
of May; unusually early and of an exceptionally large number, was the record from N. V. McCanch for 4 April 1967
when he counted 40 Whinchats just north of Gatwick Airport where migrating chats are frequently noted. Spring
passage is normally over by the end of May.

The autumn passage is on a larger scale than in spring
and usually lasts from the middle or end of July to early
October, peak numbers occurring towards the end of August
or in September. Concentrations of up to 12 are not uncommon at this time of year but the largest recorded number
in autumn was given by Bentham in 1932 when he reported
20 on Epsom Downs on 4 September. The latest record for
the county is of one seen by C. K. Dunkley on Epsom
Downs on 25 October 1968.

There is only one significant recovery of this species for the county; a bird ringed as a juvenile at Beddington on 12 August 1968 was recovered in Zaragoza province, Spain on 26 September 1969.

Redstart
Phoenicurus
phoenicurus

Moderately common summer visitor, locally distributed. Passage migrant.

The population of this species is known to have fluctuated considerably especially in southern England over the past hundred years. There was a marked decrease in number to about 1940 since when there has been some recovery (Parslow, 1967). Published records for Surrey appear to reflect the national trend. At the end of the review period the species was fairly widely distributed in park, heath and woodland where suitable nesting holes are usually available in old timber. It is generally confined to the rural areas but was still occurring in Richmond Park and spasmodically on Wimbledon Common.

Bucknill considered the species to be fairly common and referred to casual occurrences in Richmond Park, Streatham and Dulwich although he regarded it as most numerous on the sandy and alluvial sides of hills in outer Surrey. It was considered fairly common in north-west Surrey in 1935 (*SEBR*) and the *Haslemere List* (1955) referred to the species' becoming scarce before the Second World War but recovering by 1951 when at least seven or eight pairs were recorded nesting in the Haslemere area. In Richmond Park numbers had increased to a total of 20-25 pairs in 1935 and 1936 but had decreased to nine pairs by 1953 this being due, it was thought, to the removal of old timber and the consequent loss of nesting holes (*The Birds of the London Area*, 1957). The 1950s showed a continuing recovery and some fairly large concentrations were reported. In 1955 it was reported in the breeding season from 16 localities and at Wishstream, Camberley, 15 singing males were noted on 22 May. In 1956 seven or eight pairs were reported from Old Dean Common and seven pairs were located on the Surrey side of the border in Windsor Great Park. In that year the species was also recorded in 11 other localities during the breeding season. In the 1960s the highest concentrations continued to be reported from the west and north-west of the county. Between ten and 20 pairs were estimated to be on the Pirbright Ranges in 1964 and there were 16 pairs in the Ash/Cleygate/Pirbright complex of commons in 1966. It is possible however that towards the end of the period there was some decline in numbers. In the centre of the county it occurs regularly at East Horsley, Oxshott and Ashtead and in the east in suitable woodland along the North Downs and at Limpsfield Chart. Bucknill described how the species frequently nested in garden nest boxes in the nineteenth century but this habit has not been reported in recent years.

Main spring passage takes place during April but there are occasional March records, the earliest being 20 March 1961 at Frensham. Autumn passage is in the period August-October, peak numbers being in September and the latest recorded occurrence is of a male bird caught by a cat at Dulwich on 1 November 1966.

There is one ringing recovery for the county; a bird ringed as a juvenile at Ewhurst on 27 September 1965 was recovered in Portugal on 1 November in the same year.

Black Redstart
Phoenicurus ochruros

Very scarce summer visitor. Passage migrant and occasional winter visitor.

This species is one of the few that have colonized Britain in this century. It was first recorded nesting in Britain in 1923 and has bred regularly since 1939, numbers reaching a peak in 1945. Its many strongholds included bombed sites of the City of London (Fitter, 1965 and Parslow, 1967). It was first recorded as breeding in Surrey in 1941 in a bombed building in Wandsworth and next in a ruined building at the Croydon airport in 1944. In 1948 and 1950 breeding was suspected but not proved on the site of the new Guildford Cathedral while in 1952 breeding was also suspected at Kingston-on-Thames. In most years from 1956 to 1965, up to three pairs were recorded definitely breeding in the county at sites in Beddington (most notably at Croydon Power Station), at the power station at Kingston-on-Thames and in Southwark. Five breeding sites were given for 1964. In 1967 a pair successfully raised at least three young at a building site at Horley (N. V. McCanch); thereafter breeding records have been confined to the Croydon area and in 1970 one pair bred while two further pairs and two other males, were recorded in the breeding season in this general area.

In Britain the species appears to be dependent on large buildings (usually industrial) in association with waste or open ground and its rise and fall as a breeding species in London is thought to have been partly linked with the appearance and gradual disappearance of bombed sites in and after the Second World War.

As a passage migrant it has been widely reported throughout the county although records prior to the mid-1930s were irregular and few. From 1950 it was regularly reported on spring migration usually over the period—the last week in March to the end of April. Most autumn reports have occurred in October. There have been a few winter records, notably at Beddington SF where in certain winters in the period 1938-51 odd birds were recorded for periods from one to three months and over-wintering may have occurred (*The Birds of the London Area*, 1957). In the last decade of the review period however, winter records were confined to late November birds in 1960 and 1961 at Holmethorpe and Epsom respectively.

Nightingale
Luscinia
megarhynchos

Moderately common summer visitor. Passage migrant. Although the Nightingale is still common in certain localities there is no doubt that the species has declined appreciably as a breeding bird in the county. What is open to doubt however is the full extent and range of the decline.

Bucknill accorded it the status of 'abundant summer visitor' and gave it as fairly common as near to the centre of London as Wimbledon and Richmond Park and even present in some years at Balham, Battersea Park and Clapham Junction. Further he regarded the Godalming area as the area where the species was most abundant in the county. Recalling his schooldays at Charterhouse (in the 1880s) he described the sale to the Charterhouse boys by the local lads of literally dozens of Nightingale eggs every Sunday in summer. Rusticus (1849) had referred to every coppice containing numbers and every garden its two or three pairs in the neighbourhood of Godalming. It is possible that these early references give a slightly false impression of the species' abundance and there may be room for doubt on the specific identification of the 'Nightingale eggs'. On the other hand not for nothing would hordes of bird catchers make trips in early summer way out into rural Surrey in search of the most prized song bird.

Dixon (1909) regarded the Nightingale as still a common bird in Surrey. Bentham found it numerous around Itchingwood Common in 1912 and very numerous at Brockham and on Holmwood Common in 1918. Beadell (1932) described it as well distributed ('many nests found') around Warlingham. *The Birds of the London Area* (1957) referred to its gradual displacement from areas close to London with the spread of the suburbs, recording however, that it was still breeding on Wimbledon Common in 1950 and regarding it as still common in the belt of country between the southern fringe of London (Walton, Epsom, Purley) and the North

Downs as well as on the downs themselves up to about the 400 feet contour.

There are indications that the species generally declined in the county in the 1950s and 1960s but some of the evidence is rather conflicting and it would be unwise to postulate a sharp decline at a particular point. It is possible however, to give some local changes of status over varying periods. By 1970 the species had become relatively scarce in the London fringe of the North Downs area. Again in May 1933, P. A. D. Hollom in a survey covering an area of six square miles south-east of Addlestone (6″ O.S. Sheet 11) found 26 singing males (*BB*, 28:81-2), whereas J. A. Sage in a survey over the same ground in 1968 and 1969 found none at all. In 1960, 11 singing males were located on Ashtead Common but by 1969 none was present there. However, in an area of 96 acres of scrub on Bookham Common, where the species was absent in 1964 and 1965, one territory was recorded in 1966 and the number of territories increased annually so that five were given for 1970. L. J. Raynsford reported that 'within the general pattern of decline 1969 was a more encouraging year' and in 1970 recorded 28 in song on the periphery of Dunsfold Airfield and 26 in song on Rodborough and Witley Commons. In 1970 the Surrey Bird Club organized a 'Nightingale Week' in an attempt to plot all singing males in the county. A total of 163 birds was recorded with the main concentration in the south-west of the county around Dunsfold/Alfold and Witley, Rodborough and Milford. Only partial coverage of the county was obtained but it included two-thirds of the sites which had been recently active. If allowance is made for those missed and ground not covered, the likely county population stood in the range of 200-300 pairs.

The species requires fairly dense cover such as bramble, thorn thicket and rose scrub for nesting and will adapt, where this cover is present, to agricultural land with thick hedgerows, common or downland or open woodland. The most favoured area—Dunsfold/Alfold is largely agricultural and consists of rough meadowland with small fields and high, thick, thorn hedges.

A bird ringed as a nestling at Pyrford on 14 June 1926 was recovered at Leatherhead on 20 August 1929.

Although direct evidence of passage migrant status is lacking there is little doubt that passage birds do occur in the county.

Bluethroat Extremely scarce vagrant.
Cyanosylvia In 1900 Bucknill had traced one specimen each of the Red-
svecica spotted and White-spotted races (*C. s. svecica and cyane-*
cula) both then in the Charterhouse Collection. In the present
century there have been only two acceptable records—both
in the 1960s. One, of indeterminate race, was seen at Beddington on 22 September 1963 and the other a bird of the
year of the White-spotted race was trapped and ringed by
L. G. Weller at Ewhurst on 30 August 1965.

Robin Abundant resident. Passage migrant.
Erithacus The Robin is widespread and common throughout the whole
rubecula county being abundant in woodland (particularly oak), a
familiar garden bird and absent only from the most heavily
built-up areas. There is no evidence to suggest that its overall
status has changed in the present century. In the 19 Common
Birds Census areas in the 1960s this species came second
in order of abundance with 1,132 out of a grand total of
11,078 recorded territories in 84 census plot years. It was
absent only from Clapham Common and the highest density
was recorded in oak woodland on Bookham Common with
an average number of 8.5 territories per ten acres (Griffin,
1970). This is not an uncommon level for stands of deciduous woodland and has been found, for instance, in 11
acres of woodland in Stoke Park, Guildford.

Some shift of population probably takes place in the
autumn and winter with birds tending to move away from
woodlands into gardens and other ground in search of food.
There have been reports also of local temporary increases
particularly in September suggesting movement or passage,
though the origin of birds is not known. Ringing returns
indicate either migration or hard weather movements. An
adult ringed at Godstone on 7 February 1959 was recovered
at Bridgewater, Somerset, 125 miles to the west, on 23 May
in the same year. A bird ringed at Ewhurst on 7 August
1965 was recovered at La Bernerie (Loire Atlantique), France,
on 16 January 1966 and a particularly interesting recovery
was of a juvenile bird ringed at Ewhurst on 31 July 1966
recovered at Klosters, Switzerland on 18 April 1969.

Bucknill referred to the habit of the species of singing at
night particularly in spring and this is still frequently
reported in the county.

Grasshopper Moderately common summer visitor. Passage migrant.
Warbler The secretive and skulking nature of this species makes it a
Locustella difficult bird to study but its reeling song does fortunately
naevia compensate somewhat for its shy nature and provides the

main evidence for its presence and distribution in the county. Bucknill described it as a regular summer visitor present on most furze-clad commons and recorded from almost every part of the county. In the first decade of the century Bentham heard birds reeling at Cutt Mill, Hankley, and Hedgecourt and found a nest in thick heather on Thursley Common in 1908. Bunyard (*BB*, 13:228) considered it very plentiful in 1919 but in 1923 he blamed fires for having driven it from many of the Surrey commons. In 1934 the *South Eastern Bird Report* reported the species as widely distributed on the west Surrey commons. On Epsom Common 15-20 pairs were present in 1938 but these were reduced to four pairs by 1948 (*The Birds of the London Area*, 1957). The species does however appear to be subject to considerable fluctuations in numbers and in the early 1950s the Surrey population was at a low ebb. The *Haslemere List* (1955) described it then as a very uncommon visitor and in 1955 it was reported from only Frensham and Thursley Commons (CNHS, 1959) while in north central Surrey it could be regularly found only on two sites, Ashtead and Bookham Commons. The 1960s however saw a gradual improvement in the number and range of its occurrences and by the end of the review period it had become locally very common and widespread. In 1969 over 44 singing males were reported from at least 32 different areas with concentrations of up to ten pairs on Ashtead Common and at Oxshott and five pairs in the Thorpe/Virginia Water area; 1970 was an even more successful year with records of 140 singing males in 47 localities. Breeding was recorded on Banstead Downs for the first time in nine years and a large concentration (at least 12) was found on the periphery of Dunsfold Airfield.

The species' habitat requirement is a fairly open area of waste, meadow or commonland with a rank growth of grass, bramble, heather or such vegetation with hedges, scattered bushes or low trees for song posts. It seems to be much less associated with gorse than in earlier days. Both wet and dry situations are used if other conditions are right. On a national scale young conifer plantations are now considered to be one of its most important habitats (Parslow, 1967) and the species is quick to exploit this habitat to the full in Surrey. One such area of forestry land at Prince's Coverts, Oxshott, has held a population varying from four to ten pairs or more from 1957 to 1970 with birds moving to newly cleared areas as the trees grew in height and became too dense. Examples of wet grass association were reported in 1970 from Peasmarsh and water meadows at Broadford, Burpham and Unstead. Typical dry association localities reported in 1970 were Clandon Downs, Guildford, Hindcombe Bottom, Merrow Downs (four or five in song on 13 May 1970) and Stoke Park (Guildford).

The species is not normally recorded until after the middle of April. Early dates have been 7 April 1969 on Esher Common and 3 April 1970 on Reigate Heath. In autumn it has been recorded up to the end of September (one was on Ashtead Common on 30 September 1969).

Great Reed Warbler
Acrocephalus arundinaceus

Extremely scarce vagrant.

Prior to 1900 there was only one definite record of this species for the county: a bird shot at Ockford Pond, Godalming, in the spring of 1858. Over a century was to pass before the species was again recorded, this time at Frensham Great Pond where a bird stayed from 5-19 June 1965 and was trapped and ringed (*BB*, 59:294). Surprisingly, another bird appeared on the Great Pond on 29 May in the following year; this too was trapped and ringed and stayed till 6 June (*BB*, 60:324).

Reed Warbler
Acrocephalus scirpaceus

Moderately common summer resident. Passage migrant.

The occurrence and distribution of this species is more than usually restricted owing to its preference for aquatic habitats where the Reed (*Phragmites communis*) grows. It is therefore limited to the fringes of lakes, gravel pits, sewage farms and riversides and this last habitat has been severely restricted in recent years because of the growing practice by River Boards of completely clearing river banks of vegetation. Bucknill considered the species rather scarce but described it as nesting sparingly on the upper reaches of the R. Wey, on the R. Thames and on the R. Mole between Betchworth and Cobham where in his day the banks were high with reeds, bushes were uncut and the stream was unnavigable—a very different picture from that of the neat and bare riversides of the 1960s. In the first half of the present century Bentham recorded small breeding populations at Albury, Godstone, Leigh Mill, Vachery and Wire Mill Ponds and at Beddington and Epsom SFs. The *Haslemere List* (1955) reported that a small population nested in *Phragmites* at Frensham Great Pond every year until 1939. The pond was drained during the war, the reed died and its Reed Warblers left. After the refilling of the pond in 1954 the *Phragmites* again appeared and Reed Warblers were back again in that year. By the end of the 1960s there were thriving colonies at both the Great and Little Frensham

Ponds. The species has certainly declined in numbers in areas close to London since 1950 but this appears to be linked with a loss of suitable habitats. Small populations were still persisting in the late 1960s at Pen Ponds, Richmond Park and on a small reed-fringed pool at Barn Elms Reservoir. In outer Surrey at the end of the review period breeding colonies were present at Frensham, Guildford SF, Hamm Moor, Papercourt and Thorpe GPS, on the Tillingbourne at Abinger, Albury, Gatton and Gomshall, Silvermere Lake and, in the extreme south-east of the county, at Wire Mill Pond. A few other localities had at least occasional pairs in the breeding season.

Although breeding is usually restricted to Reed there have been records of nesting in osier beds, in vegetation dominated by Reedmace (*Typha latifolia*) as at Guildford SF and in 1967 L. J. Raynsford recorded a successful nest in brambles at Frensham.

As a summer migrant the Reed Warbler is one of the latest to arrive. Although 'firsts' in April are not uncommon most birds do not appear till the first weeks of May. The earliest record for the county was on 14 April 1935 at Warlingham. Last dates are usually recorded in October and the latest record was of a bird singing at Frensham on 22 October 1969.

Birds ringed at Frensham have been recovered in Portugal in September and Spain in October. Recoveries also reflect the passage of birds through the county to other parts of the British Isles and of the movement between colonies in the county from one year to the next.

Marsh Warbler
Acrocephalus palustris

Extremely sporadic summer resident and passage migrant. The first record of this species in the county was at Richmond 24 April—8 May 1906 but the record was not unreservedly accepted and was put in square brackets by *British Birds* (1:84). There were however no reservations for a record from G. W. Kerr who found two successive nests with eggs in an osier bed near Thorpe in June 1907 (*BB*, 1:186). The *South Eastern Bird Report* has a record of a nest of this species found in the lower part of a bramble bush surrounded by rushes and coarse grass at Bookham in 1934 but it is not clear whether this record was fully authenticated.

The next record was in 1958 when Bentham located a bird he identified by song and field description as a Marsh Warbler, on 23 June at Gatton Park. Two different birds were seen subsequently and at least one of them was seen by a second observer. Behaviour suggesting the birds were feeding young was noted and on 11 July, Bentham described what he was convinced was a juvenile bird.

In 1961 a male *Acrocephalus* warbler took up territory at Guildford SF for about a fortnight and two experienced watchers, R. K. Murton and N. J. Westwood, observed that habitat, song, appearance and behaviour were typical of the Marsh Warbler.

The last record of the species in the review period was of a bird trapped at Walton Reservoirs by the Hersham Ringing Group on 9 July 1966. It was caught in rank willowherb and thought to be a bird of the year.

Sedge Warbler
Acrocephalus schoenobaenus

Moderately common summer resident. Passage migrant. This species is less restricted than the Reed Warbler in its choice of habitat although its distribution and numerical strength in Surrey at the end of the review period was similar to that of the Reed Warbler. It has certainly decreased as a breeding species since 1900 when Bucknill described it as an abundant summer visitor breeding freely along the banks of the Rivers Mole, Thames, Wandle and Wey and small streams and as present at Dulwich and in Wimbledon Park. Information on its breeding distribution in the first half of the present century is sadly lacking. Bentham recorded that on 1 June 1907 the marshes at Wire Mill Pond were alive with singing Sedge Warblers but that there was a great falling off in numbers in later years. Venables (1933) reported that it bred in the small marsh in the south-east corner of Frensham Little Pond and all along the south shore of the Great Pond. In 1969 breeding was still taking place at Frensham Little Pond but Common Birds Census figures for the Great Pond area showed a declining trend in the last half of the 1960s with territories established as follows: 1964: three, 1965 and 1966: six, 1967 and 1968: two and 1969: nil.

During the late 1950s and 1960s breeding has been recorded at Barn Elms, the sewage farms at Beddington and Hersham, Chertsey Meads, the gravel pits at Frimley and Thorpe, various sites near Weybridge (including Brooklands and Hamm Moor), the R. Wey at Eashing, Godalming, Pyrford and Sutton Place, the Enton and Cutt Mill Ponds, Gatton Park and Gatwick. However breeding has been far from continuous at many of these sites and in 1969 was recorded at only seven, the total estimated numbers of pairs being less than 30. In that year national Common Birds Census figures reflected a serious reduction in common with the Whitethroat but the records for 1970 indicated some recovery in numbers. In 1970 the Wey Valley appeared to be holding the largest number of breeding pairs and J. J. Wheatley assessed the probable breeding strength as follows: Broadford: a colony of several pairs, Unstead: at least one pair on water meadows, Millmead, Guildford: four or five pairs, Stoke water meadows, Guildford: five to ten pairs and Guildford SF: two or three pairs. There have been no breeding records from the South Recording Area since 1962.

First arrivals are usually recorded in the second half of April—the earliest dates are 6 April 1951 (at Godstone) and 7 April 1953 (at Frensham). Dispersal of young and passage begins in August and, throughout August and September good numbers frequently build up at favoured feeding areas such as sewage farms and gravel pits. In 1961 at Hersham SF there were 40 birds present on 5 August; a peak of c. 70 was reached on 2 September, numbers had dropped to ten on 10 September and the last bird was recorded on 7 October. A late record was of one bird at Hamm Moor on 22 October 1969.

The recapture of a bird ringed on 6 September 1967 at Swillington Ings, Yorkshire, at Egham six days later demonstrates that birds breeding in other areas pass through the county on passage.

Aquatic Warbler *Acrocephalus paludicola*

Extremely scarce vagrant.
The Aquatic Warbler has been recorded once in the county; a juvenile bird was trapped and ringed at Beddington SF on 20 September 1959 (*BB*, 53:424).

Blackcap *Sylvia atricapilla*

Common summer visitor, regularly over-wintering. Passage migrant.
This species is widely distributed and common throughout the county in suitable habitats including large gardens and parks and is more likely to be found in built-up areas than its near 'cousin' the Garden Warbler. Its status relative to the Garden Warbler's during most of the review period is not clear. Bucknill had considered the Blackcap to be the more numerous species. In 1912 Bentham considered it to be not so abundant as the 'numerous Garden Warbler' and in 1920 believed that there were more Garden Warblers than Blackcaps in the Elstead area. J. E. Harting, in a lecture in 1910, stated that the Blackcap was seldom or never seen in the Weybridge area which was certainly not the case in the 1960s. A report in the *South Eastern Bird Report* gave it as less common than the Garden Warbler in the Limpsfield

district in 1934. The Common Birds Census studies in Surrey 1960-69 showed the two species roughly equal in distribution but with numerical advantage to the Blackcap. There were 155 territories of Blackcaps in 13 of the 19 areas studied compared with 82 territories of Garden Warblers in 12 areas. The areas in which the two species held territory nearly coincided; this indicated the considerable extent to which both species utilize the same habitat (woodland or copse with undergrowth) (*per* D. Griffin, 1970). At Ashtead in the late 1960s the Blackcap nested one year and the Garden Warbler the next in almost identical situations at a tennis court overgrown with brambles. However, during the same period, in Prince's Coverts, Oxshott where the ground cover was thick and impenetrable and the tree height up to ten feet or more, the Blackcap was scarce and the Garden Warbler a comparatively common nester. Thus it can be seen that the Garden Warbler tolerates denser scrub than the Blackcap and in some localities, as for instance where there are young conifer plantations with scrub and bramble, rose and thorn left to grow unchecked, Garden Warbler breeding densities can be high. The Garden Warbler can tolerate the absence of trees whereas the Blackcap appears to require at least a partially sylvan setting for breeding.

The species was first recorded wintering in Surrey in 1937 when a female suddenly appeared on 12 February and fed daily on chipped peanuts at a garden bird table in Haslemere till about 20 March (*SEBR*). There were no further records of wintering until 1959 when a female was seen in Leatherhead on 25 December. From that year to the end of the review period odd birds have been seen in most winters.

The first spring records are usually in March though it is often difficult to judge whether they refer to migrant birds or over-wintering birds on the move. The main arrival is usually from the middle to the end of April. The main autumn passage is in September, with stragglers seen in October and occasionally November.

Two ringing recoveries are of interest; a bird ringed as a juvenile on 13 September 1958 at Chaldon was recovered in the Basses-Pyrénées, France on 21 October 1959 and a female ringed at Guildford on 19 October 1959 was recovered on 16 February 1961 at Morengo, Algeria.

Garden Common summer visitor. Passage migrant.
Warbler The status and habitat preferences of this species relative to
Sylvia borin the Blackcap are discussed under Blackcap. The Garden

Warbler was widely distributed throughout the county at the end of the review period. There are however few records before 1950. Bentham described the species as numerous or very numerous in the first quarter of the present century in such localities are Addington, Elstead, Leigh Mill (Godstone), Leith Hill, Ockley, Selsdon Woods and Wonersh. In 1934 it was reported as sparsely distributed in central and eastern Surrey (SEBR); however it seems unlikely that its general status in the county has undergone much change in the present century.

The species is later to arrive than the Blackcap and there is only one known March record for the county—on 27 March 1954 on Epsom Common. Usually birds begin to appear in the third week of April with main passage lasting through the first half of May. Departure and autumn passage is in the period August to October (latest date 14 October 1965 at Ewhurst) and at the end of the review period there were no records of birds over-wintering in the county.

Good numbers of Garden Warblers have been ringed in the county; in 1965 for instance L. G. Weller ringed 87 at Ewhurst (compared with 44 Blackcaps) and P. G. Davis ringed 30 nestlings in that year in the Haslemere area. Recoveries of the species have been few, with less than 50 in the national statistics by the late 1960s. The only foreign recovery of a Surrey-ringed bird was in fact the first for Britain from Norway. It was ringed fully grown on 24 August 1965 at Ewhurst and recovered at Tønsberg on 5 May 1969.

Whitethroat
Sylvia communis

Very common summer visitor. Passage migrant. Of the warblers summering in the county this species is second only to the Willow Warbler in abundance; it is widespread except in the most built-up areas of London. Its habitat preference is for open areas of common or waste ground with thick patches of ground vegetation such as bramble, thorn, rose, nettle, gorse and heather. It will also tolerate agricultural land where the hedges are thick enough, or there are sufficient marginal areas to give it the cover it needs. Bucknill regarded it as abundant in the rural areas but there are insufficient data prior to 1960 to determine what population changes, if any, had taken place between 1900 and that year. With the advent of the Common Birds Census in 1961 it became possible to make quantitative assessment of some of our common breeding birds such as the Whitethroat. In the studies in Surrey the Whitethroat came tenth in order of abundance with 464 territories estab-

lished in a grand total of 11,078 territories of all species
recorded in 19 areas over 84 census plot years (Griffin,
1970). It was present in all areas studied with the exception
of agricultural downland at Leatherhead (an area with little
or no ground or secondary cover) and Clapham Common
with a similar deficiency. The highest density was recorded
on Ashtead Common in 1968 with 3·4 pairs per ten acres.
Ashtead Common is open commonland (on clay) with
patches of thick ground cover of bramble and gorse and
probably represents the species' optimum habitat. In all the
areas studied where Whitethroats were present there was a
severe drop in numbers of breeding pairs in 1969 with
numbers of recorded territories down to a quarter or less of
those of previous years. This crash was nationwide and no
full explanation of it has been postulated. However, numbers in 1970 showed some signs of recovery and gave cause
for hope that the 1969 drop marked only a temporary set-
back.

The species is usually first recorded in the second week
of April (earliest date—6 April 1961) with peak numbers
passing through in the last week of April or in early May.
Autumn passage is mainly in August and September with
occasional stragglers sometimes recorded in October. A late
record was for 22 October 1963 at Ewhurst.

There have been foreign recoveries from France and
Portugal. A bird ringed as a nestling at West Byfleet on
26 May 1923 was recovered at Sernache do Bon Jardine,
Portugal on 4 October 1929 and another so ringed at Fren-
sham Ponds on 26 June 1923 was recovered at Limoges,
France in September 1923. Two fully grown birds ringed
in summer months at Ewhurst were recovered—one at
Alvites, Portugal on 2 Sepember 1962 exactly a month after
ringing and the other on 7 October 1952 at La Gironde,
France in the year of ringing. Another fully grown bird
ringed at Haslemere on 6 August 1962 was recovered at
Sacavem, Portugal on 28 September 1962.

Lesser Common summer visitor. Passage migrant.
Whitethroat Bucknill described this species as not as numerous generally
Sylvia as the Whitethroat although more abundant in some locali-
curruca ties and this description held good at the end of the review
period. The species is widely reported in the county but is
relatively scarce on the sandy heathlands north of the Hog's
Back. It adapts more readily to agricultural country than the
Whitethroat and is found in thick hedgerows with scattered
trees as well as on common and downland with scrub, so

32 *Grasshopper Warbler.* An expanding species in the county but much more often
heard than seen; nests are rarely found (*S. N. Dalton*)

long as taller bushes are present to provide song posts. L. J. Raynsford (*SBCQB*, 8, *February* 1959) pointed out its liking for an association with Ash (*Fraximus excelsior*) (tree or sapling) in its choice of road or trackside thicket.

In the Haslemere district the species was reported as very scarce in 1934 except in the hedgerows and on the Weald clay where it was quite common while in 1945 it was described as well distributed and slightly more numerous than the Whitethroat (*SEBR*). Bentham also considered it to be more numerous than the Whitethroat in the Hedgecourt Pond area in 1914. In 1939 Bentham found 12 nests on Ashtead Common, the highest concentration recorded in the county.

In the early 1960s breeding season records submitted to the Surrey Bird Club totalled 20-25 annually. The records in the second half of the decade were less than half this number although it is far from clear that this can be taken as an indication of a decline. In any case the breeding population is known to fluctuate considerably from one year to another (Parslow, 1967) and no long term changes in the national status have been detected. The Common Birds Census studies in Surrey show it to be less widespread and more thinly distributed in the county than the Whitethroat. In the period 1960-69 24 breeding territories were recorded in 84 census plot years in nine areas out of the 19 studied, the largest concentration being on agricultural land (Wealden clay) at Haslemere.

The first arrivals are usually recorded in the third and fourth week of April, with stragglers still passing through in early May. Autumn passage lasts from August to September, there being occasional October records. There have been no foreign recoveries of Surrey-ringed birds.

Extremely scarce and local resident. **Dartford**
The Dartford Warbler has long been the subject of con- **Warbler**
siderable interest in Surrey and has been regarded with *Sylvia*
something akin to affection by many generations of ornitho- *undata*
logists. For this reason its fortunes have been fairly well documented and it is possible to describe in some detail its history in the county.

In Britain and in Surrey in particular, the species is on the northern fringe of its European breeding range and is subject to considerable fluctuations in numbers. As far as Surrey is concerned, it sometimes becomes extinct following adverse weather or retreats through loss of habitat and then gradually recolonizes, to start the cycle again. In the present century the species has largely been confined to the western

33 *Red-backed Shrike*, carrying Bumble Bee. Formerly common, now fewer than half a dozen pairs are recorded annually (*D. M. T. Ettlinger*)

heather commons but has occurred sporadically in the north-east of the county prior to 1940.

In the nineteenth century peak numbers were probably present around 1850 after which a slow decline commenced (Raynsford, 1963). In 1900 Bucknill considered it to be a somewhat rare species but thought it might be described as abundant in several places. In the environs of London it was regarded as extinct on Walton and Reigate Heaths in 1901 (*Zool.*) but it was recorded again in the former area in the years 1912-15. A nest was found on Putney Heath in 1910 after some years of watching and the species was present there until at least 1913.

In its south-western stronghold on the commons at Hankley and Thursley/Elstead, Bentham estimated the population at about 20 pairs in 1908. There was a very severe winter in 1916/17 and the species was all but wiped out in the county. Bunyard (*BB*, 13:228, 17:200) could find no birds in 1919 and it was not till 1922 that he could report that birds were nesting again but fire destroyed large tracts of the habitat in that year and the species had disappeared again in 1923. In 1927 Bentham found a pair on Walton Heath and breeding was proved there in 1928 but the birds were apparently eliminated again by the hard winter of 1929/30. However, the species made a remarkable comeback in the early 1930s and a census taken by L. S. V. Venables and H. Thompson in south-west Surrey in 1933 produced an estimated population of 80-90 pairs with 40 pairs on one common alone. The species nested on Chobham Common in 1929-34 (P. A. D. Hollom) and in 1935 the *South Eastern Bird Report* described the bird as comparatively abundant in north-west Surrey and 12 pairs were seen and eight nests found in an area of less than one square mile.

The species also recolonized old haunts in the north-east of the county. Bentham found two nests on Walton Heath in 1935 and by 1938 eight pairs were present there. Only two immature cocks were found in 1939 at this site but three pairs bred on nearby Headley Heath. A pair had also bred on Wimbledon Common in 1936. This burst of nesting activity however was to mark the species' last appearance in the north-east of the county. A series of hard winters from 1939/40 to 1941/42 followed and much destruction of habitat finally put an end to this population and apart from stragglers seen on Epsom Common in the winter of 1937/38 none has been recorded in that area since then. The occupation by the military authorities during the Second World War greatly damaged the habitat in west Surrey and following the hard winter of 1939/40 the Dartford Warbler probably became extinct in the county once more.

Breeding again took place in 1953 in two localities in the south-west; from then on there was a steady build-up and in 1961, despite the loss of over 500 acres of suitable heathland through fire, a minimum of 35 pairs were established in west Surrey, centred principally on three traditional heathland sites in the south-west but with records from new areas and from the north-west where the habitat was recovering after previous fires. The position at the end of the 1961 breeding season was therefore good; there was plenty of available habitat and the species was poised to regain its 1930 status but tragedy was to strike at the species yet again. The next disaster was described by L. J. Raynsford (*SBCQB*, 21 *March* 1962) in the following words:

'A spell of hard frost commenced 14 December 1961. Coldest days 18 December local minus 19 degrees Fahrenheit, 25 December local minus 18 degrees F. and 28 December minus 15 degrees F. Dartford Warblers seen on 27 December were lively and vociferous. Snow fell on 31 December starting in the early hours, about five inches everywhere at dawn and followed by another fall of three inches. A spartan observer who ventured on one of the principal commons described the scene as a vast white blanket humped here and there by bent-over gorse. For three days the canopy was unyielding, as is explained by the following temperatures (F.): 1 January: maximum 27—minimum 10, 2 January: maximum 30—minimum 22, 3 January: maximum 34—minimum 14. Then a steady thaw set in. As soon as the snow disappeared the first reconnaissances were carried out. No Dartford Warblers were seen or heard. Two Woodlarks were seen in three patrols and it was an event even to hear a Wren. No Dartford Warblers seen again 1962. It was surmised that most ground or near-ground roosting birds were literally imprisoned by the snow and starved to death. The corpse of one Dartford Warbler was found in a sandstone crevice.'

It is reasonably certain that this snowfall on the last day of 1961 killed all the Surrey breeding population of Dartford Warblers at that time and no further records at all were received during the next eight years. Then in 1969 evidence of breeding was recorded in an area north of the Hog's Back where earlier in the year two pairs had been seen. No further records were received from this site in 1970 but a cock was heard and seen at a different site in May and a second bird was seen in this same area but no breeding evidence was recorded. In 1971 in one locality an agitated bird was watched on 27 June carrying food to various spots as if feeding dispersed young.

At the end of the review period therefore the species was poised in a precarious position and attempting once more to make a home in Surrey.

The preferred habitat of the Dartford Warbler in Surrey appears to be well-grown Heather (*Calluna vulgaris*) of at least two feet in height representing eight to ten years of growth. Venables (1937) examined at least 80 nests in west Surrey all of which were in Heather in this stage of growth, the nest being supported below the surface of the vegetation in the fork of the heather stem or on a gorse spray or even the lower branches of a pine sapling. The habitat in this stage of growth is of course very vulnerable, fire risk being a continual hazard although it must be stressed that without this burning the habitat would completely disappear under a climax vegetation of birch and pine. L. J. Raynsford has drawn attention to a comparatively new hazard to the Dartford Warbler's habitat—the invasion of the commons by birch scrub. The point of intolerance in the species is probably reached when five foot saplings exceed 75 to the acre (*SBCQB*, 17 *March* 1961).

When the species is thriving resident birds remain on the commons throughout the winter and thus, of course, they often fall victim to severe spells of weather. There is however some evidence of dispersal to the south coast in the autumn (*Bird Migration*, 2:83) and there seems little doubt that Surrey has in the past been recolonized by birds from other less vulnerable areas in Hampshire and Dorset.

Willow Warbler
Phylloscopus trochilus

Abundant summer visitor. Passage migrant. This is the commonest summer visitor and is found in suitable habitats almost throughout the county; it is particularly abundant in deciduous open woodland, heathland with birch and sallow and plantation land where young trees offer thick ground cover. It also breeds in parks and large gardens where sufficient ground vegetation is allowed to flourish.

In 19 Common Birds Census areas studied from 1960-69 the Willow Warbler came eighth in order of abundance (and 'top' of the summer visitors) with 517 territories out of a grand total number of 11,078 in 84 census plot years. It was absent only from farmland at Chessington, cultivated downland at Leatherhead and from Clapham Common. The highest recorded density was on Holmbury Hill, a dry area of heather and pine with heavy birch scrub penetration where a density of 3·5 pairs per ten acres was recorded (Griffin, 1970). At Park Down, Banstead eight territories in 8·8 acres of hawthorn scrub were recorded in 1970, this giving a density of nine pairs per ten acres. In another good habitat on 96 acres of scrub and grassland at Bookham Common over the period 1964-69 recorded territories have been as follows: 20, 14, 19, 27, 21 and 26.

It is first recorded in most years in March but the main arrival takes place in the first and second weeks of April and passage continues into May. Peak autumn passage is in August and last records are usually at the end of September or in the first or second weeks of October. Occasionally birds are recorded in the winter months, as for instance one at Sutton on 11 November 1931 and one at New Haw on 19 February 1967.

Two birds ringed at Guildford and Haslemere in August were recovered three weeks later in north central Spain and north-eastern Spain respectively. One bird ringed in the nest at Haslemere was recovered the following year from north Portugal in September. Two August-ringed birds from Haslemere were recovered in subsequent years from the Pennines in Yorkshire.

Chiffchaff
Phylloscopus
collybita

Very common summer visitor, frequently over-wintering. Passage migrant.

The Chiffchaff is widely distributed and common in suitable habitats throughout the county. It is a bird of mature woodland where there is secondary growth of ground vegetation in which it can nest but it will readily colonize small copses and gardens that offer the right combination of ground cover and tree height. It is far less numerous than the Willow Warbler in Surrey and has noticeably different habitat preferences.

There is no evidence of any changes in status in the present century. Details from the Common Birds Census in Surrey show that the species was regularly present in five areas out of 19 with a total registration of 101 territories in 84 census plot years compared with 517 for the Willow Warbler. The largest concentration was recorded in 40 acres of oakwood on Bookham Common where registered territories varied from one to seven (average four) over the ten years 1960-69 (Griffin, 1970). Two to four singing males were, in the late 1960s, normally present in 20 acres of mixed matured woodland with underscrub in Stoke Park, Guildford and areas such as this seem to hold the highest densities.

The species regularly over-winters in Surrey. It did so in Bucknill's time but the number of recorded instances greatly increased in the 1960s and at the end of the review period odd birds were recorded annually in winter at sewage farms or in wood or scrub with an aquatic association.

The Chiffchaff is one of the first summer visitors to arrive but it is impossible to separate early passage birds in February from over-wintering individuals. It is usually recorded in March, often in the first week but peak numbers generally occur in the last week or in early April. The species is often observed in falls after nights of heavy passage, as for example 200 counted at Silvermere on 27 March 1955. Autumn passage lasts from August to October with largest numbers occurring in the second half of September. At times of passage the species is not confined to woodland and readily resorts to scrubland, gardens and sewage farms.

Birds showing characteristics of the Scandinavian race (*P. c. abientinus*) are occasionally reported, usually in autumn although Bentham provided one spring record from Walton Heath on 25 April 1948.

The few recoveries that have been recorded of Surrey ringed birds give some indication of the species' migration route to Africa through Spain and Portugal. A bird ringed at Chessington on 20 September 1959 was recovered a fortnight later at Estremadura, Portugal and a bird ringed at Thorpe in August 1966 was retrapped at the Biological Station on the Coto Donana, Spain on 23 October of the same year.

Wood Warbler
Phylloscopus sibilatrix

Moderately common summer visitor, locally distributed. Passage migrant.

The Wood Warbler is the least common of the leaf warblers nesting in Surrey. It is dependent on open woodland which has no more than a thin cover of ground vegetation and because of this requirement its distribution in the county is local although widespread. Its greatest concentration probably occurs in woodland on the Lower Greensand from Limpsfield in the east through the Leith Hill area to the south-western woodlands at Haslemere. In these areas L. J. Raynsford has pointed out that the preferred nesting site is usually in an association of ground vegetation dominated by Bilberry (*Vaccinium myrtillus*) (*SBCQB*, 17, *March*

1961). The species is also found in the beech woods of the North Downs, from the Shirley Hills in the east to the Sheepleas in the west, where ground cover is sufficient. Bilberry is of course absent from these chalklands. The species also occurs in small numbers on the clay and gravels of north and central Surrey as at Arbrook, Ashtead, Bookham and Oxshott Commons and until at least the 1950s, Richmond Park and Wimbledon Common.

There is very little in the published literature from which to assess any status changes in the present century but apparently there has been some contraction of range especially on the fringe of London and a number of writers have pointed to considerable fluctuations in numbers from year to year. Probably the largest breeding numbers have occurred around Haslemere, where in 1963 eight nests plus three occupied territories were found within a radius of one mile. P. G. Davis ringed the following numbers of nestling Wood Warblers in this area from 1962-66: 19, 32, 58, 57 and 60; this indicates an appreciable local population. Hydon Heath, also in the south-west of the county, is another stronghold of the species regularly studied by L. J. Raynsford who reported four to ten pairs in the area throughout the 1960s. His records also point to a fairly high percentage of unmated singing males in some seasons. In the 19 Common Birds Census areas studied in Surrey from 1960-69 only five Wood Warbler territories were recorded, three of them being at Haslemere.

The species is not usually recorded till the middle of April and passage lasts into May. There are no autumn records later than the end of September.

Two ringing recoveries are of interest. An adult female was ringed at Hydon Heath on 31 May 1958 and was found breeding again within 120 yards of its 1958 nest in June 1959 and a bird ringed as a nestling at Haslemere on 6 July 1967 was recovered at San Marcello, Pistoia, Italy on 29 August 1967.

Yellow-browed Warbler *Phylloscopus inornatus*

Extremely scarce vagrant.
This species has been authentically recorded only twice in the county—both records in the present century and both times in gardens. F. H. Frohawk saw and heard a bird in his garden at Sutton on 10 October 1930 (*BB*, 24:159) and Mrs J. Cordero provided satisfactory details of one seen in her garden at Reigate on 28 September 1960.

Goldcrest Common resident. Probable winter immigrant.
Regulus The Goldcrest is well distributed as a breeding species in
regulus the county and is locally very common particularly in
conifer plantations or areas where there are clusters of pine
trees. It is especially common along the North Downs and
in the greensand areas of Leith Hill and Holmbury St Mary;
it also occurs as a common resident in gardens in some areas,
as for instance at Ashtead and Guildford where conifers
are a common feature of the gardens.

Numbers of this species are dramatically reduced as a
result of hard winters. The Goldcrest was 'unusually
numerous' in Surrey in the winter of 1911/12 (Bentham)
but was decimated by the winter of 1916/17 and apparently
took several years to recover. Similarly numbers were very
low immediately after the winter of 1962/63 but by 1965 the
population was showing signs of recovery. 'Above average'
numbers were reported from many areas in 1967 which
was regarded as an exceptional year for Goldcrests.

Some shift of populations takes place in winter. The
resident birds are augmented by, it is thought, immigrants
from the North and the Continent. The extent to which
resident birds move to other areas in winter is impossible
to assess and ringing returns have not as yet thrown any
light on this matter.

Winter flocks of 20-30 are sometimes seen and flocks of
50 plus at Chessington and Oxshott in November 1968 are
the largest on record for the county.

Goldcrests will come to garden bird tables particularly
when weather conditions are severe. In 1956 a bird was
reported taking suet from the hand. In winter birds are
often reported searching for food on the heaths and commons, well away from trees.

Firecrest Scarce winter visitor.
Regulus The first definite record of this species in Surrey was of
ignicapillus one 'obtained' and exhibited at Wimbledon on 31 December
1905 (*BOC Bull.*, 1906). Since then there have been approximately forty records, fifteen of which have been in the last
decade of the review period which may be a reflection of
intensive recording rather than of increased numbers. There
was an exceptional number in 1969, with singles at Chessington on 1 January, at Ewhurst on 21 March, at Stone-
leigh on 4 April and at Addington on 13 October.

Nearly all records are of single birds though on three
occasions two have been seen together. They are often
recorded with Goldcrests—for example there were two with

40 Goldcrests at Selsdon in 1958. Records are fairly evenly distributed over the months October to April, the earliest date being 2 October and the latest 10 April.

Common summer visitor. Passage migrant. **Spotted**
Although subject to some fluctuations in numbers this **Flycatcher**
species breeds regularly and widely in the county in various *Muscicapa*
habitats including commonland, woodland, farmland, parks *striata*
and gardens. It was present in ten out of 19 Common Birds
Census areas in the 1960s (Griffin, 1970). There is no evidence of any marked change of status during the period
under review.

First arrivals in Surrey are usually recorded in the last
week of April or the first week in May but exceptionally
in 1966 there were no records before 17 May (at Stoke Park,
Guildford). The earliest record was one at Frensham Great
Pond on 10 April 1970.

Spotted Flycatchers often use nest boxes and some birds
return to the same box year after year; there are records
of nesting immediately on arrival and in one case the nest
was completed and an egg laid within 48 hours. Bentham
drew attention to the late nesting by the species in 1920
when he recorded a pair feeding young just out of the nest
at Godstone on 29 August (*BB*, 14:132) and A. M. Edwards
found a recently dead fledgling on 4 October 1960 at
Milford.

After the breeding season family parties are frequently
reported and movement is evident from the end of July.
On 28 August 1956, 53 birds were observed passing in one
hour at Tattenham Corner and influxes of up to c. 50 birds
have been recorded from various localities in July and
August. Records for September are all of much smaller
numbers and the latest recorded date for the county appears
to be 1 October at Guildford SF in 1961.

Recoveries of Surrey-ringed birds include two in Portugal
and three in Spain, all recovered in September or October
and all but one in the year of ringing.

Scarce passage migrant. **Pied**
The Pied Flycatcher was seldom recorded in the present **Flycatcher**
century before 1940 but since then it has been seen on *Muscicapa*
passage annually. There have been about a hundred records *hypoleuca*
for the county in the period under review spread over April
—May (a third of the records) and August—September
(two thirds). A late date was of a male at Nonsuch Park
on 3 October 1955 and in 1970 there was the exceptional
record of one at Barn Elms on 6 December. Most records

are of single birds although occasionally two are seen at one time. On 27 August 1954 five birds were present in the county on the same day as follows: one at Addington, one at Richmond Park, one at South Norwood and two at Barn Elms Reservoir. Essentially a night migrant the bird is likely to appear when on passage in any suitable open space—rural, suburban or urban; there are for example, recent records from the inner London commons as at Clapham and Tooting Bec.

Before the period under review the species was recorded as nesting on rare occasions and there is one authenticated record of successful breeding in the county—at Peckham in 1812. In the review period the only territorial behaviour recorded is of a male which sang daily in one locality from 9 May to 13 June 1948 after which date it was not seen again (*BB*, 42:121).

Red-breasted Flycatcher *Muscicapa parva* Extremely scarce vagrant.
There have been four records of this eastern European breeding species in Surrey, all within the period 1951-58. The first was of a bird seen by E. L. Crouch at Ockham on 10 June 1951 (*BB*, 45:258). Other records were of a female at the edge of a wood overlooking the R. Wey at Eashing on 25 May 1954, an extremely shy bird observed on several occasions between 31 August and 6 September 1955 at Beddington SF and a bird which was watched for 20 minutes in a garden at Banstead on 18 August 1958.

Dunnock *Prunella modularis* Abundant resident.
This species is well distributed throughout the county except in densely built-up areas.

It is difficult to assess any possible change of status during the period under review. Bucknill gave it as a 'familiar resident throughout the county' observing that 'it keeps largely to the neighbourhood of dwelling houses' but at the end of the review period the species was common in gardens, parks, farmland with hedgerows, common land and open woodland. Populations do not appear to be markedly affected by hard winters; the species was apparently unaffected by the hard winter of 1962/63 (*SBR*, 11:28).

In the Common Birds Census in Surrey in the 1960s the Dunnock was found to be the fourth commonest breeding species recorded in the 19 study areas. Only the Blackbird, Robin and Blue Tit were more numerous.

In five of these areas the species constituted over 10 per cent of the breeding bird population. On commonland at Ashtead the Dunnock was the commonest of all, constituting over 17 per cent of the total breeding population. In woodland at Ashtead and Walton densities of one pair to three or four acres were found although densities elsewhere rarely exceeded one pair per ten acres (Griffin, 1970).

There is some evidence of small movements at migration periods. Power (1910) mentioned parties usually of four to six moving slowly westwards from garden to garden in the month of October while in 1957 an increase associated with north west movements was noted at Dulwich during October in the early mornings and parties of 11 and 22 were recorded moving west in the area in the same month. There is one ringing recovery for the county which is not local—a bird ringed at Bradwell, Essex on 25 August 1961 was recovered at Newdigate, Dorking on 2 April 1962.

Meadow Pipit

Anthus pratensis

Moderately common resident, locally distributed. Passage migrant and common winter visitor.

As a breeding species in Surrey this species is restricted to open grassland or heathland but even within this habitat its distribution in the county is curiously patchy. It occurs on some of the more open commons such as Ditton and Epsom but the growth of trees has caused it to cease breeding on commons where it was once plentiful as at Littleworth (Esher) and Limpsfield. It is common on the heathland around the Frensham Ponds but is comparatively scarce in other heathland areas as at Hindhead. It occurs in places along the North Downs, as for instance at Banstead and Merrow but is absent from other downland areas apparently equally suitable. Headley Heath has had a long record of breeding Meadow Pipits. Bentham found a large number there in 1931 and despite great pressure on the habitat a small breeding population was still present in the 1960s. The banks of reservoirs and patches of rank, damp grass on sewage farms are also regularly favoured for breeding.

In 1957 the London Natural History Society made a special study of the species within the society's recording area. Altogether upwards of 39 pairs were found to be present (19 of which were proved to be breeding) in the Surrey section of the area, the largest concentration being reported from Headley Heath (14 pairs). Some evidence was adduced for a contraction of the breeding range in Surrey due to urbanization and loss of habitat (Homes, Sage and Spencer, 1960).

In the 1960s the Meadow Pipit was recorded in only four

out of 19 Surrey Common Birds Census areas, as follows: Banstead (downland): 22 territories over three years, Weybridge (farmland): one territory, Walton Reservoirs (grassland): 7 territories (over five years) and Frensham (heather common): 60 territories over six years.

Where it is abundant the Meadow Pipit is one of the commonest hosts to the Cuckoo. Of 50 nests found near Frensham in 1968 P. G. Davis found six containing Cuckoos while of four nests found on Hankley Common in June 1960, L. J. Raynsford found three with Cuckoos' eggs.

As a passage migrant the species is recorded regularly in the autumn usually in small flocks or singly moving in a generally southerly direction. At Worcester Park in 1968 ssw movements were observed from 23 September to 15 October, with a maximum movement of 120 birds between 0900 and 1000 hours on 30 September and on 26 October 1969 small parties flew south throughout the morning, again in that year movement was seen throughout September to mid-November at Ewell, with a maximum of 123 flying south or sw in two hours on 26 September. Spring passage also occurs but is less often observed although a build-up of numbers is frequently recorded at sewage farms and on reservoir banks in March and April. Exceptionally heavy passage was indicated in 1960 when on 27 March at Beddington sf a conservative estimate of numbers was 2,000 and about the same time nw movements were seen at Addington, Guildford and Sanderstead. At Thorpe in 1970 between 150 and 180 birds in all were counted moving nw in small flocks between 0730 and 1100 hours on 4 April.

The species winters in the county in appreciable numbers and sewage farms are particularly favoured feeding places as the birds are able to find insect food on the effluent filters (rarely frozen) and on the open flooded fields and settling beds. Concentrations of up to 500 have been regularly reported from Beddington sf and of up to 200 at Earlswood, Epsom, Ripley and Hersham sfs. Roosting is seldom recorded but a regular winter roost of up to 40 birds was observed in the 1960s in Tufted Hair Grass (*Deschampsia caespitosa*) at Prince's Coverts, Oxshott.

Although good numbers of Meadow Pipits have been ringed, there are few recoveries. A bird ringed as a nestling at Frensham on 21 June 1966 was retrapped at Farnham on two occasions in December of the same year. Another bird so ringed at Frensham in June 1961 was recovered

on 9 January 1962 in the Algarve, Portugal, this suggesting
that at least some of our nesting birds migrate to the south
in winter.

Extremely scarce vagrant. **Richard's**
Bucknill cited one doubtful record for the early nineteenth **Pipit**
century. There have been two records in the present century *Anthus*
both at Beddington SF. The first was of a single bird on 17 *novaesee-*
and 18 April 1958 (*BB*, 51:171) and the second was of two *landiae*
birds on 23 and 24 October 1970, one staying till 26 (*BB*,
64:362).

Common summer visitor, widely distributed. Passage **Tree**
migrant. **Pipit**
The distribution of this species in the county is limited by *Anthus*
its habitat requirement which is open common, down or *trivialis*
scrubland with scattered trees and ground cover of heather,
grass or Bracken. It is common along the North Downs and
on most of the commons of north, central and west Surrey
and it is a species that has readily adapted to cleared woodland replanted with conifers as at Redlands (Dorking) and
Prince's Coverts (Oxshott) although this being a transitional
habitat, is deserted when the young trees exceed four or
five feet in height. In a study of Tree Pipit territories on
the greensand commons of west Surrey, Venables (1937)
found that it required a tree at least 15 feet in height for a
song post, this being a limiting distribution factor and that
of 57 nests studied, 29 were in thick well-grown heather,
17 in half-grown heather recovering after fire and 11 in an
earlier and thinner transitional stage of heather growth.
Generally speaking the species is more widespread and
occurs in greater numbers than the Meadow Pipit; the
latter species is absent for example, from many parts of the
North Downs where the Tree Pipit is common while on
the heathlands of the west and north west of the county
the Tree Pipit outnumbers the Meadow Pipit in all but the
Frensham and Thursley areas.

The species was in territory in six out of 19 Common Birds
Census areas studied in Surrey 1960-69. A total of 45 territories in 84 census plot years was recorded, the largest
number being at Holmbury Hill with 20 over three census
years. At Frensham over a period of six years, six territories
were recorded on heather common, compared with 60
Meadow Pipit territories. (*per* D. Griffin).

As with many other species the published records do not
permit an adequate appraisal of status changes in the
present century. Dixon (1909) mentioned breeding at Dul-

wich, Wimbledon, Streatham and Norwood but development and public pressure on the remaining suitable habitats around London have certainly pushed the species further out; by 1970 it was no longer breeding in Richmond Park. In the Addlestone/Weybridge area in 1932 P. A. D. Hollom found the habitat occupied by the species to be much less specialized than in more recent times, the occupied habitat then, extended to hedgerows and trees in association with meadowland. The growth of scrub over the last few decades of the review period has also ousted the species from some of its previous haunts, as for instance Bookham Common where prior to 1940 at least 12 pairs used to nest, numbers decreasing to one singing male by 1957 (G. Douglas). The species was absent from this area till 1968 when a pair took up territory in an area partially burnt by fire. A singing male was present in 1969 but breeding was not proved.

As a passage bird it is usually first recorded in the first or second week of April (early dates were one on 19 March 1933 (*The Handbook*, 1:195) and two at Holmethorpe SPS on 31 March 1966) and departing birds are usually on the move from August to October. The latest record is of one flying south at Worcester Park on 7 October 1969.

There are no records of Surrey-ringed birds being recovered but one bird, ringed as a nestling at Marley, just over the Surrey/Hampshire border, on 29 June 1962 was recovered in Portugal on 20 September of the same year.

Rock/ Water Pipit *Anthus spinoletta* — Scarce though regular winter visitor and passage migrant. Three races of this species have been recorded in Surrey— the (British) Rock Pipit (*A. s. petrosus*), the Water Pipit (*A. s. spinoletta*) and the Scandinavian Rock Pipit (*A. s. littoralis*). Both races of rock pipit breed mainly on rocky coasts and islands, their names (above) very generally indicating breeding range; the Water Pipit breeds in mountainous country in central and southern Europe eastwards to Asia Minor.

There are many difficulties in separating the three races; in winter plumage *littoralis* is hardly distinguishable from *petrosus* and in spring plumage *littoralis* resembles *spinoletta*. But spring plumage could develop even before January (*spinoletta*) and from the end of January (*littoralis*); on the other hand the change to breeding plumage could begin as late as the time of departure in March/April (Johnson, 1970). It is also possible to confuse *petrosus* and *spinoletta* in winter plumage. The species is doubtless often overlooked and most of the records for the county come from the well-watched places such as Beddington and Guildford sfs. From the above it can be seen that the species presents many problems to ornithologists and recorders. No attempts can be made at assessing the races' status during the review period and the reader must bear in mind when following this account, the increased incidence of bird watching and recording in the county and the increasing knowledge and competence of observers, particularly during the last decade or so of the review period.

In 1900 Bucknill had traced one or two specimens of the Rock Pipit (*A. s. petrosus*) which had been killed in the county but neither the Water Pipit nor the Scandinavian Rock Pipit was known to him as a bird of Surrey. The occurrence of the three races in Surrey during the review period are summarized below:

Rock Pipit
A. s. petrosus

The first definite record which can be traced for the review period is of one bird seen by Bentham at Beddington sf on 8 December 1928. Until the 1950s the Rock Pipit was not regularly recorded in Surrey except at Barn Elms Reservoir. Records for the county fall between 27 September and 6 April and passage is apparent in October and November and again in March. Some birds over-winter and the fact that a bird ringed at Hersham sf on 15 January 1966 was retrapped there on 7 January 1967 suggests that some return to the same site each year. Most of the records have come from the reservoirs—Barn Elms, Island Barn and Walton and the sewage farms at Beddington (in particular) and Hersham. Other localities where records have been made include Frensham Ponds, Holmethorpe sps and Leatherhead sf. The Rock Pipit seems to favour reservoirs more so than the Water Pipit and can be seen feeding on insects, vegetable matter and small snails in the brickwork of the banks. Single birds are usually seen in winter but sometimes more and a party of c. 12 was on the tow path at Barn Elms on 9 January 1968. Records suggest that the Rock Pipit is slightly more numerous than the Water Pipit in the county.

Water Pipit
A. s. spinoletta

The race was first distinguished in Surrey by D. Goodwin on 11 December 1949 at Woking sf (*BB*, 43:294) and has been recorded annually since 1955; records have steadily increased and in the 1960s it was proved to be regularly over-wintering at several sites. Records for the county fall between 10 October and 5 May. As an autumn passage migrant it generally occurs a little later than the Rock

Pipit. At Beddington sf, where a special study was made of Water Pipits occurring during the winter of 1967/68, numbers up to 13 were counted when the only really extensive check was made. Beddingon and Guildford sfs together account for over two thirds of the records, those for Beddington being biassed towards over-wintering and Guildford towards spring passage. Other localities where the Water Pipit is recorded with some regularity include Abinger watercress beds, Barn Elms Reservoir and Unstead sf. A late bird at Island Barn Reservoir on 3 May 1959 was in full summer plumage.

Scandinavian Rock Pipit *A. s. littoralis* There are only two records of this race in Surrey; A. D. Prowse identified birds on the basis of the colour of underparts at Beddington sf on 15 and 16 March 1966 and 5 April 1967 (Johnson, 1970).

Pied/White Wagtail *Motacilla alba* Pied Wagtail: Common resident. Probable winter immigrant. Passage migrant.
White Wagtail: Scarce but regular passage migrant.
The Pied Wagtail (*M. a. yarrelli*) is the commonest and most widespread of the wagtails in the county. It is able to live in close association with man and is found both in town and country. It is commonly found breeding in habitats close to water as at gravel pits, sewage farms, in parks and on river/stream courses. Breeding is also frequently reported from completely dry habitats, in gardens and around or in large building complexes, such as Charterhouse School. Nests are usually in a natural hollow or crevice in wall or tree and not infrequently in buildings such as garden sheds and barns; it even nests in large machinery. The largest breeding concentrations are reported from sewage farms. During the early 1960s for instance between ten and 20 pairs regularly nested at Hersham sf, the nests being located in the clinker walls of the sprinklers, in trees, buildings and abandoned cars. There is no evidence to suggest that the status of the species as a breeding bird has changed during the present century but, as with many of our commoner birds, precise information is lacking.

In autumn and winter birds congregate into fairly large flocks and numbers up to several hundreds are not infrequently reported from sewage farms, watercress beds and less frequently, open agricultural land. The numbers recorded suggest that the resident population is swollen by immigrants, probably from the North, into the county during the winter months. Passage birds, particularly in autumn in September and October, are occasionally reported—sometimes in flight, singly or in small parties; often passage is recognized by the appearance and sudden dispersal of large flocks. One of c. 300 recorded at Epsom SF on 1 October 1955 had moved on by the afternoon of the same day. In hard weather the effluent beds and sprinklers of sewage farms, which are usually kept frost free, are particularly favoured feeding sites.

Roosts have been found in a variety of situations including open commonland and reed beds at Frensham, sallow bushes on Bookham Common, laurel bushes and bamboo at Virginia Water and in artificial sites such as greenhouses and other buildings. The largest roost recorded in the county has been at the Oxshott brickworks where on 10 February 1962 c. 617 birds were counted as they flew into the roost (D. K. Withrington). Pre-roost flight behaviour has been observed at Hersham SF where at dusk the birds congregate around the filter beds before flying off in small parties to the chosen roost site (Parr, 1963).

There are two foreign recoveries of the Pied Wagtail from Surrey; a fully grown bird ringed at Ewhurst on 25 September 1962 was recovered at Mirandela, Portugal on 7 February 1963. This bird may well have been a migrant passing through the county when it was trapped but the second recovery of a bird ringed as a nestling in May 1916 and recovered in Garonne, France in March 1917 suggests that some birds of the local breeding population migrate southwards in the winter.

The White Wagtail (*M. a. alba*), the Continental race, is a scarce but regular passage migrant through the county. It has been recognized in the county since the nineteenth century and Bucknill referred to it as a rare visitor; there is a sprinkling of records for the first half of the present century but since the early 1950s it has been recorded annually, usually in the spring in small numbers over the period March to May. In the autumn this race (*M. a. alba*) is more difficult to separate from birds of the local form (*M. a. yarrelli*) but subspecific identification is occasionally claimed and accepted with qualifications.

Grey Wagtail
Motacilla cinerea

Moderately common resident. Winter visitor and passage migrant.

This species has certainly increased in numbers and firmly established itself as a breeding bird in the present century. In 1900 Bucknill regarded it as essentially a winter visitor and knew of only one definite breeding record—at Wimbledon Common in 1893. Dixon (1909) cited a breeding record from Barnes Common in 1897 and breeding was recorded at Farnham in 1901 (*Zool.*, 1902). Bentham located a pair at Oxted in 1906 and in the same year L. B. Moritz found a pair at Hammer Pond, Thursley (*SBCQB*, 22, *June* 1962). Following this there appears to have been a gradual increase and after 1910 breeding was reported from Bramley, Frensham, Tilford and Pyrford. In 1922, R. E. Moreau commented on the increase stating that prior to 1920 he had never seen Grey Wagtails in 'his corner' of south west Surrey but after an absence of two years abroad he found four pairs near bridges on an eight-mile stretch of the R. Wey. (*BB*, 16:189). From about 1930 one or two pairs were recorded every year on the R. Mole near Leatherhead and more recently pairs were noted on the R. Thames at Molesey Lock (*The Birds of the London Area*, 1957). In 1953 no less than seven pairs had established territories on the Tillingbourne Stream with its attendant ponds between Westcott and Gomshall. In 1960 records were submitted to the Surrey Bird Club of at least 22 pairs from 17 localities and in the following year it was estimated that the Surrey population exceeded 35 pairs. The hard winter of 1962/63 affected the species severely and the breeding population was considerably reduced. In one area where ten pairs had bred in 1961 there were only two pairs in 1963 and other breeding sites had none (*SBCQB*, 27, *September* 1963). By 1970 the species had recovered its numbers but the records are not sufficiently detailed to indicate whether the population of the early 1960s had been equalled or exceeded.

In the breeding season the species is generally confined to the banks of small streams and rivers, preferably near falling water and most frequently using the superstructures of bridges or other artificial overhangs for nesting. Breeding has also been recorded at sewage farms which provide the same type of habitat.

In winter the species resorts to sewage farms, watercress beds and the edges of reservoirs and lakes. Numbers are usually under ten but exceptionally, larger concentrations are sometimes recorded and c. 20 at Beddington SF in January and again in October and December 1961 is the largest.

This species is known to migrate through the British Isles and many casual records are submitted of birds apparently on migration, often from places remote from water and particularly in the autumn.

Scarce summer resident. Passage migrant.

Yellow Wagtail *Motacilla flava*

The Yellow Wagtail group of races is a subject of much complexity and controversy. One of the problems is the occurrence within the breeding range of one race of birds resembling those found breeding typically in another usually far distant area. For the purpose of this brief summary it has been assumed that all Yellow Wagtails breeding in Surrey belong to the British race (*M. f. flavissima*) except where certain records from Beddington are concerned.

In 1900 the Yellow Wagtail was a common summer visitor; it was nesting freely at Frensham and was numerous in other parts of the county. Numbers breeding in the present century have varied considerably but at the end of the review period the Yellow Wagtail's range was virtually restricted to the north-east of the county. Its decline in numbers and contraction of range seem to have been particularly rapid in the 1960s.

In the first two decades of the present century the species was apparently still breeding in some numbers in heather around Frensham Little Pond. In 1907 Bentham found six pairs in that area and referred to large numbers in the area in the following year. There are however no published records from the Frensham area after 1919 and it would appear that breeding had ceased there by the early 1920s. Another breeding site in heather was on Horsell Common in the early years of the century. In 1902 six pairs nested on Wimbledon Common and breeding was reported in Bracken in Richmond Park up to 1912. The *Haslemere List* (1921) described it as a local nesting species but the only breeding locality in south-west Surrey at that time appears to have been around Shalford. Bentham found a nest there in 1918 and up to five or six pairs continued to breed in the Shalford/Wonersh area throughout the 1920s. What might have been a relic of that population appeared in 1944 when a pair was found at Unstead SF and a small breeding population continued there till 1956 when long grass in which the birds were nesting was cut (CNHS, 1959). A small colony was located near the R. Wey at Stoke (Guildford) in 1947 but by 1960 the only breeding pairs reported in the west of the county were at the adjacent Guildford SF and none was reported from that area in the remainder of the review period. In the north and east of the county the breeding population has been confined latterly to sewage farms, gravel and sand pits and the grass fringes of reservoirs. Breeding at Beddington SF and Barn Elms Reservoir had already been recorded in 1900 (*The Birds of the London*

Area, 1957). Breeding continued intermittently at Barn Elms until the mid-1950s and was still occurring at Beddington in 1970. Breeding pairs at Beddington reached a peak in 1958 and 1959 at c. 35 pairs and declined in the 1960s. At least 20 pairs were present early in the breeding season in 1970. Epsom and Hersham SFS supported small breeding populations in the 1950s as did a gravel pit area on the site of the present Queen Elizabeth II Reservoir and the population at this last site persisted for a number of years in the early 1960s on the grassy banks of the completed reservoir. By the end of the 1960s recorded breeding pairs were less than six and in 1969 restricted to Beddington SF, Thorpe and the Walton/Weybridge area. The position in 1970 was, however, more hopeful with six pairs recorded at Thorpe in addition to the good number at Beddington mentioned above. A remarkable record also in this year was of two pairs nesting, on waste ground near Vauxhall Bridge, at least two young being raised.

Early migrants are often recorded in the last week of March or early April but main passage is usually from mid-April to mid-May and at this time numbers at favoured localities can be large, as for instance c. 50 at Beddington SF on 15 April 1966. From about mid-July birds tend to congregate at good feeding areas such as gravel pits and sewage farms where large numbers have been recorded roosting in reeds and similar aquatic vegetation. At Thorpe GPS in 1965 roosting numbers built up to a peak of 110 birds on 5 September and birds were present there till the end of September. Some birds linger into October and there have been records of wintering birds. One was seen at Chase on 12 December 1953 and there were records of one or two birds wintering at Beddington in 1956/57, 1959/60 and 1960/61.

There have been a number of interesting recoveries of this species. A bird ringed as a nestling in Kent in June 1964 was recovered roosting at Hersham SF in September of the same year indicating that there is a widespread dispersal of local birds from their breeding localities and prior to migration. A bird ringed at Guildford on 5 June 1933 was recovered on passage at Leon (Landes) France on 20 September in the same year and a bird ringed at Thorpe in August 1965 was trapped in its wintering area at Thies, Senegal on 1 December 1965.

Birds showing characteristics of the Blue-headed race (*M. f. flava*) were regularly reported in the last two decades of the review period, usually on spring passage in April or

May. At Beddington sf in 1966, 1969 and 1970 a male showing the characteristics of *flava* was apparently paired with a female *flavissima*, while in 1970 a female showing characteristics of *flava* was mated with a male *flavissima*.

There are less than seven records of the occurrences of this race before 1950. Parslow (1967) described how birds of a pale blue/grey-headed type, apparently identical to Sykes' Wagtail (*M. f. beema*) a race that normally breeds in Western Siberia, have been recorded breeding in some years in south-east England. The breeding population at Beddington sf was discovered to contain some birds of this type as well as 'variants' in 1957 and 1958.

B. S. Milne made detailed studies of this colony and his work lent support to the theory that the degree of variation found in the Yellow Wagtail in south-east England was due to hybridization between yellow-headed types and grey-headed types rather than the result of gene-flow from drifted migrants. The history of one of the birds ringed in this study is of particular interest. This bird ringed as a juvenile Yellow Wagtail (*M. f. flavissima*) on 21 July 1956 at Beddington was retrapped there as an adult male *beema* type in July the following year and later recovered near Ovar, Portugal on 15 September 1958. For further information on this subject readers are referred to papers by Williamson and Milne: (*BB*, 48:382-403 and *BB*, 52:281-95).

Waxwing
Bombycilla garrulus

Irregular winter visitor.
This species is subject to periodic irruptions triggered off, it is thought, by over-population in northern Europe.

In the present century invasions have occurred in Britain in the following winters: 1903/4, 1913/14, 1921/22, 1931/32, 1936/37, 1943/44, 1946/47, 1948/49, 1949/50, 1959/60, 1965/66 and 1970/71. Only two or three birds were recorded in Surrey in 1913/14 and similarly the county appears to have been only marginally affected, if at all, by further invasions in the 1920s and 1930s. Up to 17 birds were recorded from Banstead, Banstead Downs and Surbiton over the period January to March 1944. The 1946/47 invasion was the largest one ever recorded up to that time, with up to 12,000 birds recorded in Great Britain (*BB*, 41:2-9, 4-40). At least 90 birds were recorded in the county, the species being seen from December 1946, when two birds were in Richmond Park, to 8 April 1947, when there were six on Wimbledon Common. The largest flock was of 32 at Effingham on 21 January 1947 but the birds were particularly numerous in the suburbs of London where they fed on berries of rowan, privet, cotoneaster and hawthorn. Numbers in the 1949/50 invasion were considerably smaller and the largest flock in Surrey was of 12 or more on hawthorn in a suburban garden at Wimbledon on 16 December 1949. In 1959 the largest number in the county occurred in March and April when up to 20 were present on Bookham Common.

The 1965/66 invasion was again on a large scale, evident in the county from the very early date of 19 October 1965 when one was seen on Oxshott Heath and records were received up to 1 May 1966. Between these two dates the birds were well distributed throughout the whole county although the greater number was seen in the London area. Peak numbers were seen in the second half of December when 380 were recorded in the county.

Birds are sometimes recorded singly or in small parties in non-invasion years.

Great Grey Shrike *Lanius excubitor* Regular winter visitor and passage migrant in very small numbers.

Records in the first two decades of the present century were few but from then on the species was seen increasingly often, until by the 1950s it was regularly recorded in the county. It usually appears in the period November to April although there are a number of October records and two for May and June. (One was of a bird on Ham Common on 15 and 20 May 1920 and seen again there on 13 June and the other was of a bird first seen on 26 March 1956 at Addington and still present on 9 June (H. E. Pounds).)

The species has wintered on the Thursley/Ockley complex of commons in at least eight of the winters of the 1960s and up to three birds were recorded there in the winters of 1964/65 and 1965/66. Other outer Surrey localities where the species has been recorded, usually as a singleton, in more than one season are Bisley, Caterham, Chobham Common, Headley Heath, Walton Heath and Witley Common. In the London area there are fairly frequent records from Richmond Park, Mitcham and Wimbledon Commons and Beddington SF (*The Birds of the London Area*, 1957).

Birds that are probably on passage are occasionally reported, as for instance on Thursley Common where they occurred on 12 and 13 March 1967 and 4 and 6 April 1968 in seasons in which they had not been recorded as wintering. However wintering birds can be elusive and winter territories can be very large, sometimes extending over several square miles as the species requires open common/

waste ground with scattered trees (dead ones are particularly favoured) or artificial high perches providing good vantage points.

There has been one record of this species in the present century—a bird seen by W. P. Izzard on Banstead Downs on 21 May 1956 (*LBR*, 21 : 36). Bucknill cited a record of a pair at Dorking in June 1886 but added 'as the specimens were not identified in any other way than by observation, the record cannot be considered as wholly satisfactory'!

Lesser Grey Shrike *Lanius minor*

Extremely scarce spring vagrant.
This species has been recorded in the county on four occasions in the present century, all since 1950. One was seen on Bookham Common on 26 and 27 May 1951 (*BB*, 45 : 258), an immature bird was in Richmond Park from 13 April to 5 May 1953 (*BB*, 46 : 305-6), one was recorded at Addington on 13 May 1960 and the fourth was at Oxshott on 8 June 1970 (*BB*, 64 : 365).

Woodchat Shrike *Lanius senator*

Very scarce summer visitor and passage migrant.
The history of the Red-backed Shrike in Surrey in the present century is of a sad decline which became catastrophic from the mid point of the 1960s. In 1900 it was regarded as a common summer visitor, nesting in all suitable rural districts and Dixon (1909) described it as breeding as close to central London as Dulwich, Barnes, Putney, Wimbledon and Richmond. Its numbers, even in the first quarter of the present century, were subject to fluctuation. C. Russell of Shere noted a marked decrease in 1912 (*BB*, 6 : 301) and P. F. Bunyard found the species breeding commonly in 1919 in places where at one time it had almost disappeared. He also found the species plentiful in 1920 and 1921 but in 1923 when there was a cold early spring, birds did not remain to breed in any numbers in their usual haunts. (*BB*, 13 : 226-31, 17 : 198-205) Bentham had recorded numerous nests in the early years of the century. In 1906 he regarded it as numerous around Oxted and on Ranmore Common; in 1910 there were two or three pairs in the Titsey Wood area and he had other frequent breeding records from north-east Surrey. The species has also been shown to be particularly faithful to a single nesting area. Miss P. Bond recorded a continuous series of breeding in or near her garden in Haslemere from 1921-39.
Breeding in the inner suburbs of London continued until the 1950s. It was last recorded breeding at Dulwich in 1949;

Red-backed Shrike *Lanius cristatus*

it bred regularly on Mitcham Common until 1956 (with a maximum of five pairs there in 1936) and it bred for the last time on Wimbledon Common in that year. The decline in these suburban areas was thought to be attributed to loss of habitat through building and development although this cannot have been the full explanation as many suitable areas remained without shrikes.

In 1960 the BTO sponsored a national enquiry into the past and present status of the Red-backed Shrike in Great Britain and the story revealed by its findings was one of a marked decline in numbers and a shrinking distribution in the present century. It was considered that destruction of habitat or predation could not fully account for the decline. The report drew attention to a theory advanced by S. Durango, that the decline was an effect of long-term climatic changes resulting in an increase in the temperature of the Holarctic region over the last hundred years, giving, in the more maritime areas of Europe, wetter summers and a consequential decline in the large insect prey of the shrike (Peakall, 1962). By 1960 Surrey was one of the four south eastern counties supporting 69 per cent of the British breeding population and by 1966 this proportion had increased to 85 per cent of the population (Parslow, 1967)

In 1960 D. B. Peakall (*SBR*, 8 : 30-2) undertook a detailed survey of the breeding of the Red-backed Shrike in Surrey. The decline of the species in the inner London suburbs has already been referred to above. In the outer suburbs a decline, albeit less abrupt, had also set in by 1960 but nesting was still recorded at Ashtead, Banstead Downs, Coulsdon, Ditton Common, Esher, Fetcham Downs, Leatherhead and Reigate although breeding had ceased in at least 12 localities where it had previously occurred. The situation in outer Surrey was even more depressing with breeding still taking place in only two areas in 1960—Chobham and Witley Commons. The county situation in the post 1960 period showed a slight recovery followed by a catastrophic drop from 1965 to the end of the decade as the following figures, being the total number of pairs recorded as present or proved or suspected of breeding, illustrate: 1961: 17, 1962: 18, 1963: 19, 1964: 18, 1965: 9, 1966: 4, 1967: 2, 1968: 3/4, 1969: 5, 1970: 3. A similar decline has been recorded from one of the species' foremost strongholds in Hampshire (Ash, 1970) and it would seem that the survival of the species as a breeding bird in southern England is in jeopardy.

The optimum breeding habitat appears to be open common or heathland with scattered bushes such as hawthorn and dog-rose. Densities of breeding pairs can sometimes reach fairly high levels in favoured areas and one such example was recorded at Leatherhead in 1961 when M. Cadman identified seven pairs on 12 acres of overgrown allotments and scrub. Also Bentham had a record of ten pairs breeding at Tadworth in 1946, three nests being found over a distance of 200 yards.

The bird is not usually seen till May although there is one very early record of a male seen on a Surrey heath on 3 April 1948 and in 1926 a nest containing five young about four days old was found on 3 May, this being then the earliest breeding record in the British Isles (*BB*, 20:150). The species departs early and there are very few September records although the latest recorded occurrence of the species in the county is 3 December 1869 (*Birds of Surrey*, 1900).

Two ringing returns are of interest. A bird ringed as a nestling at Guildford on 6 July 1958 was trapped on the Island of Kos in the Dodecanese, Greece on 25 September of the same year and illustrates the easterly migration route taken by the species. Also in 1958 two birds that were found paired and breeding on Witley Common had been ringed as sibling nestlings in a brood in the same spot in the previous year.

Starling
Sturnus
vulgaris

Abundant resident. Passage migrant and winter immigrant. This species could well be the commonest resident bird. It breeds in all parts of the county wherever it can find a crevice or hole in which to make its nest. It is able to live quite happily in close association with man using buildings for nesting and having food provided by scraps in gardens and has thus kept pace and probably increased in numbers as urban development has spread out from London and around the larger towns. Bucknill considered the species to be in an expansionist period at the start of the century 'when the eaves of every modern red brick house usually (held) a pair or two' but he did refer to the first nesting record in Richmond Park in 1875 so it is possible that its increase had been comparatively late in the nineteenth century. In certain rural areas breeding densities are often lower than suburban areas because of a shortage of nesting holes but wherever these are numerous as in mature woodland or parkland, the species is very common.

The population is vastly increased in the winter by immigrants from the Continent. Starting in late September spectacular movements are regularly seen moving west or wnw on broad fronts across the whole county, peak numbers usually occurring shortly after dawn; however, at times of heavy passage, movements can last all day with flocks varying in size from small parties of five or so to many thousands. In 1968 at Worcester Park autumn passage was recorded from 9 October to 6 November with a maximum of 2,300 west in one hour 40 minutes on 31 October. At the same site in 1969 passage lasted from 23 September to 24 November with a peak of 3,000 west on 5 November. Return passage in the spring is seldom reported and probably takes place in a less conspicuous manner, starting possibly direct from roosts and therefore difficult to separate from normal roost dispersal movements. Hard weather movements are occasionally reported and one of Bentham's records referred to a continuous flight se of parties of 12 to 500 in very cold weather over Epsom Downs on 5 January 1929.

In 1925 and the early 1930s E. M. Nicholson showed that most birds using London roosts are resident and the catchment area extends at least 14 miles from St Paul's Cathedral, the birds using well defined flight corridors across the suburbs to and from the roosting areas. Very little work has been done on roosts outside the London area but the following have been reported: Five hundred birds were roosting in the reed beds of Pen Ponds, Richmond Park on 28 October 1962 and also in that year a very large roost was located at Ockham in woodland, this being estimated at c. 10,000 on 27 July numbers rising to c. 42,000 in August and c. 600,000 by 16 December. Another large roost of numbers rising to 250,000 in September and reputed to have been established 30 years previously was reported from an area south of Reigate in 1967. Some temporary roosts are occasionally noted as for instance at Prince's Coverts (Oxshott) where juvenile birds take up temporary roosts in young plantations in the late summer.

The Starling is frequently ringed and recoveries provide evidence of the origin of some of our winter visitors. One bird ringed at Beddington on 25 December 1938 was recovered near Moscow on 20 June 1941 and other winter-ringed birds have been recovered from Belgium (two), France (one) and Germany (six). Another bird ringed on 5 October 1959 in ussr was recovered at Selsdon on 7 February 1960 and one, ringed as a juvenile on 26 June 1965 in Belgium, was recovered at Earlswood on 18 October in the same year.

Scarce resident. **Hawfinch**

Cocco-
thraustes
cocco-
thraustes

The Hawfinch is generally recognized as a shy and elusive species and this fact has made it difficult both in the past and in more recent times to assess its real status in the county. In 1900 it was regarded by Bucknill 'as generally resident throughout the county and in many places as quite a plentiful species'. Dixon (1909) considered it to be resident in Burgh Heath, Combe Wood, Croydon, Ewell, Mortlake, Richmond and Wimbledon and *The Birds of the London Area*, 1957 was still able to describe it as of regular occurrence at Dulwich, Putney, Tooting Bec Common and Wimbledon. Bentham recorded the species usually in ones or twos on several occasions in every year from 1906 to the mid-1950s particularly at Limpsfield, on the eastern North Downs, at Reigate and Walton Heath. He regarded the species as common around Tadworth early in the century but later described it as very scarce. Guy Mountfort (1957) gave its status in Surrey as local but well distributed, particularly in the beech woods and thickets on the downs and in orchards. He described it as most numerous in the Caterham, Farnham, Guildford, Haslemere and Woking areas. Impressions from field workers at the end of the review period were of a sad decline in status in the last two decades of the period; for instance it was then far from common in the Guildford area. No more than two cases of proved breeding were reported in any year of the 1960s.

During the winter months birds congregate in flocks and in certain seasons stay faithful to a particular area where food is available. The largest winter concentration so far recorded was given by Bentham for 1919 the year in which he saw two flocks of 150 and 100 feeding on Holmwood Common on holly berries. In the late 1930s and early 1940s parties were regularly recorded in the grounds of the Haslemere Museum—the maximum number of birds being 50 on 5 April 1938 and 19 February 1942. The largest winter flock in more recent times was reported from a Hornbeam wood near Earlswood where a flock built up to c. 100 birds in February 1966 and then declined to small numbers by May. Hornbeam seeds are in fact a favourite food of the Hawfinch but there are regular reports of birds taking cherry stones, yew berry kernels, cotoneaster berries, holly berries and haws. Although there is no evidence to show that the Hawfinch is anything but sedentary in Surrey, the large numbers recorded in winter and early spring in some years suggest that Continental birds might be involved.

Greenfinch Very common resident. Winter immigrant and passage
Chloris migrant.
chloris This species is widespread and common in the county and
is probably the most abundant finch in the suburbs of outer
London and the larger country towns, where parks and
gardens provide nesting sites. It is a species that readily
comes to bird tables and there is little doubt that it has
benefited since the Second World War from the increasing
practice of putting out seed. It is common too in the more
rural parts of the county but less so here than the Chaffinch.
Apart from its increase in suburban London and the residential areas of our larger towns there is little evidence to
suggest any change in status in the present century. Bucknill described it as a common resident breeding freely on
commons, in hedges and orchards in all parts of the county.

In autumn and winter birds congregate in large flocks
and resort to sewage farms, stubble fields and other areas
that provide good feeding conditions. Seeds of Bur Marigold
(*Bidens spp.*), docks (*Rumex spp.*) Persicaria (*Polygonum
persicaria*) and rose are particularly favoured. Bentham
reported flocks of up to 500 in the early years of the century
and flock sizes of this order were frequently reported during
the 1960s, the largest being 1,000 at Unstead sf on 24
December 1961.

There is evidence that winter sees a good deal of shifting
of populations of Greenfinches with influxes into the county
from other areas of Britain and the Continent and some
movement of resident birds to the south. Diurnal westerly
movements of small parties of birds are occasionally reported in October and early November and it would appear
that these movements represent immigration of Continental
birds. These movements, however, never reach the scale of
those recorded for the Chaffinch (see under that species).

At least three birds ringed in the autumn or winter in
the county have been recovered in northern France in the
same or a subsequent winter and similarly, birds ringed in
France and Belgium (in February and April) have been
recovered in Surrey. On the other hand the Greenfinches
in one type of area in the county would appear to be
largely sedentary as was demonstrated in a study of the
dispersal of birds feeding in the winter months during the
period 1959-66 in gardens in Sanderstead where it was
estimated that a total of up to 1,000 Greenfinches fed during
the winter. Of 79 recoveries of birds ringed as part of the
study only 13 had travelled more than four miles. Further-
more these were shown to have dispersed in all directions

with three birds being recovered over 60 miles to the north east. The conclusion was reached that for the most part the local Greenfinches in the Sanderstead area pursued a routine annual cycle, spending spring and summer at their breeding haunts in the hedgerows and large gardens, dispersing to corn stubbles and suburban seed-bearing localities in autumn and early winter and invading suburban gardens where food is offered, in January when the natural supply runs out (Cornelius, 1968).

Certain Greenfinches in the county (particularly at Brockham) have been observed with an abnormal reddish plumage tint and after a study of this phenomenon it was concluded that it arose from the birds' feeding on some food rich in red carotene during the late summer (Washington and Harrison, 1969).

Goldfinch
Carduelis
carduelis

Common resident, summer visitor and passage migrant. At the turn of the century this was a comparatively rare breeding species in Surrey. In common with the whole of England there had been a big decrease in Surrey in the nineteenth century with a significant increase during the early part of the twentieth century. There are several references to increases in the early 1920s or before. The bird is now a widespread and common species particularly fond of large gardens, orchards, commonland or downland with scattered bushes of thorn. It is, however, less common in the heather country of the west and north-west of the county.

The largest flocks are usually recorded in the autumn when family parties join together to feed on thistles and similar seed plants on the open commons and waste ground. Two hundred and fifty were recorded at Addington in August/September 1961, 200 at Farnborough North GP on 8 October 1965 and c. 250 at Farleigh Downs on 4 September 1967. Occasionally large flocks are recorded in April, as for instance 200 at Thursley on 27 April 1964 and 100 at Leith Hill on 24 April 1965. Winter flocks are usually of smaller numbers—50 or so. Sometimes the species congregates with Linnets and Siskins. Roving flocks are often recorded feeding on alder seeds and are regularly seen along the rivers and streams of the county. Diurnal migration is occasionally reported in the autumn, as for instance a sw movement on 14 October 1967 at an average rate of ten per hour for three hours at Barn Elms Reservoir and in the period 23 September to 21 November 1969, sw or sww passage was recorded on c. 40 bird days at Worcester Park.

Ringing returns show that there is a dispersal of Surrey-ringed birds to and through north-west France and down the western seaboard of France (Les Landes) to the north-east corner of Spain. Of nine birds ringed in autumn (August—October) and recovered abroad three were recovered in north-west France, two in Les Landes and four in the north-east corner of Spain.

Siskin
Carduelis
spinus
Common winter visitor. Passage migrant.

There is no evidence to suggest any great changes in the status of the Siskin in the county during the period under review. Bucknill gave it as 'occurring rather irregularly in most parts of the county but in some places and in some seasons in considerable numbers'. This held good to a large extent at the end of the review period. Perhaps the species could be described as rather less irregular although there were still fluctuations in numbers.

Bucknill further showed that the species very occasionally nested in the county although suggestions have been made that these records may have referred to escaped birds (*The Handbook*, 1:62). There are no breeding records for the review period although a bird was reported singing at Weybridge as late as 9 June in 1924 and display and courtship were observed in one locality in March and April, 1960 (the birds were not located in early May). Nevertheless in 1970 an adult pair was observed in the Weybridge area from July to September—a hopeful sign.

The species does breed in very small numbers in a few southern counties and increasingly so, the nearest breeding area to Surrey probably being the New Forest (Hampshire). Surrey is the only county mentioned in *The Handbook* where full song is regular by wintering birds (February to April) and this was increasingly reported in the 1960s. Bentham heard Siskins singing on a warm sunny Christmas Day early in the century.

The extreme dates for winter visitation during the review period are 16 September and 3 May. Small numbers passing west have been seen October to December in some years and southwards movement has been recorded for December. Many birds do not arrive until November and in some years only small numbers are seen before December. In some areas birds are seldom seen before the turn of the year. From January onwards flocks of 20-40 are commonly reported from various localities and flocks of up to 100 are sometimes seen; occasionally there are larger numbers. In some cases numbers build up during the early months of the year and in others, numbers rapidly increase (or good numbers appear) in March and April, occasionally reaching 100 or so, presumably as part of spring passage migration.

An analysis of records for the last decade of the review period gives no obvious patterns of numbers and distribution and there are no indications of 'invasions'. If very broad criteria are used, only the winter of 1966/67 was consistently 'good' and only the winter of 1964/65 was consistently 'poor'. Exceptional records during this period were as follows: in 1969 the largest flock recorded in the year was before Christmas—150 plus were at Virginia Water on 13 December; in February 1962, there were few records and the numbers were small; in 1963 there were greatly increased numbers during the cold spell and several flocks of the order 30-50 were widely reported; in addition 450 (the highest number given in the whole review period) were recorded at Wisley Common on 24 March and there were 150-200 in Oxshott Woods on 8 April.

The species appears to 'settle in' to some areas, notably Frensham where it is regularly recorded, numbers of the order of 50 sometimes appearing early in the winter. However more usually flocks rove around the county searching for food (primarily tree seeds) and are commonly seen on Alder and birch. It frequents the R. Mole and R. Wey. In 1968 there was a report of its becoming increasingly numerous in gardens at West Humble, near Dorking where the favourite food is the seed of Lawson's Cypress (*Chamaecyparis Lawsoniana*). The Siskin had in fact established itself as a garden bird a few years earlier when it was discovered that Siskins were coming into gardens to feed on fat in the Hersham/Walton/Weybridge area. In some cases birds fed exclusively on this food and in others they went on to bird seed. On one day in late March 1969, 137 Siskins were counted feeding at the same time in one small garden in Weybridge (G. H. Gush *in litt.*).

Fat baiting has been a considerable aid to ringing enterprises and some interesting results have been obtained. In the first place Bullock (1967) has shown the extent to which 'fat' fattens up the birds prior to spring migration and he discovered a remarkable loss of weight during the day, the birds only carrying a small surplus over to the following day but a marked general trend of increasing weight. Towards the time for departure, a decided preference for bird seed took the place of the 'insatiable appetite' for fat.

Secondly, intensive ringing had produced many recoveries and these have given some indications of movements. The species breeds widely on the Continent and recoveries of Siskins ringed in Weybridge during the months February, March and April—in France, Germany, Holland, Italy, Spain, Sweden and Switzerland in subsequent winters indicates that birds do not necessarily return to Britain each year. On the other hand one bird ringed in Weybridge in March 1966 was retrapped there in the same month of the three following years. There were 11 recoveries from Belgium, eight of them in October; these birds may or may not have been on their way to Britain. One ringed at Rybatschi, Kaliningrad, USSR on 3 October 1966 was retrapped at Weybridge on 18 February 1967 and birds ringed in Germany in October and November have been retrapped in Weybridge in spring. Two further Weybridge-ringed birds were recovered, presumably at their breeding grounds, in Norway and Sweden in June and May respectively.

Linnet
Carduelis
cannabina

Very common resident. Passage migrant and winter immigrant.

The Linnet is a widely distributed breeding bird in the county present on the commons, heaths, downs and on agricultural land. It also occurs in large gardens and the parks of suburbia but it is markedly less common in these habitats than the Greenfinch. It frequently breeds socially in thickets of thorn, bramble or gorse. Venables (1937) examined 17 nests on the heaths of west Surrey all of which were placed in a small bush or sapling in mature heather, the nests often being below the surface of the heather on the lower branches of the supporting tree. In the 1940s young conifers (four-five feet in height) were found to be a favourite nesting site in the Horley district. Heather-placed nests have been frequently found on Chobham Common.

Apart from a possible increase in the first two decades of the present century thought to be due to the cessation of bird catching (*The Birds of the London Area*, 1957) there is no evidence for the major part of the review period of any significant change of status, only the temporary effects of hard winters.

In autumn and winter the species forms flocks often several hundred strong and these concentrate in areas where weed seeds are available. In the first half of the present century Bentham frequently recorded flocks of up to 200 and exceptionally up to 700 on the North Downs. Beadell (1932) referring to the Woldingham Area in the 1930s described huge flocks of 'thousands' in the stubble fields 'at times'. Maximum numbers in winter flocks recorded at the end of the review period were in the order of 300-400.

Small parties of up to 30 birds are frequently recorded from late September to early November flying in a general westerly or southerly direction usually in association with other migrating passerines. In 1969 ssw movements over Worcester Park were recorded between 23 September and early November. In the previous year the peak movement at Worcester Park was on 11 October when 113 flew south between 0800 and 0930 hours.

Ringing returns show that many of Surrey's breeding birds migrate to France and Spain in winter. Birds ringed as nestlings at Woldingham and Whitmoor Common have been recovered from La Gironde and Lot et Garonne, France respectively. Two fully grown birds ringed at Walton Reservoir on 29 September 1968 were trapped by bird catchers in Les Landes on the west coast of France on 26 October of the same year.

Twite
Carduelis flavirostris

Very scarce winter visitor.
As this species resembles the Linnet it may well be that it is occasionally overlooked and again because of this resemblance reservations must apply to certain of the early records. There is an unsupported record of one at Clapham Common on 1 January 1918, W. A. Shaw noticed one in the Haslemere area just before Christmas, 1919 and there was one at Thursley in February 1933. Stanley Cramp identified two, probably both females, at Barn Elms Reservoir on 28 October 1946 and records have been published in the *Surrey Bird Report* in six of the last twelve years of the review period. There is a wide scatter of areas and dates (within the period 25 October to 27 March). Single birds only were involved except in 1960 when four were at Farleigh on 29 December.

The status of the species in the county before 1900 is uncertain.

Redpoll
Carduelis flammea

Common resident. Passage migrant and winter immigrant.
The Redpoll is now a comparatively common breeding bird in the county, widely distributed but limited to areas of open common/heath or downland with scattered bushes or small trees to provide nest sites. It has been recorded nesting in large gardens as at Haslemere and Oxshott and is another species that has benefited from the provision of suitable habitat in the form of young conifer plantations. It seldom breeds on agricultural land.

The status of this species in Surrey at the end of the

review period was appreciably different from that in 1900 when Bucknill described the Redpoll as essentially a winter visitor. (Although he knew of occasional breeding records he regarded these as distinctly unusual.) In *British Birds*, breeding was reported on Wimbledon Common in 1902, near Godalming in 1926 and again on Wimbledon Common in 1908. In the period 1907-14 Bentham recorded in his diaries breeding or suspected breeding at Cutt Mill, Hedgecourt Pond, Kingswood, Limpsfield Common, Oxted and Walton Heath. At Kingswood he found six nests in 1914. It would appear therefore that the considerable expansion and extension of range which took place within the county in the first two decades of the present century continued, so that by the 1960s the species was widely reported from many parts of the county. In 1961 it was estimated that at least 32 pairs were present in the Burgh Heath/Tadworth/Headley Heath area. There is evidence that extension of range and increase were still taking place in the 1960s. The following figures of territories on an area of 96 acres of grass and scrub on Bookham Common illustrates this: up to 1962: nil, 1963: one, 1964 and 1965: two, 1966: three-four, 1967 and 1968: four, 1969: six (G. Beven).

In the autumn and winter, resident numbers of birds are reinforced by immigrants from the Continent and from the North. The species is occasionally reported in flight, usually in a southerly direction in small numbers in October. Winter flocks often in association with Siskins and sometimes Goldfinches are commonly seen feeding on birch and alder catkins along the riversides and in woods and on commons. Small flocks regularly resort to sewage farms and other areas rich in weed seeds. Bentham's records demonstrate that flocks of over 50 birds were only very exceptionally recorded in the first half of the present century; since the mid-point of the century however, flocks of up to several hundred have been frequently reported; 300 were recorded at Churt feeding on weeds on 1 February 1965 and 400-500 were present on Epsom Common in November 1969 feeding on the ground on blown birch seed. In 1970 an experienced observer estimated that up to 6,000 were present in birch woods at St George's Hill (Weybridge) during early March.

It is probable that most of the Redpolls recorded in Surrey belong to the British race (*C. f. disruptis*) but occasional reports are received of birds showing characteristics of the Continental race, the Mealy Redpoll (*C. f. flammea*). Most of these records are of odd birds in winter usually in

association with 'lesser' Redpolls. Beadell (1932) recorded
'hundreds' of Mealy Redpolls that stayed a fortnight in
May 1915 in the Celsham area although he gave no
supporting details.

Ringing returns demonstrate the influx both of birds
from northern Britain into the county and of birds from
the Continent. Birds ringed in the winter months at Cobham, Haslemere and Ripley have been recovered at Glasgow
and St Helen's (Lancashire), Norwich and Durham respectively and at least four birds ringed in the wintering
area at Haslemere have been recovered in a subsequent
autumn in Belgium (two), France and Holland.

Common resident.   **Bullfinch**
Local increases and decreases were often recorded in the *Pyrrhula*
county during the review period. For instance Bentham *pyrrhula*
gave it as increasing enormously in the Hedgecourt area in
1907, Eric Parker referred to 'scores and scores' at Feathercombe, near Hambledon in January 1948 after 'an absence
in the summer of 1947' and K. D. G. Mitchell observed
that in 1966 the Bullfinch was a rarity at Wallington where
it had been formerly common in late summer. It is thus
rather difficult to assess general status through the review
period (the species was common in the county in 1900) but
the indications are that an expansion took place in the last
decade or so in keeping with the national trend (Parslow,
1967). Towards the end of 1961 there was 'an almost spectacular increase in the number of Bullfinches in the county'
(*SBR*, 9:26) and in 1963 the records indicated a substantial
increase in numbers (even so the species was described as
distinctly scarce in the Addington, Chelsham and Farleigh
areas in this year). The Common Birds Census in Surrey
during the 1960s showed a general upwards trend in numbers
of breeding territories.

The species is generally distributed in the county in habitats providing good hedge or scrub cover. It is commonly
found in gardens and its predilection for buds of fruit trees
is well known. However this is no new phenomenon and
the Bullfinch was recorded visiting gardens in the last
century.

In winter, flocks of 20 or so are commonly recorded;
occasionally numbers in flocks reach 50 and the largest flock
recorded for the review period was of 84, feeding on chick-
weed (*Cerastium spp.*) at Lyne sf on 25 November 1967.

Ringing has produced some evidence of movements and
a Bullfinch ringed at Woldingham on 22 February 1961

was recovered at Histon (Cambridgeshire) on 8 August 1964.

Crossbill Visitor in irregular numbers, sometimes resident.
Loxia It is well known that the Crossbill (*L. c. curvirostra*) popula-
curvirostra tion in northern Europe irrupts from time to time when over-population coincides with a failure of the spruce (*Picea*) crop and that one of the consequences is the invasion of Britain by the species. With considerable tracts of Scots Pine (*Pinus sylvestris*) and a fair number of plantations of European Larch (*Larix decidua*), Surrey is one of the counties the species finds hospitable and it frequently remains to breed, albeit in very small numbers.

Parslow (1967) gave the Crossbill as markedly increased as a breeding bird in Britain and citing W. B. Alexander and D. Lack 'mainly due to immigration from the Continent and the recent planting of conifers'. As far as Surrey is concerned, breeding was recorded in most years from 1954-69; in only three years in this period was breeding doubtful (and in three others probable). This compares very favourably with the position in the earliest years of the century. Although Bucknill gave it as 'doubtless sometimes' nesting, the first record of breeding (seven pairs recorded) was in 1910 after the invasion of 1909; the species bred again in 1914 at Croydon and Weybridge, after which there was a gap until 1926 when five pairs bred. Between 1926-54 breeding was recorded in only eight years. Thus it can be seen that breeding has become more frequent in the last 15 years of the review period. An analysis of the frequency of invasions during this period shows that it was three times greater than in some earlier periods, there being gaps of at least ten years between invasions twice in the early part of the century. This latter observation supports Alexander and Lack.

The Crossbill has bred in various localities in the county including Addington, Croydon, Kew Gardens (1936 and 1967) Oxshott and Walton Heaths but the most favoured areas have consistently been the pinewoods of south west Surrey notably in the Frensham and Hindhead areas. The best year appears to have been 1931 when eight to ten pairs bred. During the years 1954-70 the number of pairs recorded definitely breeding rarely exceeded two, except in 1960 when definite breeding records were received from two localities involving five pairs and birds were recorded under circumstances where breeding possibly took place, in another eight localities.

Invasions have taken place in Surrey in the following years of the review period: 1909/10, 1927/28, 1929, 1930/31, 1935/36, 1953/54, 1962, 1963/64 and 1966/67. Invasions have been on different scales and the patterns have varied. During what are generally regarded as large scale invasions, numbers over 100 at one place were sometimes recorded, notably during the invasion of 1935/36 when Eric Parker saw many more than 100 at Hambledon and 'hundreds' were dissecting cones on Reigate Heath. During smaller invasions, flocks of 30 or so were commonly reported.

The records are not complete enough to indicate patterns of invasion for the whole of the review period. However a description and an analysis of the invasion in the 1960s is given below.

In 1962 the influx began mid-July; 130 birds were recorded 12-18 July, a peak number of over 154 was reached 2-8 August, numbers dwindled slowly and there were ten recorded in December.

In 1963 numbers were low until March when 84 were recorded. A peak number of 120 was reached in May but in June there were only c. 30 and in July—14. Afterwards numbers built up again somewhat and there were 60 plus in December.

The year 1964 thus began with abnormal numbers in the county; there were 84 in January, a peak number of 135 in March and 111 in April after which numbers dwindled rapidly and no birds were reported in June. During the remainder of the year numbers were negligible.

In 1966 evidence of Crossbills was noted in May. The main body had arrived by mid-July and a peak number of 772 was reached this month. Numbers decreased, at first rapidly then steadily and in December there were only 57 recorded.

In January 1967, similar numbers were reported and a sharp peak of c. 124 was reached in March, numbers falling to 49 in April and 11 in May. Small or very small numbers only were recorded in the rest of the year.

The 1962 invasion appears to have been short and sharp whereas the other two covered part of two consecutive years. The pattern of the 1963/64 and 1966/67 invasions were similar in some respects; the second year peaks were both in March, this suggesting reinforcement from outside the county; on the other hand the 'first-year peaks' were at rather different times of the year. Little is known about occurrences of the Crossbill in Surrey in non-invasion years early in the review period. Bucknill gave it as 'no doubt occurring annually'. There are gaps in the records for the years 1903-08 and 1915-25 inclusive but it seems likely that a very few were present in many of them. The Crossbill was certainly recorded in Surrey in almost every year from 1926 onwards.

A feature of the 1962 invasion was that the species was noted particularly in larch habitats and it was relatively absent from the areas of pine at Esher, Oxshott and Wisley. There are only two records of the species taking food other than pine and larch seeds—two were feeding on Woolly Aphis (*Eriosoma lanigerum*) on one occasion and on another a party was feeding on Whitebeam (*Sorbus aria*) berries.

Parrot Extremely scarce vagrant.
Crossbill Bucknill cited two occurrences of this species in the county
Loxia in the nineteenth century, neither record being entirely
pytyopsittacus satisfactory. During the very large irruption of Crossbills (*Loxia spp.*) into Britain in 1962 many of the birds in the northern half of the country were identified as Parrot Crossbills. The only evidence that this species penetrated into southern England came in fact from Surrey where at Wisley at least one and probably four were present 23 April—15 May. One female was trapped and ringed and its measurements answered to those of the present species (Davis, 1964).

Two-barred Extremely scarce vagrant.
Crossbill On 11 March 1948 four birds of this species (two males and
Loxia two females) were recorded in the county in an undisclosed
leucoptera locality by J. C. Owens. He described them convincingly in a letter to *British Birds* (42 : 119-20). A male was present at Frensham from 22 September to 20 October 1966 (*BB*, 60 : 331). Bucknill referred to a very few specimens including three shot in the winter of 1889 when several were recorded in Britain.

Chaffinch Abundant resident. Passage migrant and winter immigrant.
Fringilla This species is common and widely distributed and absent
coelebs only from the more heavily built-up areas. It is the commonest finch over most of the county, outnumbered only by the Greenfinch in suburban areas. In the 19 Common Birds Census areas studied in the county in the 1960s it was fifth in order of abundance following Blackbird, Robin, Blue Tit and Dunnock with a total of 724 recorded territories out of a grand total of 11,078 in 84 census plot years. It was present in all the areas except two, Ashtead Common and Banstead Downs and the highest density was recorded

at an agricultural land at Wotton with 1.8 pairs per ten acres (Griffin, 1970). County records in general do not show any marked changes in the review period but national statistics suggest that there was some decline in numbers in the early and mid 1960s following a peak in about 1950 (Parslow, 1968). The figures from the Bookham Common census areas are certainly in line with this national trend; for example in 61 acres of scrub and grassland, there were 18 Chaffinch territories in 1948 and 33 in 1949 while the mean for the period was nine (Beven, 1971).

In the autumn during the great influx of Continental passerines into and across southern England, the Chaffinch is one of the more noticeable migrants; small parties of several birds or up to 50 or more are regularly seen flying in a generally NW direction at just above house-top level usually in the two hours following dawn. F. D. Power first recorded this phenomenon at Brixton in 1902 when he noted an almost daily movement, from 7 October to 5 November. Recent examples have come from Dulwich in 1957 when 2,550 birds flying WNW were counted over the period 26 September—5 November and Worcester Park in 1968 when movement was recorded from 9-31 October, the highest count being c. 1,100 on 15 October between 0745 and 1030 hours. Return spring movement is seldom reported but in 1969 R. E. Smith recorded an east to NE movement at Worcester Park during March and April with a maximum of 60 birds on 21 March.

There is no doubt that some of these immigrants stay in the county during the winter months probably joining up with resident birds. Flocks of a few hundred are frequently recorded from suitable feeding areas such as stubble fields, under beech when the mast crop is good and at sewage farms and other places where weeds are left to flourish and seed. Bentham recorded flocks of up to 400 regularly in the early decades of the century and Beadell (1932) recorded a flock of over 1,000 in Halliloo Wood (near Warlingham) in March 1913. Flocks consisting almost entirely of the same sex are occasionally reported, as for instance that of 500 plus in Nonsuch Park on 21 March 1969 which contained only 40 males.

Large numbers of Chaffinches have been ringed in the county and recoveries indicate both the incidence of passage birds and the presence of Continental visitors. Birds ringed in the winter or at migration time have been recovered in Norway (four), Germany (three), Belgium (three), France (one), Sweden (one) and Ireland (one).

Brambling Winter visitor. Passage migrant.

Fringilla This species is moderately common in Surrey in the majority
monti- of winters, abundant locally in some of them and distinctly
fringilla scarce in the others.

Arrival is recorded in October, November and December;
one seen on 9 September 1953 in the Haslemere area was
easily the earliest recorded during the review period. Passage
south or west is occasionally seen in October. Records before Christmas are generally fewer and of smaller numbers
than in the New Year. In the autumn/early winter some
years, very few are recorded; in this period in 1906 Bentham
only saw one Brambling, while in 1960 there were records
of several flocks of up to 40 birds before the turn of the
year.

Numbers recorded in the early months of the year are
extremely variable but flocks of 100 are not uncommon in
a good year and up to 500-600 are occasionally recorded.
The Birds of the London Area, 1957 gave Beddington SF
as a locality where 'they regularly run into hundreds' and
Beadell (1932) mentioned 'thousands' in spring 1929. The
largest number known for the review is c. 1,000 in the
woods of the Royal Military Academy, Camberley in the
winter of 1953/54.

There is evidence of spring passage in late February,
March and April when influxes are sometimes recorded.
Passage is sometimes seen, as when Bentham observed 300
flying NE at Tadworth on 9 March 1930. Males are sometimes recorded in summer plumage in April. Birds are
occasionally reported as late as the first week or so of May
and exceptionally there was one on Wimbledon Common
on 12 June 1938.

Records come from various localities and very many are
of single birds only, usually in a flock of Chaffinches.
Bramblings are most commonly seen in Surrey feeding on
beech mast although they do feed on berries and seeds.
Hard weather tends to bring Bramblings into gardens when
they may visit bird tables and have been recorded feeding
on apples.

The only foreign recovery for the review period was of a
bird ringed at Haslemere on 22 March 1962 found at
Plouescat (Finistere) France on 17 February 1963. One ringed
at Texel, Holland on 28 October 1938 was recovered at
Bookham on 26 December, in the same year.

Common resident. **Yellow-**
This species is well distributed in the county in suitable **hammer**
habitats. Whilst it is found on farmland and grassland *Emberiza*
where enough cover is provided by ground vegetation, *citrinella*
hedges or bushes the most favoured habitats are on heath,
common or downland. The species was present in all the
Common Birds Census plots studied in Surrey over the
period 1961-69 except at Leatherhead and on Clapham
Common and the highest density was recorded on heathland at Frensham. An even higher density was recorded on
grassland with scrub at Bookham Common where over the
period 1963-68 there was an average of 7.7 territories yearly
(*SBR*, 16:34). The species appears to have been generally
common in the county throughout the review period; however as a bird of the countryside it has retreated in certain
areas where pressure of use or development has altered
the habitat.

Winter flocks of 20-30 are frequently recorded and occasionally as late as April; the largest flock recorded in
Surrey during the review period was c. 100 birds on downland at Ashtead on 29 December 1970.

During the severe winter of 1962/63, the species was
reported in urban areas and besides the Thames. Information is lacking on possible winter immigration, post-breeding
dispersal and movement in general. A bird ringed at Frensham 12 September 1965 was recovered at Fareham (Hampshire) 60 miles ssw on 11 February 1968. The species may
well be a passage migrant in the county but the evidence
is inconclusive.

Scarce and local resident. **Corn**
Bucknill gave this species as 'not very abundant' but **Bunting**
'tolerably plentiful both on the commons and high fallows *Emberiza*
throughout the county'. Dixon (1909) wrote that Corn Bunt- *calandra*
ings were present and probably breeding at Croydon, Epsom,
Richmond and Wimbledon and were nesting at Mitcham
and Surbiton. During the review period the species declined
dramatically in the LNHS Recording Area (*The Birds of the
London Area*, 1957). Its status in the rest of the county up
to 1950 is far from clear although it is probable that the
general decline in the country (Parslow, 1968) was reflected
in Surrey. However since 1950 breeding has been increasingly recorded in a number of localities and in some areas
there are regular small colonies as at Chertsey, Thorpe,
Wanborough and Compton. The colony on 400 acres of
arable land at Wanborough, north of the Hog's Back,

was probably in existence in Bucknill's time and it has been recorded as holding from seven to possibly 13 singing males since 1963. The species is however often polygamous so actual breeding numbers are difficult to determine.

By 1970 breeding season records for Burgh Heath, Chessington, Clandon, Ewell, Guildford and Stoke D'Abernon had been made. Its preferred breeding habitat in Surrey in present times appears to be open arable land, with fences rather than hedges and planted with cereals but it is also found on grass downland and open land near gravel pits.

Outside the breeding season the species is recorded in other localities, both singly and in small flocks. A flock at Riddlesdown in 1964/65 grew to c. 30 birds on 26 December 1964 and appeared to remain in the locality until at least 20 March 1965 when c. 20 birds were seen. The largest winter concentration recorded was a roost in sallow and reeds at Hamm Moor, Weybridge which built up to a maximum of 150 birds on 22 January 1970.

Cirl Bunting *Emberiza cirlus* Very scarce and local resident.

The Cirl Bunting breeds in a very few favoured localities in Surrey. Its status appears to be lower than in 1900 but not appreciably so. Breeding season records for the period under review have come from widely spread localities but evidence of regular breeding is generally lacking.

However, there has been a continuous record of breeding since 1954 in the area of the Hog's Back (the species showing a preference for the south side) where it was also recorded in the early years of the twentieth century. In one locality on the Hog's Back up to six males were heard singing one year in the late 1950s. In the last decade of the review period breeding was proved at Effingham, Puttenham and Ranmore and isolated singing males were recorded in various other localities during the breeding season. The species appears to require open country with some hedgerows or trees and is usually found on chalk.

There are few records outside the breeding season and these are mainly from known or possible breeding localities. A male was 'in fairly good song' at Betchworth on 4 October 1957.

Ortolan Bunting *Emberiza hortulana* Extremely scarce vagrant.

Bucknill gave one record for the last century of a specimen which had possibly escaped from captivity. The three records for the period under review are of an adult male seen on the summit of Nore Hill near Chelsham on the North Downs on 23 August, 1947 (*BB*, 40:20), an immature bird seen in stubble with Chaffinches at Epsom sf on 1 October 1955 and a pair at Epsom sf which was seen on several occasions between 3 and 10 May 1958, song being heard on one occasion.

Little Bunting *Emberiza pusilla*

There has only been one record for the county. On 31 March 1956 during a period of strong north-east winds two Little Buntings were identified at Beddington sf and a third bird seen on 3 April; three were present until 14 April, the last bird being seen on 21 April. The birds frequented a ploughed field associating with flocks of Meadow Pipits and Tree Sparrows. A full description is given in *British Birds* (50:206-08). At the same time two Little Buntings were recorded at Staines in Middlesex.

Reed Bunting *Emberiza schoeniclus*

Common resident. Probable passage migrant and winter immigrant.

In 1900 Bucknill gave this species as 'a resident breeding commonly throughout the county', generally nesting near water or in marshy ground but on occasions well away from any water. This description held good in Surrey in 1970 (except in so far as the expansion of the Metropolis had resulted in loss of habitat) and it is likely that it fitted the species in Surrey throughout the review period although as recently as 1969 Bell, referring generally to Reed Buntings breeding on dry land away from water, thought it appeared quite possible that the phenomenon was of recent origin. Local variations in populations have been recorded, notably the marked increase in numbers at the site of Frensham Little Pond when it was drained during the Second World War. Again the population at Bookham Common doubled between 1951-61.

In the last decade of the review period the species was recorded breeding in a variety of habitats with a stretch of water and/or marshy ground. It bred at gravel and sand pits, reservoirs and sewage farms, on commonland, farmland, parkland and riverside. At least 20 pairs bred in the Wey valley between Eashing and Shalford in 1964 and a similar number was present at Guildford in 1970. Density of breeding numbers is sometimes quite high near a pond or gravel (or sand) pit; there were ten pairs at Holmethorpe sps in 1962. On typical wet commonland on clay at Ashtead there was a minimum of four pairs in territory on 53 acres in 1968 and 1969.

Dry breeding habitats recorded at the end of the review period include uncultivated fields and plantation land. In some areas as at Ashtead Common, Prince's Coverts (Oxshott) and Wisley Common, Reed Buntings and Yellow-hammers overlap although the former species is invariably dominant in the wetter areas and the latter in the drier parts.

In winter, flocks of varying numbers are reported from breeding localities and elsewhere. In some years numbers in flocks recorded do not exceed 12 or so but in others numbers are up to 50. The largest flock on record for the county is c. 75 at Burpham on 20 February 1969. Roosts are seldom recorded but there were 25 plus roosting in riverside reeds at Unstead on 6 March 1969. There have been many records of birds visiting gardens in winter during the last decade of the review period. Bell (1969) referring generally to this phenomenon gave it as possibly of recent origin but Bentham observed in 1922 that the species frequented gardens in Tadworth in winter.

Immigration from the Continent to Britain takes place in October and November and it seems likely that some birds pass through or winter in Surrey. There is circumstantial evidence of this given by Bentham who, over very many years of observations, noted a sharp increase in numbers of Reed Buntings in October.

Lapland Bunting
Calcarius lapponicus

Extremely scarce vagrant.

The first recorded instance of this species in the review period was of a bird at Wimbledon Common on 3 November 1957 (*LBR*, 22:34). In the following spring a bird in partial summer plumage was seen at Beddington SF on 5 April.

Bucknill cited six occurrences in the last century.

Snow Bunting
Plectrophenax nivalis

Scarce winter visitor and passage migrant.

Bucknill described this species as a rare winter visitor. In the review period there was one recorded occurrence in 1902 but the next was not until 1944. However since 1953 the year the first *Surrey Bird Report* covered, the species has been recorded in most years. There have been about 30 records from 1953-70 all within the period 21 October to 5 March but mostly in November. The 1944 record was of an exceptionally late bird on 14 April at Ewhurst. Most records are of single birds or twos although five were seen at Kingswood on 16 January 1956 and a small flock was present at Box Hill in mid-November 1967. There are no records of birds seen for more than a few days at one place so it would seem that winter visitors are on the move. Barn Elms Reservoir and the Walton Group of Reservoirs have provided a large proportion of the records.

Abundant resident.

House
Sparrow
Passer
domesticus

Although this species is one of the most abundant in the county it is very little recorded and it was not included in the BTO Common Birds Census. The status of the House Sparrow in Surrey during the review period is therefore difficult to assess; there appears to have been a considerable decline in numbers since 1900 in the area of inner London where breeding numbers are greatest in any event but while this was attributed to the disappearance of horse-traffic in the early years of the century Cramp and Tomlins (1966) could not account for the continued decline after 1950. On the other hand with the spread of the urban development around London and the growth of many towns in Surrey it is very probable that total numbers of House Sparrows have increased. The species is generally found near buildings (of all sorts) except when it flocks and resorts to grain and stubble fields, sewage farms etc. in late summer, autumn and winter.

There are no estimates of breeding densities in the towns or suburbia of Surrey. However W. G. Teagle gave 40 birds per ten acres in Lambeth in 1950 and E. M. Nicholson (*Birds and Man*, 1951) 50 birds per ten acres in Battersea Park in the spring of 1945 and 1950.

Winter flocks observed feeding on stubble, contain up to about 500 birds. However communal roosts (when the species ceases to use the nest hole) far exceed this number. A roost of some 2,700 birds in Richmond Park was recorded in January 1936 and in recent years there have been some records of roosts of over 5,000 including one at Banstead Downs where on 22 November 1960, 18,000 were counted flying in to roost although total numbers roosting could not be estimated, a roost at Mitcham Common where numbers were estimated at 6,000 in 1958 and one of 'several thousand' at Motspur Park.

Of House Sparrows ringed in the county, the furthest recovery was of a bird ringed at Weybridge and controlled 14 miles away at Redhill. There have been local recoveries of Surrey-ringed birds which survived for seven and nine years.

Common resident, locally. Probable winter immigrant.

Tree Sparrow
Passer
montanus

Bucknill described this species as 'not a common resident', breeding very locally and with variable numbers seen in winter. Its breeding status appears to have changed little in the first half of the twentieth century. During this period it was known as a rare winter visitor in the Haslemere area, reported only from Thursley. Pounds (1952) knew of no breeding record for the eastern region of the North Downs in nearly thirty years of watching. However one large colony was recorded during this period at Beddington SF where 50 pairs were estimated in 1933.

From the records made in the 1950s it is evident that a considerable expansion took place at this time, this reflecting (and possibly anticipating) the national trend (Parslow, 1968). Up to 100 pairs were present in 1955 in the Beddington area in the breeding season. The expansion continued into the 1960s and the species was by now being reported from widespread localities. By the end of 1970 the Tree Sparrow had been recorded in all but one of the ten kilometre squares of the county (BTO Atlas Survey).

During the last decade of the review period there were several records of good-sized colonies; these include 56 pairs in ten colonies in the Banstead/Merstham area in 1968, 30 pairs at Shalford Meadows in 1965 and 70 pairs in the Walton/Weybridge/Addlestone area in 1962.

The species is often curiously attached to particular clumps or lines of trees (often by or near a river) where nesting holes are available. Nest boxes are sometimes used and a colony of six pairs used disused hollow aircraft assembly jigs at Brooklands, Weybridge.

In autumn and winter the species is more widespread and is attracted to arable fields, sewage farms and other areas where seeds are to be obtained. Birds then gather in flocks sometimes with other species notably the House Sparrow, buntings and finches. Flocks of 50-200 are regularly seen each winter and occasionally larger flocks are recorded; 400-500 have been twice recorded at sewage farms during the 1960s and the largest flock recorded during the review period was up to 700 at Addington at the end of November 1961.

There is a small amount of evidence suggesting Continental immigration in winter and ringing has indicated that some birds wintering in the county may have come south as birds ringed in winter in Surrey have been recovered in later summers in Lincolnshire and Rutland.

PRE-1900 RECORDS

Species given in *The Birds of Surrey* (1900) which have not been recorded in the Review Period 1900-1970

Species	*Bucknill's Observations Summarized*
Wilson's Petrel *Oceanites oceanicus*	Four birds in Charterhouse Collection said to have been shot in Godalming—identification correct but source not sufficiently authenticated.
Squacco Heron *Ardeola ralloides*	One in Charterhouse Collection—shot at Vachery Pond? Probably obtained between 1850 and 1880.
Glossy Ibis *Plegadis falcinellus*	One shot at Guildford 1833 and one at Woking 1867.
Golden Eagle *Aquila chrysaëtos*	An unsubstantiated record of a bird shot at Godalming in 1810.
Swallow-tailed Kite *Elanoides forticatus*	One very doubtful record for Farnham 1833.
Red Grouse *Lagopus scoticus*	Introduced unsuccessfully early nineteenth century at Bagshot Heath and Cobham.
Barbary Partridge *Alectoris barbara*	One in Charterhouse Collection—shot at Puttenham? Bird no doubt introduced or escaped from captivity.
Virginian Colin *Ortyx virginianus*	Several records c. 1840 following introduction at Windsor (Berkshire). A few introductions in Surrey itself. No permanent success.
Purple Gallinule *Porphyrio porphyrio*	Single bird Bury Hill Lake near Dorking September 1894—February 1895 when found dead. Importation suspected.
American Golden Plover *Charadrius dominicus*	A bird shot at Epsom in 1870 and in Charterhouse Collection was deemed to be the Asiatic race (*C.d. fulvus*) by one competent to judge.
Dotterel *Charadrius morinellus*	Possibly once a regular visitor. A number of specimens shot Peckham, Hindhead and Farnham but before 1854.
Red-breasted Snipe *Limnodromus griseus*	One shot near Battersea c. 1850.
Great Snipe *Capella media*	A few records not very well authenticated.

Species	*Bucknill's Observations Summarized*
Black Guillemot *Cepphus grylle*	Three undated records. One killed at Lambeth in Charterhouse Collection.
Black Woodpecker *Dryocupus martius*	Two records—one 'hopeless error'—other unsatisfactory.
Siberian Thrush *Turdus sibiricus*	Discrepancy between two accounts of specimen shot in Surrey—again identification in some doubt.
Alpine Accentor *Prunella collaris*	One killed Milford 1841 in Charterhouse Collection.
Rose-coloured Starling *Sturnus roseus*	Specimens obtained at Godalming some time after 1849, Dorking 1857 and Thames Ditton 1861.

NOTE: In 1970 the Charterhouse Collection was but a remnant (see Chapter: A Modern History of Birds and Man in Surrey).

Appendix II

SURREY BREEDING BIRDS

Birds known to have bred during this century are listed below. It is beyond the scope of this work to present a definite list of all species which have ever bred in Surrey but information relating to the period before 1900, drawn from Bucknill except where stated, is included for interest. BTO Atlas standards of proven breeding have been consistently applied to the twentieth-century material but for earlier records it has been necessary to use a certain amount of discretion in interpreting the sources.

A   Birds for which breeding has been proved since 1900

Great-crested Grebe	Coot	Wryneck
Little Grebe	Lapwing	Woodlark
Heron	*Ringed Plover* x	Skylark
Mandarin Duck x	Little Ringed Plover x	Swallow
Wood Duck x	Snipe	House Martin
Mallard	Woodcock	Sand Martin
Teal	Curlew	*Golden Oriole* x
Garganey x	Common Sandpiper	Carrion Crow
Gadwall x	Redshank x	Rook
Shoveler x	*Stone Curlew*	Jackdaw
Tufted Duck x	Stock Dove	Magpie
Pochard x	Feral Pigeon	Jay
Canada Goose x	Woodpigeon	Great Tit
Mute Swan	Turtle Dove	Blue Tit
Buzzard	Collared Dove x	Coal Tit
Sparrow Hawk	Cuckoo	Marsh Tit
Hen Harrier	Barn Owl	Willow Tit a.
Montagu's Harrier x	Little Owl x	Long-tailed Tit
Hobby x	Tawny Owl	Nuthatch
Kestrel	*Long-eared Owl*	Treecreeper
Black Grouse	Nightjar	Wren
Red-legged Partridge	Swift	Mistle Thrush
Partridge	Kingfisher	Song Thrush
Quail	Green Woodpecker	Blackbird
Corncrake	Great Spotted	Wheatear
Pheasant	Woodpecker	Stonechat
Water Rail	Lesser Spotted	Whinchat
Moorhen	Woodpecker	Redstart

Black Redstart	x Wood Warbler	Linnet
Nightingale	Goldcrest	Redpoll
Robin	Spotted Flycatcher	Bullfinch
Grasshopper Warbler	Dunnock	Crossbill
Reed Warbler	Meadow Pipit	Chaffinch
Marsh Warbler	x Tree Pipit	Yellowhammer
Sedge Warbler	Pied Wagtail	Corn Bunting
Blackcap	Grey Wagtail	Cirl Bunting
Garden Warbler	Yellow Wagtail	Reed Bunting
Whitethroat	Red-backed Shrike	House Sparrow
Lesser Whitethroat	Starling	Tree Sparrow
Dartford Warbler	Hawfinch	*Total* 121 species
Willow Warbler	Greenfinch	
Chiffchaff	Goldfinch	

Key x : not known to breed before 1900 (18)
    a.: unrecognized before 1900 but no doubt breeding
    Species shown in italics have not been proved to breed 1968-70 (12).

B Birds for which there is good evidence for breeding before 1900 but not since

Marsh Harrier	Pied Flycatcher
Hoopoe	Icterine/Melodious Warbler b.
Raven	Siskin c.
Ring Ouzel	

b.—*The Handbook,* 11:65
c.—Breeding Siskins reported by Bucknill may have been escapes (*The Handbook,* 1:62).

C Other Records

It seems likely that the Montagu's Harrier, Hobby and Golden Oriole bred at least occasionally in the nineteenth century but definite evidence is lacking. Available pre-1900 evidence for several other species including the Bittern and Bearded Tit is unsatisfactory though some, including a few of those marked x in List A, may also have bred. More recently there was an unsuccessful breeding attempt by Black-headed Gulls in 1956 and breeding has been suspected but not proved for two species not in List A, namely the Spotted Crake and Siskin.

Appendix III

ATLAS OF BREEDING BIRDS: SURREY 1968-1971

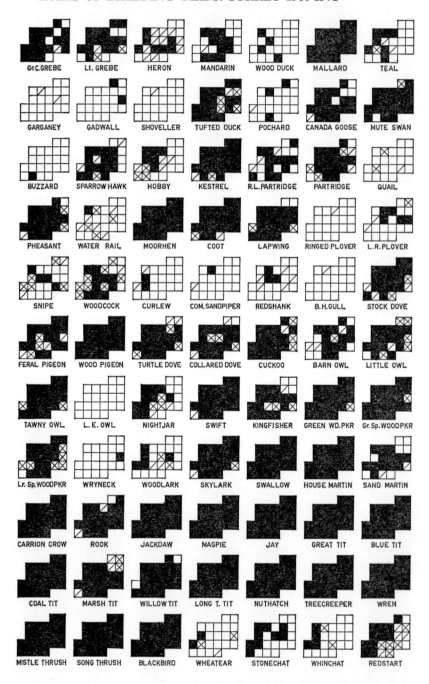

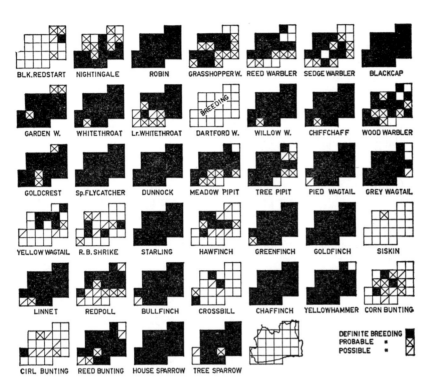

BLK.REDSTART NIGHTINGALE ROBIN GRASSHOPPER W. REED WARBLER SEDGE WARBLER BLACKCAP

GARDEN W. WHITETHROAT Lr.WHITETHROAT DARTFORD W. WILLOW W. CHIFFCHAFF WOOD WARBLER

GOLDCREST Sp.FLYCATCHER DUNNOCK MEADOW PIPIT TREE PIPIT PIED WAGTAIL GREY WAGTAIL

YELLOW WAGTAIL R.B.SHRIKE STARLING HAWFINCH GREENFINCH GOLDFINCH SISKIN

LINNET REDPOLL BULLFINCH CROSSBILL CHAFFINCH YELLOWHAMMER CORN BUNTING

CIRL BUNTING REED BUNTING HOUSE SPARROW TREE SPARROW

DEFINITE BREEDING ■
PROBABLE ＝
POSSIBLE ＝

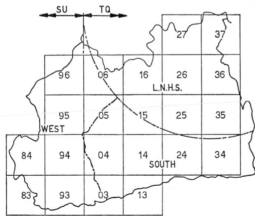

SU   TQ

27 37
96 06 16 26 36
        L.N.H.S.
95 05 15 25 35
WEST
84 94 04 14 24 34
              SOUTH
83 93 03 13

Crown copyright reserved

Appendix IV

GAZETTEER

	Grid		Grid		Grid
Abinger	TQ04	Broad Mead	TQ05	Coneyhurst	TQ04
Abinger Hammer	TQ14	Broadwater	SU94	Coulsdon	TQ35
Addington	TQ36	Brockham	TQ14	Cranleigh	TQ03
Addlestone	TQ06	Brockwell Park	TQ37	Crooksbury	
Albury	TQ04	Brook	SU93	Common	SU84
Aldershot	SU85	Brooklands	TQ06	Croydon	TQ36
Alfold	TQ03	Burgh Heath	TQ25	Crystal Palace	TQ37
Alice Holt Forest	SU84	Burpham	TQ05	Cutt Mill	SU94
Arbrook Common	TQ16	Busbridge	SU94		
Ash (& Vale)	SU85			Deepcut	SU97
Ashtead	TQ15	Camberley	SU86	Denbies The	TQ15
		Capel	TQ14	Devil's Punch	
Badshot Lea Ponds	SU84	Carshalton	TQ26	Bowl	SU83
Bagmoor Common	SU94	Caterham	TQ35	Ditton Common	TQ16
Bagshot	SU96	Chantries	TQ04	Dorking	TQ14
Balham	TQ27	Charterhouse		Dulwich	TQ37
Banstead	TQ25/6	School	SU94	Dunsfold	TQ03
Barn Elms	TQ27	Chase	SU93		
Barnes	TQ27	Cheam	TQ26	Earlswood	TQ24
Barrow Green	TQ44	Chelsea Reach	TQ27	Eashing	SU94
Battersea	TQ27	Chelsham	TQ35	East Sheen	TQ17/27
Beddington	TQ26	Chertsey	TQ06	Effingham	TQ15
Beddlestead Valley	TQ35	Chessington	TQ16	Egham	TQ07
Berrylands SF	TQ16	Chiddingfold	SU93	Elstead	SU94
Betchworth	TQ24	Chilworth	TQ04	Englefield Green	SU97
Birtley	SU93	Chipstead	TQ25	Enton	SU94
Bisley	SU95	Chiswick	TQ27	Epsom	TQ26
Blackheath	TQ04	Chobham	SU96	Esher	TQ16
Blackwater R.	SU85/6	Churt	SU83	Ewell	TQ26
Bletchingley	TQ35	Clandon	TQ05	Ewhurst	TQ04
Blindley Heath	TQ34	Clapham	TQ27		
Bookham	TQ15	Cleygate Common	SU95	Farleigh	TQ36
Bourne R.	TQ06	Cobbett Hill	SU95	Farley Green	TQ04
Box Hill	TQ15	Cobham	TQ15/16	Farnborough North	
Bramley	TQ04	Combe Bottom	TQ04	GP	SU85
Brixton	TQ37	Combe Wood	TQ27	Farncombe	SU94
Broadford	SU94	Compton	SU94	Farnham	SU84

	Grid		Grid		Grid
St Martha's Hill	TQ04	Tadworth	TQ25	Waverley	SU84
Sanderstead	TQ36	Tattenham Corner	TQ25	West Byfleet	TQ06
Seale Chalk Pit	SU84	Teddington	TQ17	West Humble	TQ15
Selsdon	TQ36	Thorpe	TQ06	Westcott	TQ14
Send	TQ05	Thursley Common	SU94	Weybridge	TQ06
Shabden Park		Tilford	SU84	White Downs	TQ14
Estate	TQ25	Tillingbourne		Whitmoor	
Shalford	TQ04	Stream	TQ04/14	Common	SU95
Shamley Green	TQ04	Titsey	TQ45	Wimbledon	TQ27
Sheepleas	TQ05	Tolworth	TQ16	Windlesham	SU96
Shere	TQ04	Tooting	TQ27	Windsor Great	
Shirley	TQ36	Twickenham	TQ17	Park	SU97
Silvermere	TQ06			Winkworth	SU94
Smallfield	TQ34	Unstead	SU94	Winterfold	TQ04
South Munstead	SU94			Wire Mill Pond	TQ34
Staines	TQ07	Vachery Pond	TQ03	Wisley	TQ05
Stanford Common	SU95	Vann Lake	TQ13	Witley	SU93
Stanwell Moor	TQ07	Virginia Water	SU96	Woking	TQ05
Stoke D'Abernon	TQ15			Woldingham	TQ35
Stonehill Common	TQ06	Waddon Ponds	TQ36	Wonersh	TQ04
Stoneleigh	TQ26	Wallington	TQ26	Woodmansterne	
Streatham	TQ37	Walton	TQ16		TQ25/26
Stringers Common	SU95	Walton Common	TQ06	Worcester Park	TQ26
Sunbury	TQ06	Walton Heath	TQ25	Worms Heath	TQ35
Surbiton	TQ16	Wandle R.	TQ26/27	Worplesdon	SU95
Surrey Docks	TQ37/38	Wandsworth	TQ27	Wotton	TQ14
Sutton	TQ26	Warlingham	TQ35	Wyke Common	SU95
Sutton Place	TQ05	Waterloo Ponds	TQ04		

BIBLIOGRAPHY

The list below gives references in the text, important sources and a selection of other relevant works.

ALEXANDER, W. B. (1945-47). The Woodcock in the British Isles. *The Ibis,* 87:512-50, 88:1-24, 159-79, 271-86, 427-44, 81:1-28.

ASH, J. S. (1970). Observations on a decreasing population of Red-backed Shrikes. *BB,* 63:185-205.

A SON OF THE MARSHES—see JORDAN, D.

ATKINSON-WILLES, G. L. (Ed.) (1963). *Wildfowl in Great Britain.* Nature Conservancy Monograph No. 3. HMSO, London.

BARLOW, I. HELEN *et al.* (1968). *A Review of the Birds of the Haslemere district.* Haslemere Natural History Society.

BARNES, J. A. G. (1961). The winter status of the Lesser Black-backed Gull, 1959-60. *Bird Study,* 8:127-47.

BEADELL, A. (1932). Nature notes of Warlingham and Chelsham.

BELL, B. D. (1969). Some thoughts on the apparent ecological expansion of the Reed Bunting. *BB,* 62:209-18.

BENTALL, R. G. (1964). An enquiry into the relative abundance of the species of birds in a Surrey oakwood and the fluctuations in their numbers during the autumn and winter months. *SBCQB,* 30:6-10.

BENTHAM, C. H. (Unpublished). Diaries 1906-68 (19 vols.).

(1959). Autumn movements of Chiffchaffs and Willow Warblers. *SBR No.* 5 *for* 1967: 24-6.

(1961). Some autumn passage movements on Epsom Downs. *SBR No.* 7 *for* 1959: 26-7.

(1967). A birdwatcher's memories of long ago. *SBR No.* 13 *for* 1965: 36-8.

(1969-70). A bird-watcher's recollections of the earlier years of the century. *SBR No.* 15 *for* 1967: 44-7, *SBR No.* 16 *for* 1968: 49-52.

BEVEN, G. (1963). Population changes in a Surrey oakwood during 15 years. *BB,* 56:307-23.

(1967). The food of Tawny Owls in Surrey. *SBR No.* 14 *for* 1966: 32-8.

(1971). Variations of bird population in scrubland on Bookham Common in relation to habitat changes, with special reference to conservation management. *SBR No.* 18 *for* 1970: 17-20.

BIDWELL, E. (1907). Heron nesting in Kew Gardens, *BOC Bull.* XIX.

BLAKER, G. B. (1934). *The Barn Owl in England and Wales.* RSBP.

BOND, PHYLLIS M. (1955). *Revised list of the birds of the Haslemere district.*

BRAZELL, J. H. (1968). *London weather.* HMSO, London.

BRITISH TRUST FOR ORNITHOLOGY (1958-63). *Bird Migration*, Vols. 1 & 2.

BUCKNILL, J. A. (1900). *The Birds of Surrey.*

BULLOCK, D. A. (1967). Siskin weights. *SBR No.* 13 *for* 1965: 33-5.

BUNYARD, P. F. (1919). Surrey field notes. *BB*, 13:226-31.

(1923). Surrey field notes. *BB*, 17:198-205.

CAMBERLEY NATURAL HISTORY SOCIETY. *Reports* 1966-67.

CARTER, M. J. (1963). Comments on PEAKALL (1962). *SBR No.* 9 *for* 1961: 27.

CHARTERHOUSE NATURAL HISTORY SOCIETY. (1959). *Birds, butterflies and moths of the Godalming district.*

CLAPHAM, A. R., TUTIN, T. G. & WARBURG, E. F. (1952). *Flora of the British Isles.* 2nd edition 1962. Cambridge University Press.

CLARKE, W. EAGLE. (1912). *Studies in Bird Migration.*

COLLENETTE, C. L. (1937). *A History of Richmond Park.*

CORNELIUS, L. W. (1968). Winter flocks of Greenfinches. *Ringers' Bulletin, Vol.* 3, *No.* 4: 15-16.

CRAMP, S. (1957). The census of Mute Swans 1955 and 1956. *LBR No.* 21 *for* 1956:55-62.

(1963). The census of Mute Swans 1961. *LBR No.* 26 *for* 1961: 100-03.

CRAMP, S. & GOODERS, J. (1967). The return of the House Martin. *LBR No.* 31 *for* 1966:93-8.

CRAMP, S. & TOMLINS, A. D. (1966). The birds of inner London 1951-65. *BB*, 59:209-32.

DANDY, J. E. (1969). *Watsonian Vice-counties of Great Britain.* Ray Society. London.

DAVIS, P. (1964). Crossbills in Britain and Ireland in 1963. *BB*, 57:477-501.

DENMAN, D. R., ROBERTS, R. A. & SMITH, H. J. F. (1967). *Commons and Village Greens.* Leonard Hill. London.

DIXON, C. (1909). *The Bird Life of London.*

DOUGLAS, G. (1951). Recent Changes in Bird Populations, *Proceedings Leatherhead and District Local History Society for 1951.*

DURY, S. (1961). *The British Isles.* Heinemann, London.

FITTER, R. S. R. (1965). The breeding status of the Black Redstart in Great Britain. *BB*, 58:481-92.

FORSTER, R. H. B. (1968). Letter concerning Perrotts Wood. *SBCQB*, 47: 15-16.

FRITSCH, F. E. (1927). The heath association on Hindhead Common 1910-26. *Journal of Ecology*, 15:344-72.

GALLOIS, R. W. & EDMUNDS, F. H. (1965). *British Regional Geology—The Wealden District.* 4th Edition. HMSO. London.

GOMPERTZ, T. (1957). Some observations on the Feral Pigeon in London. *Bird Study*, 4:2-13.

GOODERS, J. (1968). The Swift in central London. *LBR No.* 32 *for* 1967: 93-8.

GRANT, P. J. (1971). Birds at Surrey Commercial Docks. *LBR No.* 35 *for* 1970:87-91.

GRAVES, G. (1811-21). *British Ornithology.* (As quoted in BUCKNILL (1900)).

GRIFFIN, D. (1970). The Common Birds Census in Surrey. *SBR No.* 17 *for* 1969:52-70.

HAMMOND, E. C. (1968). *Wildfowl Conservation on Metropolitan Water Board Reservoirs.* Nature Conservancy report of limited circulation.

HARRISON, C. J. O. (1961). Woodlark population and habitat. *LBR No.* 24 *for* 1959:71-80.

HARTING, J. E. (1910). The natural history of Weybridge (Lecture). *Surrey Times* 24 *March* 1910.

HASLEMERE LISTS and REVIEW—see BARLOW, I., BOND, P. M. and SHAW, W. A.

HEADLEY HEATH MANAGEMENT COMMITTEE (1964). *Report* 1955-63.

HICKLING, R. A. O. (1967). The inland wintering of gulls in England, 1963. *Bird Study*, 14:104-13.

HOLLOM, P. A. D. (1956). The Great Crested Grebe in Surrey. *SBR No.* 3 *for* 1955:3-4.
(1959). The Great Crested Grebe sample census 1946-55. *Bird Study*, 6:1-7.

HOMES, R. C. *et al.* (1957). *The Birds of the London Area since* 1900. LNHS. Collins. London. A new revised edition was published by Rupert Hart-Davis in 1964.

HOMES, R. C., SAGE, B. L. & SPENCER, R. (1960). Breeding population of Lapwings, Coot and Meadow Pipits. *LBR No.* 23 *for* 1958:54-61.

JOHNSON, I. G. (1970). The Water Pipit as a winter visitor to the British Isles. *Bird Study*, 17:297-319.

JORDAN, D. (1889-96). Various works including:
(1895). *The Wildfowl and Seafowl of Great Britain.*

KEYWOOD, K. P. & MELLUISH, W. D. (1953). A report on the bird population of four gravel pits in the London area 1948-51. *LBR No.* 17 *for* 1952: 43-72.

LABERN, M. V. & HARVEY, D. H. (1970). *Conservation in Surrey—an appraisal of selected open spaces.* Working party of the Nature Conservancy, Surrey County Council and Surrey Naturalists' Trust.

LACK, D. (1956). *Swifts in a Tower.* Methuen. London.

LACK, D. & EASTWOOD, E. (1962). Radar films of migration over eastern England. *BB*, 55:338-414.

LAMBERT, G. C. (1918). Continental Jay at Cobham. *BOC Bull.* XXXVIII: 61.

LEATHERHEAD AND DISTRICT LOCAL HISTORY SOCIETY. *Proceedings* 1947-68.

LONDON NATURAL HISTORY SOCIETY. *London Bird Reports* 1951-70.

MAGEE, J. D. (1965). The breeding distribution of the Stonechat in Britain and the causes of its decline. *Bird Study*, 12:83-9.

MARR, B. A. E. & PORTER, R. F. (1965). Migration watches in 1964. *Sussex Bird Report for* 1964.

MAYHEW, H. (1851). *London Labour and the London Poor.* Vol. 1.

METROPOLITAN WATER BOARD (1961). *The water supply of London*. Metropolitan Water Board. London.

MIDDLE THAMES NATURAL HISTORY SOCIETY. *Middle Thames Naturalist* 1947-70.

MILNE, B. S. (1959). Variation in a population of Yellow Wagtails. *BB*, 52: 281-95.

MONK, J. F. (1963). The past and present status of the Wryneck in the British Isles. *Bird Study*, 10: 112-32.

MOUNTFORT, G. (1957). *The Hawfinch*. Collins. London.

MULLENS, W. H., SWANN, H. KIRKE & JORDAIN, Rev. F. C. R. (1920). *A Geographical Bibliography of British Ornithology*.

NAU, B. S. (1961). Sand Martin colonies in the London area. *LBR No. 25 for* 1960: 69-81.

NEWMAN, E. *et al.* (1849). *The Letters of Rusticus on the Natural History of Godalming*.

PARKER, E. (1929). *English Wild Life*.

(1935). *Ethics of Egg Collecting*.

(1937). *Country Year*.

(1939). *Predatory Birds of Great Britain*.

(1941). *World of Birds*.

(1946). *Countryman's Weekend Book*.

(1947). *Surrey*.

(1952). *Surrey Naturalist*.

PARR, D. (1963). A study of the bird life of Weylands sewage works, Hersham, Surrey. *LBR No. 27 for* 1962: 66-90.

(1969). A review of the status of the Kestrel, Tawny Owl and Barn Owl in Surrey. *SBR No. 15 for* 1967: 35-42.

(1970). Gull flight lines in Middlesex and Surrey in the winter of 1968/69. *SBR No. 16 for* 1968: 36-42.

PARSLOW, J. L. F. (1967-68). Changes in status among breeding birds in Britain and Ireland. *BB*, 60: 2-47, 97-123, 177-202, 261-85, 396-404, 493-508, 61: 49-64, 241-55.

PEAKALL, D. B. (1962). The past and present status of the Red-backed Shrike in Great Britain. *Bird Study*, 9: 198-216.

(1962) The post-war status of the Red-backed Shrike in Surrey. *SBR No. 8 for* 1960: 30-2.

POTTS, G. R. (1970). Recent changes in the farmland fauna with special reference to the decline of the Grey Partridge. *Bird Study*, 17: 145-66

POUNDS, H. E. (1952). *Notes on the birds of Farleigh and district and the North Downs*.

(1965). *Birds of Dulwich and its neighbourhood*.

POWER, F. D. (1910). *Ornithological notes from a south London suburb, 1874-1909*.

PRESTT, I. (1965). An enquiry into the recent breeding status of some of the smaller birds of prey and crows in Britain. *Bird Study*, 12: 196-221.

PRESTT, I. & BELL, A. A. (1966). An objective method of recording breeding distribution of common birds of prey in Britain. *Bird Study*, 13 : 277-83.

PRESTT, I. & MILLS, D. H. (1966) A census of Great Crested Grebe in Britain 1965. *Bird Study*, 13 : 163-303.

PURLEY COUNTY GRAMMAR SCHOOL NATURAL HISTORY SOCIETY. *Annual Reports* 1961-68.

PYCRAFT, W. P. (1907). Sea Eagle in Surrey. *Knowledge*. London.

RADFORD, M. C. (1966). *Birds of Oxfordshire and Berkshire*. Longmans. London.

RAYNSFORD, L. J. (1961). Effect on bird population of heathland habitat by encroachment of silver birch scrub. *SBCQB*, 17.

(1963). A short history of the Dartford Warbler in Surrey. *SBR No 9 for 1961* : 31-3.

REYNAULT, W. E. (1906). Occurrence of Firecrest at Wimbledon. *B.O.C. Bull.* XVI.

ROBBINS, R. W. & DÉAR, H. R. (1932). Chapters on birds in *Oxted, Limpsfield and Neighbourhood*, edited by L. G. Fry.

ROYAL COMMISSION ON COMMON LAND (1958). *Report*.

RUSTICUS—See NEWMAN, E.

SAGE, B. L. (1960). The spring migration of the Common Gull through the London area. *LBR No. 23 for 1958* : 69-74.

(1964). The gull roosts of the London area. *L.B.R. No. 28 for 1963* : 63-8.

SANKEY, J. (1966). *Chalkland Ecology*. Heinemann. London.

SARGENT, J. (1908). Black-throated Diver in Richmond Park. *BOC Bull.* XXI.

SAVAGE, C. (1952). *The Mandarin Duck*. London.

SHARROCK, J. T. R. (1970). Scarce migrants in Britain and Ireland during 1958-67, Part 3. *BB*, 63 : 11-16.

SHAW, Rev. W. A. (1921). *List of the birds of the Haslemere district*.

SHERLOCK, R. L. *et al.* (1960). *British Regional Geology—London and the Thames valley*. 3rd edition. HMSO. London.

SOUTH, S. R. (1971). Ducks in Windsor Great Park. *Middle Thames Naturalist No. 23 for 1970* : 3-5.

STAFFORD, J. (1962). Nightjar enquiry 1957-58. *Bird Study*, 9 : 104-15.

(1963). The census of heronries 1960-61. *Bird Study*, 10 : 29-33.

STAMP, L. DUDLEY & HOSKINS, W. G. (1963). *The Common Lands of England and Wales*. Collins. London.

STEVENSON, E. P. (1914). Kingfisher on River Wandle. *Selbourne Magazine* : 196.

SUMMERS, D. D. B. (1969). Common birds in Surrey. *SBR No. 15 for 1967* : 31-5.

SURREY COUNTY COUNCIL (1969). *Open Spaces in Surrey*. Surrey County Council.

SURREY NATURALISTS' TRUST. *Annual Reports* 1965-70.

SWANN, BRENDA (undated). *The registration of rights of common*. Central Committee on Commons Registration.

VENABLES, L. S. V. (1937). Bird distribution on Surrey greensand heaths: the avifaunal-botanical correlation. *Journal of Animal Ecology*, 6:73-85.

VENABLES, P. (Unpublished MSS deposited at the Haslemere Museum). Bird Life of Frensham Ponds, dated July 1933. Records of duck etc at Frensham Ponds 1931-34, undated.

VESEY-FITZGERALD, B. (1949). *British Game*.

WASHINGTON, D. & HARRISON, C. J. O. (1969). Abnormal reddish plumage due to 'colour-feeding' in wild Greenfinches. *Bird Study*, 16:111-14.

WELLER, L. J. & J. J. (1964). Ringing Sand Martins in Surrey. *SBR No. 10 for 1962*:30-2.

WESTWOOD, N. J. (1961). The pattern of Snipe migration at Guildford sewage farm over seven years. *SBR No. 7 for 1959*:22-6.

(1962). The pattern of wader migration at Guildford sewage farm. *SBR No. 8 for 1960*:24-9.

WHITGIFT SCHOOL SELBOURNE SOCIETY. *Annual Reports*

WILLIAMSON, K. (1955). Migration drift 1953-69 and the Yellow Wagtail complex. *BB*, 48:382-403.

WITHERBY, H. F. & NICHOLSON, E. M. (1937). On the distribution and status of the British Willow Tit. *BB*, 30:358-64.

WITHERBY, H. F. *et al.* (1938-41). *The Handbook of British Birds*. 5 vols., with later revisions.

WOOLDRIDGE, S. W. & GOLDRING, F. (1953). *The Weald*. Collins. London.

WOOLDRIDGE, S. W. & HUTCHINGS, G. E. (1957). *London's Countryside*. Methuen. London.

The following were also abstracted:
British Birds 1907-70
Surrey Bird Reports 1954-70
South Eastern Bird Reports 1934-47

Index

Index

Page numbers in **bold type** are the key references to the Systematic List. As an easy-to-use key, they represent the **first page** (only) on which the **family**, **species** or **race** indexed appears, in its **particular section** in the list. Other references in the list are shown in non-bold type as those for the rest of this work.